MW01231515

200 Years of Ricardian Trade Theory

Ronald W. Jones • Rolf Weder
Editors

200 Years of Ricardian Trade Theory

Challenges of Globalization

 Springer

Editors
Ronald W. Jones
Department of Economics
University of Rochester
Rochester, NY
USA

Rolf Weder
Faculty of Business and Economics
University of Basel
Basel, BS
Switzerland

ISBN 978-3-319-60605-7   ISBN 978-3-319-60606-4   (eBook)
https://doi.org/10.1007/978-3-319-60606-4

Library of Congress Control Number: 2017957064

Printed on acid-free paper

This Springer imprint is published by Springer Nature
The registered company is Springer International Publishing AG
The registered company address is: Gewerbestrasse 11, 6330 Cham, Switzerland

*To James Mill—for encouraging
David Ricardo to write his book*

Preface

The Ricardian trade theory is, and has always been, very important to us. It is fundamental to almost everything done in international trade theory. And the insights that can be derived from it even for the current discussion about globalization are invaluable. Here is a man, David Ricardo, who—200 years ago—had to be encouraged to write down his thoughts in a book on the principles of economics. What he wrote in the inconspicuous Chapter VII "On Foreign Trade" on a few pages is ingenious—also from today's perspective.

Reducing the world economy to two countries (England, Portugal) and two goods (wine, cloth), and explicitly distinguishing between internationally immobile factors of production (capital, labour) and internationally traded goods, made it possible to study complex issues by simplification. It allowed David Ricardo to revolutionize the thinking about the determinants and the effects of international trade. By using a numerical example of countries' labour productivities, he introduced the crucial distinction between absolute and relative differences in the countries' abilities to produce goods. This established the concept of *comparative advantage*, an expression and wisdom most people are confronted with at some stage in their life.

One of us, Rolf, recalls his own experience:

> When I studied economics at the University of St. Gallen I was intrigued by the Ricardian numerical example. In autarky, countries had to sacrifice quantities of one good in order to get more of the other good. With trade, they suddenly got more of both. This sounded a bit like magic. Many years later, when I was a Postdoc at Simon Fraser University, I took the graduate trade course offered by a Professor Jones from the University of Rochester. I was immediately fascinated of the way he was thinking about Ricardian trade theory (and international trade, in general). This was economics at its best. I remember how much I liked the "Augmented Ricardian Trade Model"[1],

---

[1]Jones, R. W. (1980). Comparative and absolute advantage. *Swiss Journal of Economics and Statistics (SJES)*, *116*(2), 272–288

and I was eager to apply the Ricardian idea to my own research on home-market effects.[2]

Even though we also have been using other models in our research (Heckscher-Ohlin, Specific Factors, models with imperfect competition), the Ricardian concept was always there and affected our thinking about international trade. Examples of later work of ours on the basis of Ricardian trade theory are Jones and Ruffin (2007, 2008)[3] and, in applying it to the demand side, Weder (2003).[4] Thinking in terms of absolute and relative differences in international trade is so fundamental. And that is what David Ricardo emphasized in his elaborations on his numerical example 200 years ago. Thus, Ricardo gave us a lot of pleasure in our continuous discussion about trade—particularly also when one of us (Ron) regularly came to the University of Basel, teaching part of the graduate trade course.

Therefore, when the two of us realized, a few years ago, that in 2017 the Ricardian trade theory would become 200 years old, we immediately agreed that this should be celebrated. An international conference on Ricardian trade theory came to mind. We started to plan the conference in summer 2016 when we met at the University of British Columbia in Vancouver. The topics would have to include the main contribution of Ricardian trade theory, the reason for Ricardo's findings and the significance of the theory in today's research in international trade and discussion on globalization.

The conference "Celebrating 200 Years of Ricardian Trade Theory" was held on May 12, 2017, at the University of Basel in Switzerland. It was great. We all enjoyed the scholarly discourse. The contributions, comments and discussions are described in *Part II* of this book—in order to make these elaborations on the Ricardian trade theory also available to a broad audience. This part will be of particular interest to readers who have a profound knowledge in international trade theory or have made it their profession to study international trade issues. But the contents of many chapters in this part will also be accessible and fun to read for those who may, normally, be "scared off" by economic jargon.

We, however, also strongly believe that the Ricardian trade theory is so important that it deserves to be known by anybody who is interested in what is happening in the world economy. These are, for example, students who are at the beginning of studying issues in international economics or international relations,

---

[2]See, for example, Weder, R. (1995). Domestic demand, comparative advantage, and the pattern of trade. *Swiss Journal of Economics and Statistics (SJES), 131*(3), 377–388 and Weder, R. (1995). Linking absolute and comparative advantage to intra-industry trade theory. *Review of International Economics, 3*(3), 342–354.

[3]Jones, R. W., & Ruffin, R. J. (2008). The technology transfer paradox. *Journal of International Economics, 75*(2), 321–328. Ruffin, R. J., & Jones, R. W. (2007). International technology transfer: Who gains and who loses? *Review of International Economics, 15*(2), 209–222.

[4]Weder, R. (2003). Comparative home-market advantage: An empirical analysis of British and American exports. *Review of World Economics, 139*(2), 220–247.

or practitioners who may have been exposed to fragments of the Ricardian trade theory but never really understood the value of the theory—in the sense: "Isn't this the abstract concept of comparative advantage with two countries that, unrealistically, only use labour?" *Part I* of the book thus takes the reader back to the time when David Ricardo created the idea, presents the standard Ricardian trade theory as we know it in trade and discusses today's important implications and applications.

In *Part III* of the book, we identify current challenges of globalization and discuss some of them in the light of Ricardian trade theory. We argue that even though 200 years have gone by since "On Foreign Trade" has been written, the world in which David Ricardo developed his fundamental ideas was not that different from today's world economy. We still have different countries with their own sets of regulations and cultural preferences. There also is limited factor mobility between countries, particularly regarding the mobility of labour. Brexit— i.e. the exit of Britain out of the European Union (EU)—may be considered an example of this reality. In this part of the book, we also include David Ricardo's original and path-breaking "On Foreign Trade"—i.e. Chapter VII of his *On the Principles of Political Economy and Taxation*, published on the 19th of April 1817 by John Murray Publishers in London.

Objectives of the Book

This book thus offers a comprehensive reflection on David Ricardo's ingenious theory of international trade. It is divided into three parts.

Part I presents the "birthday boy", his concept and the many applications and insights that can and have been derived from it, particularly in modern times. Part II explores important aspects of the Ricardian trade theory through the eyes and experience of leading experts on international trade theory, taking into account the latest research in the field. Part III discusses current challenges of globalization in the light of Ricardian trade theory and includes the original "On Foreign Trade" written and published by David Ricardo in 1817.

The book thus:

- Brings together relevant key features of the Ricardian trade theory and comparative advantage,
- Addresses a broad audience interested in the current and future development of international trade theory, including undergraduate and graduate students,
- Offers an intellectual journey from the emergence of the theory to its established standard version in the field of international trade and, furthermore, to its revival in the latest developments of research in international trade,
- Discusses these aspects among scholars in international trade theory and reflects on current challenges of globalization in the light of Ricardian trade theory.

An interesting feature of the book is that it includes the discussions held at the Scientific Conference that have been transcribed (Chaps. 8, 11, 14 and 18). This allows, to some extent, for an authentic replication of the questions and answers among the speakers, discussants and chairs at the conference on various aspects of Ricardian trade theory and international trade, in general.

Targeted Audience

The book brings together everything we believe is important on the subject of the Ricardian trade theory and which usually is scattered over many textbooks in economics and international trade, books about the history of economic thoughts, scientific articles in trade and, of course, David Ricardo's all-encompassing oeuvre. Anybody who is interested in Ricardian trade theory, in comparative advantage and in international trade, in general, should benefit from the book as a whole—or at least of some chapters.

The book can be used for teaching purposes for a number of different courses in economics, international trade and globalization. In particular, Parts I and III will be interesting to and accessible by a *broad audience, including undergraduate students in history, economics, business, political science and other disciplines.* Part II is more difficult and a result of a conference with academics and renowned scholars in international trade theory. It will be especially interesting for *graduate students and faculty members*, interested in the current and future development of trade theory. Those readers who find some chapters or sections in Part II difficult to read may always go back to individual chapters in Part I which provide the foundation of these elaborations. Thus, *"everything in one place"* was an important target when designing the book. In order to make the reading for a heterogeneous audience easy, we also cross-reference from chapters to chapters of the book.

We hope readers will join us in *celebrating 200 years of Ricardian trade theory* by going back to the origin, experiencing the standardization and further development of the theory and appreciating its implications and recent revival in research pursued in international trade. Fellow economists Bruno S. Frey and David Iselin recently edited a book with the provocative title "Economic Ideas You Should Forget".[5] We can assure you that David Ricardo's idea and thus Ricardian trade theory does not belong to this category. Also, it seems that, in the field of international trade, old and new theories are complementary and not substitutes. Or, as one of us, Ron, uses to say:

In trade, we try to get it right the first time.

[5]Frey, B. S., & Iselin, D. (Eds.) (2017). *Economic ideas you should forget.* Cham: Springer International Publishing.

Acknowledgements

This book would not have been possible without the contributions and dedicated support of a number of people. We would like to thank all of them for their engagement. We are particularly indebted to the following persons:

All our colleagues who wrote chapters for the book, presented and discussed papers at the conference or chaired sessions: Harris Dellas, Jonathan Eaton, Peter Egger, Bill Ethier, Simon Evenett, Thomas Gerber, Carsten Hefeker, Andrew Lee, Antonio Loprieno, Esteban Rossi-Hansberg, Roy Ruffin, Nicolas Schmitt and Scott Taylor. Without their compliance with the very tight deadline, the book would not have been ready on time.

Hermione Miller-Moser and Christoph Schweizer who spent much effort in transcribing presentations and discussions held at the conference in order that the authors of the chapters in this book could finalize them.

Master's students, doctoral students and Postdocs (in trade) at the University of Basel who supported us in the final editorial work (formatting texts, drawing figures, giving feedback to drafts): Dragan Filimonovic, Vera Frei, Rahel Fritz, Christian Rutzer, Till Schmidlin, Madeleine Schmidt, Christoph Schweizer and Timon Sutter. Only their big effort and excellent work during the last 2 weeks before the deadline allowed us to submit the manuscript on time.

We also would like to thank Daniel Diermann, Yvonne Mery, Peter Schnetz and Jesse Weder for making and supporting us in putting together the photographs used in this book and to Claire-Lise Dovat for making the photocopying of the 3rd edition (printed in 1821) of Ricardo's book (owned by the University of Basel Library) possible.

We thank Thomas Gerber and Till Schmidlin for their great support in organizing the conference at the University of Basel on May 12, 2017, and also in advertising the whole series of events described in Chap. 1 of this book. We also thank the sponsors of the scientific conference (the Stiftung Basler Kantonalbank zur Förderung von Forschung und Unterricht der Wirtschaftswissenschaften an der Universität Basel and the Faculty of Business and Economics) for their support.

Our thanks also go to Martina Nolte-Bohres, Katharina Wetzel-Vandai and Yulija Zeh who, as members of Springer International, found interest in our idea and gave us, together with their team, their professional support in making this book a successful project.

This book, particularly the chapters we wrote ourselves, also reflects the experience we made in teaching the material in undergraduate and graduate courses in international trade over the years. We thus are also grateful to our students who, with their questions and suggestions, made us think hard how to get across these important (Ricardian) ideas.

Finally, we would like to thank Kit and Katharina for their support and patience.

Rochester, USA   Ronald W. Jones
Basel, Switzerland   Rolf Weder
July 31, 2017

Contents

Editors and Contributors

About the Editors

Ronald W. Jones is Professor of International Economics, Department of Economics, University of Rochester (USA), and the author of 180 scientific articles in international trade theory in peer-reviewed economics journals. He has also written several books, including the undergraduate textbook of *World Trade and Payments: An Introduction* (10th edition) (co-authored with Richard Caves and Jeffrey Frankel (Pearson)) and *Globalization and the Theory of Input Trade*, reflecting his Ohlin Lectures in 2000 (MIT Press).

Rolf Weder is Professor of International Trade and European Integration, Faculty of Business and Economics, University of Basel (Switzerland). He has published on international trade, European integration and Swiss economic policy in peer-reviewed journals. He is the author of a number of books (in German), including *International Competitive Advantage: A Strategic Concept for Switzerland* (co-authored with Silvio Borner, Michael E. Porter and Michael J. Enright (Campus)) and *Switzerland and the EU* (with Beat Spirig (NZZ Libro)).

List of Contributors

Harris Dellas Department of Economics, University of Bern, Bern, Switzerland

Jonathan Eaton Department of Economics, Pennsylvania State University, University Park, PA, USA

Peter H. Egger Department of Management, Technology and Economics, ETH Zurich, Zurich, Switzerland

Wilfred J. Ethier Economics Department, University of Pennsylvania, Philadelphia, PA, USA

Simon Evenett Department of Economics, University of St. Gallen, St. Gallen, Switzerland

Thomas Gerber Faculty of Business and Economics, University of Basel, Basel, Switzerland

Carsten Hefeker Department of Economics, University of Siegen, Siegen, Germany

Ronald W. Jones Department of Economics, University of Rochester, Rochester, NY, USA

Andrew Lee Cooperative State University Karlsruhe, Karlsruhe, Germany

Antonio Loprieno Faculty of Business and Economics, University of Basel, Basel, Switzerland

David Ricardo Gatcombe Park (near Minchin Hampton), Gloucestershire, UK

Esteban Rossi-Hansberg Department of Economics and Woodrow Wilson School, Princeton University, Princeton, NJ, USA

Roy J. Ruffin Department of Economics, University of Houston, Houston, TX, USA

Nicolas Schmitt Department of Economics, Simon Fraser University, Burnaby, BC, Canada

M. Scott Taylor Department of Economics, University of Calgary, Calgary, AB, Canada

Rolf Weder Faculty of Business and Economics, University of Basel, Basel, Switzerland

Chapter 1
Introduction: Celebrating 200 Years of Ricardian Trade Theory

Ronald W. Jones and Rolf Weder

Abstract We argue that it is rather unusual in economics that a theory, after 200 years, is still relevant and so important. We contribute this to the brilliance of the Ricardian idea and its simplicity. We show that the Ricardian trade theory was always present in the field of international trade, but even experienced an increase in its importance in the last 50 years. We then briefly describe how we celebrated the Ricardian Year 2017. The scientific conference on May 12, 2017 was the highlight. It is the pillar of this book. The chapter ends with a short presentation of the idea and structure of the book.

200 Years of Ricardian Trade Theory! This is very unusual. Many—or most—ideas one economist has are usually passed by, as new models or ideas *replace* the old ones. This is no different in other sciences, in physics, in biology, in medicine— even in history or political science. Original assumptions are often replaced by new ones which are considered "better". Theoretically derived relationships turn out to be refuted by real world observations. More general theories are being developed that include the original idea only as a particularity of something much "bigger" and more relevant. Or the theme in which the idea has achieved its significance in the past loses its importance in the future; the idea becomes irrelevant.

The Ricardian story is somewhat different. David Ricardo wrote about trade and markets, but 200 years later his idea and assumptions have not been replaced: The world has many countries, which was true in Ricardo's time and is still the case. As Britain recently has suggested, there is a strong possibility that there will still be many countries 200 years from now. The Heckscher-Ohlin trade model, developed by Eli Heckscher, Bertil Ohlin and Paul Samuelson in the first half of the twentieth century, puts heavy weight on countries having more inputs than just labor (Ricardo did mention more factors than labour, but his model—the Ricardian trade model—

R.W. Jones (✉)
Department of Economics, University of Rochester, Rochester, NY, USA
e-mail: ronald.jones@rochester.edu

R. Weder (✉)
Faculty of Business and Economics, University of Basel, Basel, Switzerland
e-mail: rolf.weder@unibas.ch

simplifies that labour is the only input). The important aspect of the Ricardian trade theory is, however, the concept that not all markets are global. This is what underlies Ricardo's theory of *comparative advantage*.

This book celebrates the *200th birthday* of Ricardian trade theory. But it does not only look back and celebrate what the theory has achieved in international trade. It also asks, and tries to give answers to, questions such as: "In which respect are the results found in Ricardo's trade theory still useful after 200 years, and beyond?" Our impression is that the theory even has re-gained some recognition in research in international trade in the last decades. The topic which it deals with—globalization—has surely attained a level of relevance in public discussions that hardly ever existed in the past. Thus, there are excellent reasons to put together this book—reasons that go way beyond the fact that "something" happens to become 200 years old.

In this introductory chapter, we first continue to dwell on why the Ricardian trade theory is so important, also including our own personal experience. Part of the reason is, in our view, due to the simplicity, the beauty and the "purity" of the theory. In the second section, we briefly draw balance of how we celebrated the "Ricardian Year 2017", alluding to the academic and public events in Switzerland at the University of Basel. In the third section, we present the structure and content of this book. We thereby hope that the reader becomes hungry for more. There are 19(!) other chapters in this book—including the Master's original chapter "On Foreign Trade"—which wait to be read by interested readers.

1.1 It's the Idea, and the Simplicity

One of the competing models in international trade is the Heckscher-Ohlin model. It, in a way, extended the Ricardian model by explicitly taking into account more factors of production (labour and capital in its standard version). At the same time, however, it reduced the richness of the Ricardian model by the assumption that technologies (not the techniques!) are identical in different countries. Heckscher and Ohlin did this so that they could focus on the aspect of countries' differences in the factor endowment. Having more than one factor of production, allowed for studying distributional effects within a country that arise from changes in prices of goods and thus from opening up a country to international trade. The model became famous, sometime after Stolper and Samuelson (1941) had shown that changes in prices of goods imply strong distributional effects between factors of production within a country. The model also led to a great number of analyses regarding the effects of factor mobility on production (Rybzynski Theorem)[1] and, particularly, of trade liberalization on the pattern of trade (Heckscher-Ohlin Theorem).

One of us, Ron, recalls:

---

[1]Rybczynski (1955).

> When I was a graduate student at M.I.T (early on, 1953), Professor Kindleberger and Professor Solow both remarked that a Professor at Harvard, Wassily Leontief, was soon to have published his article that very quickly stirred up a lot of professors and graduate students looking for thesis material. He had numbers (he was way ahead of 'new-new trade theory' and its importance of real numbers) that suggested, contrary to the belief by all, that the U.S. was producing goods for exports that were more labour-intensive than the goods it produced in its import-competing industries. How could this be? Great interests were placed on making sense of this in a Heckscher-Ohlin world. The numbers did not seem to attract economists that were successful in making sense of this. Some even believed it seemed to put question to the validity of the concept of comparative advantage.

Note that the Ricardian idea of *comparative advantage* was still fundamental to this—as it was called at the time—"modern trade theory": The Heckscher-Ohlin Theorem implied that, in the $2 \times 2 \times 2$ case (two goods, two countries, two factors), *relative* differences between the countries' factor endowments determined the pattern of trade. A country that is relatively well endowed with labour, has a comparative advantage in the production of the labour-intensive good and thus is expected to export this good and import the capital-intensive good. Again, it is *relative* differences and not absolute differences which matter for the pattern of trade. Jones (2008) argues that it is this aspect which had been neglected by Leontief (1953) and that this was one of the reasons for the great controversy at the time (see also Jones, 1956). One problem was that the data only referred to the U.S., *no foreign data was used* (see Chap. 6 in this book).

1.1.1 Increasing Importance of the Ricardian Idea

The empirical analyses of the pattern of trade during the last 50 years more and more revealed that allowing for technological or, more generally, productivity differences between countries is crucial for an accurate explanation of the observations. In other words, the assumption of identical technologies in the Heckscher-Ohlin model seemed inconsistent with observations. This created further recent support for the Ricardian model. Feenstra (2016, p. 48) concludes: "So we are back in a world of Ricardo, where technological differences are a major determinant of trade patterns."

It may thus not be surprising that more efforts have been undertaken in order to empirically analyze the Ricardian trade theory in the last 15 years. An important breakthrough was achieved by Eaton and Kortum (2002) who generalized the model to, among others, a large number of countries as discussed in Chaps. 6 (Jones), 7 (Taylor) and 12 (Eaton) in this book. In the meantime, a number of empirical studies, such as Costinot, Donaldson, and Komunjer (2012), have used this approach to test the Ricardian trade theory. The empirical analyses before were important, but focused on the two-country case (see Chap. 5 and also Chap. 12 in this book).

Moreover, the "new-new trade theory" based on firm-level increasing returns to scale and heterogeneity in productivity, such as Melitz (2003) and Eaton, Kortum, and Kramarz (2011), can be interpreted to be closely related to the Ricardian trade theory. The reason is that, in these theories, international trade leads to a special-ization in the direction of relatively productive firms. Even though specialization now takes place within industries and among firms, general-equilibrium effects of trade liberalization on the average wage rate and their impact on specialization may, in our view, be considered as fundamentally Ricardian. The relatively more productive firms end up exporting, whereas the relatively unproductive ones dis-appear (or may only produce domestically).

We both have been heavily relying on Ricardo in our teaching and, to some extent, in research. In teaching, this is not only the case for undergraduate courses in international economics in which comparative advantage and the Ricardian gains from trade through specialization typically have their role. It is also true for our graduate courses in trade. Some may argue that the Ricardian trade theory is quickly explained on this level—Feenstra (2016) uses three pages in his graduate textbook (pp. 1–3)—and then move on as there is, indeed, a lot of new material to be taught. As mentioned above, one may reply that this implies at least an indirect confrontation with Ricardian trade theory which is operating in the background of these new developments. And sometimes, if the Dornbusch-Fischer-Samuelson (1977) model is introduced, Ricardo may explicitly come back in these courses and textbooks. Remark: The wide use of the Dornbusch-Fischer-Samuelson article is another big reason to support Ricardo.

But there is a lot that can and, in our view, should be discussed. One of us, Rolf, typically "forced" (or gave the opportunity to) his graduate students to go back to the origin and read Ricardo's "On Foreign Trade"—to appreciate the discovery of comparative advantage and to reconstruct the implementation in the standard Ricardian trade theory (see Chap. 3 in this book). We both have been discussing many applications and extensions of the model with the students: The implications of nontraded goods, for example, the effects of technological changes or the extension with an internationally mobile factor of production. We presented the so-called "Augmented Ricardian Trade Model" (Jones, 1980) or discussed the recent paper by Samuelson (2004) and the "The Technology Transfer Paradox" (Jones & Ruffin, 2008). We relied on some of the insightful discussion by Krugman (1996) on "International Competitiveness" (see Chap. 5 in this book).

We both always appreciated the simplicity (and also the beauty) of the Ricardian model with two or N goods. Some may think that, particularly for the graduate level, the model is too simple—that it simplifies the reality too much or that it is just not enough demanding for the graduate audience. We, instead, kept emphasizing that it encourages us to understand relationships—which are, in principle, very complex and important—much better. One can see why and when a technological improvement in the foreign country positively or negatively affects the real wage rate of the home country. The fact that there are different cases to be distinguished (complete or incomplete specialization) helps, in our view, to understand the economics behind it. In this sense, the model with a continuum of goods is more restrictive.

1.1.2   Simplicity of the Ricardian Idea

In addition to the idea, it is also the *simplicity* of the Ricardian (and of any other good) model that we believe is important for its appreciation by and survival in the research community. Some years ago, we discussed what motivates us in research and whether it is possible to realize if one has found out something which could be important. We came to the conclusion that one usually doesn't, but that very often we are driven by trying to improve our understanding. To simplify things usually helps. We recall Ron's answer in an interview some years ago about his 1965 paper (Jones, 1965): "I was trying to make the trade literature easier than it has been; trying to make things more simple. This always has been a driving force of what I have been doing." And he added: "I think I have a comparative advantage in that I know if I do not know. This is important."

The argument that it is the combination of the idea and the simplicity which is crucial for the permanent success of the Ricardian trade model can, in our view, be nicely illustrated with Fig. 1.1 and Eq. (1.1). Figure 1.1 shows the World Production Possibility Frontier for two countries—Home and Foreign (*)—that produce quantities of two goods (i = 1,2,), y_i and y_i*, in the trade equilibrium.[2] We suppose that the home country has a comparative advantage in good 1. In other words, it uses relatively less labour in the production of good 1 than the foreign country. This is formally captured by the following inequality:[3]

$$\frac{a_{L1}}{a_{L2}} < \frac{a_{L1}^*}{a_{L2}^*}.$$ (1.1)

Fig. 1.1 The world production possibility frontier

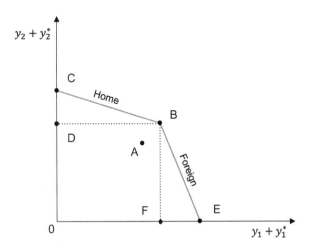

[2]See also the "World Transformation Schedule" used in Caves, Frankel and Jones (2007, p. 63).
[3]Note that a_{Li} (a_{Li}*) captures the amount of labour per unit of output in industry *i* in the home (foreign) country.

Looking at Fig. 1.1, this implies that the triangle *CDB* reflects what Home can produce if point *D* were its origin and triangle *BFE* reflects what Foreign can produce if point *F* were its origin. The figure adds these two diagrams: If both countries only produce good 2, *OC* would be the total world production. The relatively smaller slope of *CB* (compared to *BE*) shows that Home has a comparative advantage in producing good 1 as assumed in Eq. (1.1). If the world demand for good 1 were to become larger, Foreign will start to produce some of good 1 (point on *BE*). If both countries are completely specialized in that good in which they have a comparative advantage (Home in good 1, Foreign in good 2), the world would produce and consume in point *B*. If one country is much larger than the other, it would still have to produce both goods in trade. If consumers in the two countries have a strong preference for one of the two goods the equilibrium may involve one country producing both goods and the equilibrium would thus be on the lines *CB* or *BE* on the World Production Possibility Frontier.

How would the equilibrium on the World Production Possibility Frontier compare with autarky, i.e., a situation in which each country consumes only what it produces by itself? An equilibrium in autarky is illustrated by a point such as *A*. The comparison between *A* (autarky) and *B* (trade with complete specialization) easily conveys the message that there are gains from trade by both countries to be made: With given resources the world achieves a higher consumption point through international trade by moving from *A* to *B*. If each country specializes in that good in which it has a comparative advantage, the world is better off. Resources are used more efficiently.

Note that this can also be seen by slightly transforming inequality (1.1):

$$a_{L1}a_{L2}^* < a_{L2}a_{L1}^*. \tag{1.2}$$

By multiplying terms, we can transform Eq. (1.1) into Eq. (1.2) which provides an analogy to Fig. 1.1: Specialization according to comparative advantage (Home produces good 1, Foreign good 2) implies that the world's total amount of labour used per unit of output is smaller than in the opposite case. The product of the two respective labour coefficients is smaller than otherwise. Both Fig. 1.1 and inequality (1.2) illustrate the efficiency gains that can be realized through specialization and international trade (see also Chap. 4 in this book). Inequality (1.2) suggests that such criteria may be found if there are many goods and many countries (see Chaps. 6, 7 and 12 in this book).

More generally, countries gain from trade by specializing in only those few goods which they are relatively best at. All the other goods they import. This Ricardian idea is fundamental—and in a way complex and demanding to understand. But, as shown above, it can be explained in rather simple and straightforward terms. This is particularly important if we economists have to explain what we mean with words to a broad audience and if we want to be sure that we are not only heard, but also understood. Simplicity also matters from this perspective.

1.2 Celebrating 200 Years of Ricardian Trade Theory in 2017

The scientific conference "Celebrating 200 Years of Ricardian Trade Theory" on May 12, 2017, was for sure the highlight of 2017, at least for us. It was also the foundation of Part II of this book. However, we were strongly convinced, when discussing the idea of a celebration, that the general public should also be addressed. The Ricardian trade theory is too important and too relevant for a discussion only within an academic circle, especially in today's world. Therefore, a whole series of lectures and panel discussions throughout the year was envisioned. Table 1.1 gives an overview of the public events and themes organized at the University of Basel in Switzerland.[4]

In the following, we briefly explain how the events relate to the Ricardian trade theory and what insights could be gained from these events and the discussion they included (until this book went into print).

1.2.1 Prelude: Ricardo's Modern Book

The series started with the *Prelude* "David Ricardo's Modern Book – A Small Retrospective" at the University of Basel Library. A small group of interested people from many disciplines and with different backgrounds attended the presentations by Thomas Gerber and Rolf Weder. The audience was eager to hear about Ricardo's personality, his life and, of course, his book and Chapter VII "On Foreign Trade". It was interesting to hear from Thomas how insecure and also

Table 1.1 200 years of Ricardian trade theory—a series of events in 2017

Prelude	April 5, 2017	David Ricardo's Modern Book – A Small Retrospective
Ouverture	April 19, 2017	Globalization: Quo Vadis?
Act I	May 12, 2017	Scientific Conference "Celebrating 200 Years of Ricardian Trade Theory"
Act II	July 20, 2017	From the Outsourcing of Production to the Dislocation of R&D?
Act III	October, 2017	Globalization, Renewable Resources and the Environment
Act IV	November 30, 2017	From Multilateralism to Regionalism—or the Other Way Round?
Epilogue	December 14, 2017	David Ricardo's Contribution and the Challenges of Today

[4]The series of events has been designed and organized by Rolf Weder and Thomas Gerber who is a PhD student in economics at the University of Basel. Till Schmidlin (research assistant) made all the posters and flyers. The idea of calling the individual events "Prelude", "Act I–IV" and "Epilogue" may have been influenced by Rolf's reading of Samuelson's (2004) paper.

Fig. 1.2 David Ricardo's modern book in a showcase with documents. Source: Poster of event and own picture of the showcase in the University of Basel Library, April 2017

modest David Ricardo was when developing and exchanging his thoughts with James Mill and Thomas Malthus before the publication of his book (see Chap. 2 of this book). In a letter to Mill, he wrote on October 24, 1815 "Oh that I were capable to write a book".[5] As it turned out he was.

Rolf stressed, among others, Ricardo's emphasis, in his original writing, on a country's exports as a "means" to buy imports with a lower amount of resources than would be required to produce them at home. The audience recognized the link to today's contrasting statements in politics, but obviously enjoyed the following remark in a letter David Ricardo wrote to Mill, with regard to the burden of writing his book—a burden which most in the audience were very able to relate to:

> You observe justly that having friends staying with us unsettles our regular habits. I find it very materially to interfere with my pursuits. Reading or writing, when one has an object in view, should be followed systematically, and at no distant intervals, for after a time our thoughts are turned into new channels and we cannot easily recall the ideas which were only beginning to be indistinctly formed in our minds. I have scarcely been a week without visitors since I have been in the country, and to that I ascribe the imperfection of the little that I have done in the writing way.[6]

Also a showcase with extracts from "On Foreign Trade", pictures, hand-written documents and, most importantly, the original third edition of "On the Principles of Political Economy and Taxation" was presented at this Prelude (see Fig. 1.2).

---

[5]Sraffa (2005), Vol. IV, p. 314.
[6]Sraffa (2005), Vol. VI, pp. 315–316.

1.2.2 Ouverture: Globalization: Quo Vadis?

On April 19, 2017 the *Ouverture* "Globalization: Quo Vadis?" was held in the Aula of the University of Basel. The date was important. Ricardo's book *On the Principles of Political Economy and Taxation* came out in London *exactly* on April 19, 1817, published by John Murray.[7] There was a panel discussion about the experience and issues of globalization among a number of representatives of different Swiss industries, of labour and of the government. The debate was lively. The audience appeared in large numbers to this event. Figure 1.3 gives an impression of the announcement and the attendance.

Note that Switzerland has a comparative advantage in industries such as the chemical-pharmaceutical industry or the machinery and electronic industry: It, however, has a comparative disadvantage in textiles and also in agriculture. Whereas the Swiss textile industry was significant more than 50 years ago, it underwent a strong shrinking process because other countries entered the market and there was no protection against rising imports. Switzerland was a member of the Multifibre Arrangement (MFA), but never applied its instruments (Weder & Wyss, 2013). In agriculture, however, protection has traditionally been large with some product segments (e.g., trade in cheese) being liberalized some years ago.

Representatives of the machinery and textile industries (Klaus Endress and Ueli Forster), of the agricultural sector (Hansjörg Walter), of labour (Beat Kappeler), the government (Marie-Gabrielle Ineichen-Fleisch) and of economics (Rolf Weder) discussed, under the guide of Daniel Hanimann (a former TV moderator) about

Fig. 1.3 Globalization: Quo Vadis? Panel discussion on April 19, 2017. Source: Own poster and picture of the event in the Aula of the University of Basel

---

[7]This is the time when John Murray Publishers also published Jane Austen's last works "Persuasion" and "Northanger Abbey" (December 1817) and when the Waterloo Bridge was opened (June 1817).

trade policy, how the textile industry adjusted to rising imports, why the agricultural sector enjoys protection, why the machinery industry is, despite its export success, under constant pressure and how labour that moves between the industries is affected by all of this and how it reacts to it.

The discussion reflected very much the issues raised by the Ricardian trade theory. The flexibility of the labour market was considered to be a key factor for the success and the adjustment of the Swiss economy. The employees in the textile industry adjusted well to the structural change because it was gradual, not abrupt, and because people found other jobs in the nearby precision mechanics and machinery industries. Note that Ricardo himself, implicitly emphasized that trade liberalizations should be implemented gradually to give individuals enough time to adjust. The protection of the agricultural industry was defended due to the preservation of a certain degree of aggregate self-sufficiency required by law.

Also, it was argued that the observed criticism in Switzerland (and elsewhere) against globalization is much more a critique against the free movement of people than against free trade in goods and services. And sometimes, globalization is made responsible for issues which are only loosely related to international trade, but are more a consequence of technological changes such as digitalization—as emphasized by the State Secretary Mrs. Ineichen-Fleisch. Overall, participants agreed that specialization and international trade remains very important, particularly for a small country such as Switzerland, and that it is generally also supported by the Swiss society. However, it remains crucial that structural changes can be digested by the affected people. This requires that the changes do not happen too quickly and that those who lose a job (in one industry or firm) may, also in the future, get temporary support until they have found a new engagement (in another industry or firm).

1.2.3   Act I: Scientific Conference

Act I, the Scientific Conference "Celebrating 200 Years of Ricardian Trade Theory", was the highlight. It took place on May 12, 2017 at the University of Basel in Switzerland. We were pleased about the support of our colleagues. Their immediate and positive replies to our inquiry and their willingness to actively participate at the conference encouraged us in our endeavor (Fig. 1.4).

The conference turned out to be a success. The presentations were great, the discussion was interesting and the audience was engaged. Part II of this book will give a detailed account of the content and interaction among the participants. We were also pleased to see many colleagues, Master and PhD students as well as Postdocs attending and discussing.

We welcomed everybody to the conference and emphasized that this was a bit like a dream becoming true when looking into the round of all distinguished colleagues in international trade, meeting at the same time at the same place for the same reason. Taking the perspective of the person celebrating the jubilee, we

Fig. 1.4 Scientific conference on May 12, 2017, at the University of Basel. Source: Own poster and picture of the participants at the conference

stated that Ricardo would probably have been surprised to see a group like this meeting 200 years after his writing. "Me, a book?".

1.2.4   Act II: Dislocation of R&D? A Panel Discussion

Act II followed on July 20, 2017. The idea of the provocative title "From the Outsourcing of Production to the Dislocation of R&D?" was to attract the interest of people from the region of Basel. The pharmaceutical-chemical industry is a key player in the region. The income traditionally depends to a large extent on the success of this industry. Even though companies such as Novartis, Roche, Lonza, Syngenta or Clariant have been investing considerable amounts in research and development (R&D) in their "home base region", they also support R&D locations abroad all over the world. As a large share of production has been outsourced or offshored over the last decades, people living and working in the region are worried about the fate of the region with respect to R&D activities.

Professor Bradford Jensen from Georgetown University—who has been successful in publishing a number of papers in international trade—informed about his preliminary results of a research project that investigates the globalization of R&D in manufacturing and services. Panelists from Novartis and the local government (Stephan Mumenthaler) and from Lonza (Allison Haitz) shared their own experience and point of view with the speaker and the audience (Fig. 1.5).

Note that the Ricardian trade theory basically implies that an increased fragmentation of the value chain in the chemical-pharmaceutical industry would lead to a finer division of labour between countries. Suppose production and R&D activities can be performed in different locations without that huge additional (fixed) costs arise. This could—in principle—be positive for the region of Basel. If it has a comparative advantage in R&D, but much less in production, the fragmentation

Fig. 1.5 From the outsourcing of production to the dislocation of R&D? Source: Own poster and picture of the event on July 20, 2017 at the University of Basel

helps securing R&D activities at this location. If, however, strong links between production and R&D exists, the verdict may be different.[8] Interestingly, the discussion at the event implied that for some R&D (particularly in the pharmaceutical industry) nearby production seems to remain crucial.

1.2.5 Act III, IV and Epilogue

After the delivery of this manuscript more events took place in the Ricardian Year 2017. Act III focused on the environmental issues of international trade with the title "Globalization, Renewable Resources and the Environment" offered by Professor M. Scott Taylor. This is an interesting subject from the perspective of the current challenges of globalization. It is, however, also interesting from a Ricardian perspective. For many of his analyses, Scott Taylor uses the Ricardian trade model as a foundation (see also Chap. 7 in this book). An example is the Ricardian Gordon-Schaefer model with a Ricardian production possibility frontier which is endogenous to the stock of a resource (see, e.g., Brander & Taylor, 1997).

Act IV was dedicated to a discussion of "Multilateralism versus Regionalism" on November 30, 2017. The question was whether multilateralism based on the multilateral world trade organization (WTO) may gain some momentum as regional agreements tend to be overburdened with regulatory elements that are not directly related to international trade. A panel with trade economists and representatives from the Swiss government and from the WTO was expected to bring light into this matter. Finally, the idea of the "Epilogue: 200 Years of Ricardian Trade Theory" on

---

[8]See, for example, the fragmentation approach by Jones and Kierzkowski presented in Jones (2000).

December 14, 2017 was to look back from the perspective of today's challenges of globalization. The event included the presentation of this book.

1.3 Structure and Contents of the Book

The book is structured into three parts. In the following, we briefly outline the idea of the three parts and present the structure and contents of each chapter.

1.3.1 Part I

Part I "David Ricardo and the Ricardian Trade Theory: 1817 to Today" includes four chapters, i.e., Chaps. 2–5.

In Chap. 2, Thomas Gerber provides insights into David Ricardo's personality, his life, his time and his principles. We find out about Ricardo's thoughts and discussions with respect to the writing of his *On the Principles of Political Economy and Taxation*.

Chapter 3 (Thomas Gerber and Rolf Weder) leads the reader through the original Chapter VII "On Foreign Trade" and discusses some of the key statements David Ricardo made in 1817 from today's perspective.

In Chap. 4, Rolf Weder presents the standard Ricardian trade model based on two, many and a continuum of goods and discusses a number of today's implications and applications of the model in Chap. 5.

1.3.2 Part II

Part II "Scientific Conference 'Celebrating 200 Years of Ricardian Trade Theory' on May 12, 2017 at the University of Basel in Switzerland" includes 13 chapters, i.e., Chaps. 6–18, written for or based on the scientific conference held at the University of Basel in Switzerland. The chapters are very different in length and can be ordered according to the four sessions of 1.5 h each held at the conference.

Session 1 focuses on "The Main Contribution of the Ricardian Trade Theory" and answers questions as: What is the central feature of the theory? Why is it so important? In which way has it shaped international trade theory? It includes Chap. 6 (paper by Ronald W. Jones), Chap. 7 (comments by M. Scott Taylor) and Chap. 8 (discussion chaired by Harris Dellas).

Session 2 focuses on "Mill and Ricardo: The Genesis of Comparative Advantage". It aims to answer questions as: What was the state of the discussion before Ricardo? Was it him who discovered the concept of comparative advantage? Why did David Ricardo come up with this ingenious idea? It includes Chap. 9 (paper by

Roy J. Ruffin), Chap. 10 (comments by Antonio Loprieno) and Chap. 11 (discussion chaired by Carsten Hefeker).

Session 3 focuses on "Putting Ricardian Trade Theory to Work in 2017: Current Empirical Analyses" and answers the following questions: In which way can the theory be empirically tested? What are the results? In which way is the Ricardian trade theory part of this? It includes Chap. 12 (presentation by Jonathan Eaton), Chap. 13 (comments by Peter H. Egger) and Chap. 14 (short discussion chaired by Nicolas Schmitt).

Session 4 focuses on "Aspects of Trade Policy and Challenges for Research in Trade" and includes a panel discussion. It includes Chap. 15 (presentation by Wilfred J. Ethier), Chap. 16 (presentation by Simon Evenett), Chap. 17 (presentation by Esteban Rossi-Hansberg) and Chap. 18 (panel discussion with these three colleagues, chaired by Rolf Weder, and presented by Andrew Lee).

Note that all the chapters, except Chaps. 6 and 9, in Part II are based on transcribed presentations and discussions which were, however, revised by all authors for this book. Names of those in the audience who asked questions are mentioned in the chapters. The chapters thereby convey the lively atmosphere at the conference, include personal notes by the speakers and thus include a "bonanza" of ideas. They are, in our view, a wonderful source of exchanged perspectives, personal experience and expertise.

1.3.3   Part III

Part III "Back to the Future: Challenges of 2017 and the Original Idea of 1817" includes two chapters, i.e., Chaps. 19 and 20.

In Chap. 19, Ronald W. Jones and Rolf Weder start with some current challenges of globalization and then reflect on some of them in the light of the Ricardian trade theory. They emphasize the churning process, the effects of factor mobility and the importance of countries.

In Chap. 20, David Ricardo presents his original "On Foreign Trade" published in 1817 as chapter VII of his *On the Principles of Political Economy and Taxation*.

References

Brander, J. A., & Taylor, M. S. (1997). International trade and open access renewable resources: The small open economy case. *Canadian Journal of Economics, 30*(3), 526–552.

Caves, R. E., Frankel, J. A., & Jones, R. W. (2007). *World trade and payments. An introduction* (10th ed.). Boston: Pearson.

Costinot, A., Donaldson, D., & Komunjer, I. (2012). What goods do countries trade? A quantitative exploration of Ricardo's ideas. *The Review of Economic Studies, 79*(2), 581–608.

Dornbusch, R., Fischer, S., & Samuelson, P. A. (1977). Comparative advantage, trade, and payments in a Ricardian model with a continuum of goods. *The American Economic Review, 67*(5), 823–839.

Eaton, J., & Kortum, S. (2002). Technology, geography, and trade. *Econometrica, 70*(5), 1741–1779.

Eaton, J., Kortum, S., & Kramarz, F. (2011). An anatomy of international trade: Evidence from French firms. *Econometrica, 79*(5), 1453–1498.

Feenstra, R. C. (2016). *Advanced international trade*. Princeton, NJ: Princeton University Press.

Jones, R. W. (1956). Factor proportions and the Heckscher-Ohlin theorem. *The Review of Economic Studies, 24*(1), 1–10.

Jones, R. W. (1965). The structure of simple general equilibrium models. *Journal of Political Economy, 73*(6), 557–572.

Jones, R. W. (1980). Comparative and absolute advantage. *Swiss Journal of Economics and Statistics (SJES), 116*(2), 272–288.

Jones, R. W. (2000). *Globalization and the theory of input trade*. Cambridge, MA: MIT Press.

Jones, R. W. (2008). Heckscher-Ohlin trade flows: A re-appraisal. *Trade and Development Review, 1*(1), 1–6.

Jones, R. W., & Ruffin, R. J. (2008). The technology transfer paradox. *Journal of International Economics, 75*(2), 321–328.

Krugman, P. R. (1996). *Pop internationalism*. Cambridge, MA: MIT Press.

Leontief, W. (1953). Domestic production and foreign trade; the American capital position re-examined. *Proceedings of the American Philosophical Society, 97*(4), 332–349.

Melitz, M. J. (2003). The impact of trade on intra-industry reallocations and aggregate industry productivity. *Econometrica, 71*(6), 1695–1725.

Rybczynski, T. M. (1955). Factor endowment and relative commodity prices. *Economica, 22*(88), 336–341.

Samuelson, P. A. (2004). Where Ricardo and Mill rebut and confirm arguments of mainstream economists supporting globalization. *The Journal of Economic Perspectives, 18*(3), 135–146.

Sraffa, P. (2005). *The works and correspondance of David Ricardo* (11 Vols.). Indianapolis: Liberty Fund.

Stolper, W. F., & Samuelson, P. A. (1941). Protection and real wages. *The Review of Economic Studies, 9*(1), 58–73.

Weder, R., & Wyss, S. (2013). Do vertical linkages limit protectionism? Switzerland in the multifibre arrangement. *The World Economy, 36*(10), 1261–1277.

Part I
David Ricardo and the Ricardian Trade Theory: 1817 to Today

Part I takes the reader back to David Ricardo as a person and to his writings, and discusses extracts from his "On Foreign Trade". It presents the standard Ricardian trade theory and shows important implications and applications from the perspective of today's world economy.

Portrait of Ricardo: Copy from Henderson/Davis (1997): The Life and Economics of David Ricardo. Springer Verlag, page V.
Signature: Copy from Sraffa (2005): The Works and Correspondence of David Ricardo. Vol. X. Liberty Fund, page 108.

Chapter 2
David Ricardo: His Personality, His Times and His Principles

Thomas Gerber

Abstract This chapter introduces the reader to the life and the early work of David Ricardo. The first section gives a brief portrait of Ricardo as successful businessman, political economist and Member of Parliament. The second section elucidates Ricardo's emerging theory of international trade in the light of war, social distress and the Corn Laws. Finally, the third section traces the transition from Ricardo's early work to his main opus *On the Principles of Political Economy and Taxation*.

Whoever concerns themselves with David Ricardo's personality, his biography or his achievements is intrigued by the man, who is regarded as one of the key figures in the history of economic thought. Obviously, there have been some critical refutations of many of his theoretical considerations, a prominent example being the famous labor theory of value, which many would say should be relegated to a museum of economic theory. Yet on the other hand, there is the ingenuity and brilliance of his contribution to trade theory, a theory that stands firm as one of the great masterpieces in the history of economic thought and still serves as point of reference in the discipline of international trade theory. Moreover, the man who created the first (real) system of political economy not only pointed the way to modern economics with his methodological approach and his use of mathematical and tabular expression, but also created and shaped the field itself.

The man, who was able to do that, is presented in the first section of this chapter. Ricardo excelled in three different careers; we thus have a brief look at each of them. In the second section the focus lies on Ricardo's times; it shows in which circumstances his early theories developed. Mainly, we have a look at two important trade debates. The last section finally shows the transition to his main opus and most influential contribution *On the Principles of Political Economy and Taxation*.

T. Gerber (✉)
Faculty of Business and Economics, University of Basel, Basel, Switzerland
e-mail: thomas.gerber@unibas.ch

© Springer International Publishing AG 2017
R.W. Jones, R. Weder (eds.), *200 Years of Ricardian Trade Theory*,
https://doi.org/10.1007/978-3-319-60606-4_2

2.1   Life and Personality

Little in the matter was expected from young David, who was born as 1 of 17 children in London on April 18, 1772.[1] His father Abraham Israel Ricardo was a businessman—a stockbroker, who moved from Amsterdam to London around 1760. David Ricardo's grandfather and uncles were likewise engaged in the financial market in Holland. It thus appears almost as a predefined path for him to commit his abilities and his strengths early on to the same branch of activity. Not much is known otherwise of those years as a boy and young teenager. Ricardo was sent at the age of 11 for educational purposes to Amsterdam. When he returned 2 years later, he soon started to work with his father at the London Stock Exchange. He had just turned 14.

Ricardo's father, described by his brother Moses as, " a man of good intellect, but uncultivated" (Vol. X, p. 5),[2] allegedly put some early pressure on Ricardo. In a letter by Maria Edgeworth to her mother, she quotes Ricardo in these words:

> My father gave me but little education. He thought reading, writing and arithmetic sufficient because he doomed me to be nothing but a man of business. (Colvin, 1971, p. 266)

Moses further talks about David Ricardo's father as someone who based his opinions in religion, education or politics upon those of his forefathers without questioning or reassessing them (Vol. X, p. 5). The lack of education, at least as felt by Ricardo, and an uncritical contemplation of things were two constituent elements for Ricardo in his later life. The wavering doubts as to abilities, visible in his letters in the forefront of the publication of *On the Principles of Political Economy and Taxation* bear witness to feelings of vulnerability. They accompanied Ricardo throughout his life. These doubts, however, were mainly dedicated to the "arrangement" of his texts and the rhetorical aspects of his verbal expression. Uncritical— the other aspect of the father's uncharming description—is surely a term that does not match with Ricardo's almost rigorous methodological approach and his inner quest to find the true principles of political economy in the absence of dogma and tradition.

The truth concerning Ricardo's education and his father might however be more differentiated than it seems to be at first glance. In the *Memoir* Moses declines the idea, supposedly around at the time, that Ricardo was of "very low origin" and "that

---

[1] A more detailed account on David Ricardo's biography can be found in the early sketches of his life by his brother, Moses Ricardo, from 1824 (Vol. X, pp. 1–13, see footnote 2), his acquaintance J. R. McCulloch (1825) or in the more recent biographies by Weatherall (1976) or Henderson and Davis (1997). Consult further Sraffa's (Vol. X) biographical notes on Ricardo and King's (2013) work on Ricardo's life and work.

[2] Note that the main source of Ricardo's writings is the eleven-volume edition of "The Works and Correspondence of David Ricardo" (edited by Piero Sraffa and Maurice Dobb). Throughout the text only the volume and the page are cited (for example: Vol. IV, p. 15). The selected quotations in the text should be attributable to the authors from the context.

he had been wholly denied the advantages of education." (Vol. X, p. 4). Abraham Ricardo's name stood not only "for honour and integrity" but was also "able and willing to afford his children all the advantages which the line of life for which they were destined appeared to require." (ibid). The myth of educational deprivation, which was even put forward to a certain degree by Ricardo himself, is thus not entirely true. Ricardo may have lacked an academic background, unlike the other political economists of the day; nevertheless, he was born into a well-to-do family.

2.1.1   Ricardo as a Businessman

With his entrance into the business world, David Ricardo began the first of three careers at the age of 14. His father did not hesitate to "place great confidence" in Ricardo's abilities, even equipping him with "such power as it is rarely granted to persons considerably older than himself." (ibid). The true test not only of his capabilities in business but also of his character development was yet to come. The latent conflict with his father finally erupted when Ricardo turned 21. His love for and later marriage to Pricilla Ann Wilkinson, a Quaker, led to a break with his Sephardic Jewish heritage and ultimately with his mother and his father. Apparently his parents could not accept Ricardo's chosen wife with her Christian beliefs. Thus as a very young man, he not only lost the support of his parents, but found himself suddenly standing on his own two feet as an independent businessman.

Yet Ricardo, having already shown aptitude, had managed to make a name for himself under his father's care. For the first steps on his own, he received financial help from other members of the Exchange. From that point on, Ricardo's path toward becoming one of the richest people in England opened up fast. In those early years he worked mainly as a stock jobber, an activity that ensured the liquidity of the market, due to the fact that jobbers were always ready to sell or buy their assets at a certain price. As Weatherall (1976) pointed out, the main quality of a nineteenth century jobber was good sense and a remarkably accurate anticipation of the fluctuations of the market. Because time was the crucial aspect in selling or buying an asset, this sense of the market divided a good jobber from a bad one. And Ricardo apparently was a very good one.

After his start as a jobber, Ricardo became a broker, and ultimately a contractor. The government needed to borrow money (loan) for their expenditures. Thus they issued various forms of financial securities. A contractor could bid for these securities. In order to do that he needed financiers willing to back him with the necessary amount of money. With this money the contractor could make a competitive bid against other contractors. This auction was enhanced by the Chancellor of the Exchequer. Once a contractor had won the competitive bidding, he sold these securities in smaller portions to minor investors and thus earned money. The art of bidding was to find the lowest price compared to that of competitors but one that was also acceptable to the bidder (see Vol. X, pp. 75–80).

Ricardo seemed to have the gift of calculating that price very convincingly. He won against other competitors in 1807 and for five consecutive years starting in 1811. The largest amount of money that Ricardo made as a contractor was in 1815 when the war between France and England reached its final stage. The bidding took place a few days before the Battle of Waterloo, which, because of its uncertain outcome, dragged prices down to a very low level. The news of Wellington's victory brought not only joy to English citizens but also "the largest single profit" (Vol. X, p. 83) made by Ricardo due to the rising prices of the purchased assets.

In his years in business David Ricardo showed a remarkable ability to make money. This is owing, as some quotes reveal, to his abstract, pragmatic and logical thinking. He did not particularly speculate, as Mallet wrote, and generally aimed to "realise a small percentage upon a large sum." (Higgs, 1921, p. 206). He was also rational enough to correctly perceive people's eagerness to over- or underestimate events and developing circumstances. Bowring, a fellow political economist, states that Ricardo observed "that people in general exaggerated the importance of events." (Vol. X, p. 73). And Moses talks not only about his brother's "quickness at figures and calculation" or "his coolness and judgment" but sees in Ricardo's gaining of tremendous wealth the area in which he best demonstrated his "extraordinary powers" (Vol. X, p. 6). Hollander explained Ricardo's achievements in the financial world later in these words:

(...) the most conspicuous fact was a remarkable degree of what might be described as mental disassociation. Ricardo was able to view—to the extent that no economist before or since has attained—a complex phenomenon, to single out therefrom one primary element and to trace its ultimate course free from the modifying or counteracting influence of opposed forces. (Hollander, 1911, pp. 74–75)

Part of this statement could easily be applied to Ricardo's second career, as it is what made him brilliant there as well.

2.1.2 Ricardo as a Political Economist

In 1799, David Ricardo experienced an impact that later developed into to a crucial force, for it was personal tragedy that led Ricardo and his wife to Bath. Priscilla had given birth to a stillborn child and in their attempt to overcome the loss, they went to a sanitarium there. One day, when Ricardo was walking through the fashionable town, he must have entered a bookstore or a library. There he came upon a copy of Adam Smith's "Wealth of Nations". This first contact with Smith's monumental contribution marks the beginning of another major aspect of Ricardo's life—an aspect in which he would show as much talent and genius as in business—that of political economy.

Ricardo was to stay in business for another 16 years but his leisure was surely marked by a new all-consuming activity. After making a huge fortune in the aftermath of the Battle of Waterloo in 1815, Ricardo started to explore in depth the new science of political economy. He bought an estate in Gloucestershire called Gatcombe Park and withdrew more and more from his activities on the Stock Exchange. Nonetheless, Ricardo managed to increase his fortune in those latter years through investments in some assets (e.g., French National securities and land). But he mainly devoted his time to political economy.

Some of his friends were worried that Ricardo might spend his time otherwise. A friend states in a letter with some irony: "So you have given up the Stock Exchange, and taken to farming" (Vol. VI, p. 149). Ricardo was quick to answer and admitted his enjoyment of the "calm repose of a country life" (Vol. VI, p. 150), describing himself as only sufficiently interested in the procedures of farming. What he was really doing though was working on his masterpiece, albeit with difficulty, as this letter from 1815 shows:

> You observe justly that having friends staying with us unsettles our regular habits. I find it very materially to interfere with my pursuits. Reading or writing, when one has an object in view, should be followed systematically, and at no distant intervals, for after a time our thoughts are turned into new channels and we cannot easily recall the ideas which were only beginning to be indistinctly formed in our minds. (Vol. VI, pp. 315–316)

Another facet of Ricardo's personality shines through this excerpt. Eventually becoming the father of three sons and five daughters, Ricardo was a very sociable person and had any number of guests and parties at Gatcombe. During these years he also kept a house in London at 56, Upper Brook Street and regularly stayed there for a few months at a time. Sometimes the weather in Gatcombe helped him concentrate, but the frequent presence of guests was not conducive to his work:

> I have hitherto had little temptation to desert my work for the pleasure of walking or riding, as the weather has been almost uniformly bad—yet I have not been able wholly to seclude myself from morning intruders. (Vol. VII, p. 54)

Despite interruptions, most of his time in these years was spent thinking and writing about fundamental economic principles.

2.1.3 Ricardo as a Politician

As early as 1815, James Mill, an intimate friend of Ricardo's, asked of him nothing more than his devotion to politics. "You now can have no excuse", Mill writes in a letter "for not going into parliament, and doing what you can to improve the most imperfect instrument of government." As a political economist Ricardo was, in Mill's perception, a clear asset to parliament, which was generally, as depicted by Mill, in a poor state. Ricardo would therefore not only "have no match" and be "a very instructive" and "a very impressive speaker" on the subjects of political economy, but also be one of the rare politicians that stand firm on ethical and moral grounds. Mill writes: "I do question whether another man would be found in it (the parliament), not ready to sell his country" and attributes Ricardo as "thoroughly honest" and as somebody that would do nothing that is "not purely and genuinely thought right." (Vol. VI, p. 253). Thus began David Ricardo's third career in 1819, when he became a member of parliament, i.e. a politician.[3]

Mr. Brougham, a fellow politician, saw in Ricardo someone who "had dropped from another planet." (Vol. V, p. 56). Evidently his approach to solving the problems of the time was—given his background as a theorist—a bit different. It would though be wrong to reduce Ricardo to an "ultra-abstract economist", who failed to offer practical and useful advice (Milgate & Stimson, 1991). Ricardo was of course talking in parliament about important economic policy questions; currency issues, taxation or governmental expenditure. He also addressed numerous other questions, on which he held a liberal view (the right to protest, religious tolerance). At the end of his political career (due to his early death) the perception of him changed. Brougham wrote later:

> There was something about him, chiefly a want of all affectation as well as pretension in everything he said or did, that won the respect of every party. (...) Few men have, accordingly, had more weight in Parliament; certainly none who, (...), might be said generally to speak against the sense of the audience, ever commanded a more patient or more favourable hearing; and, as this was effected without any of the more ordinary powers of oratory or of entertainment possessed by others, it might be regarded as the triumph of reason, intelligence, and integrity over untoward circumstances and alien natures. (Vol. V, xxxii–xxxiv)

And Mallet, his friend, wrote about Ricardo as a politician:

> Ricardo was a bold man; and he was bold because he reasoned thoroughly with himself, and carefully examined the opinions which he adopted. (...) His knowledge of mankind, and of political society was chiefly acquired in books, and wanted the test of experience; but although he was a thorough reformer, and an advocate for universal suffrage, and vote by ballot, no man was less of a revolutionist in principle: he was, on the contrary humane, considerate and just in all his views. (Higgs, 1921, pp. 209–210)

2.1.4 Ricardo as a Person

Throughout his whole life, Ricardo's character was described as amiable. It is at least surprising that a man, who was not only tremendously successful in his different careers but who also took some firm stands against prevailing opinions or circumstances, attracted little real criticism. On the contrary, in one of the most famous (and rare) descriptions of his personality, Maria Edgeworth, wrote:

> Mr. Ricardo, with a very composed manner, has a continual life of mind, and starts perpetually new game in conversation. I never argued or discussed a question with any person who argues more fairly or less for victory and more for truth. He gives full weight to every argument brought against him, and seems not to be on any side of the question for one instant longer than the conviction of his mind on that side. It seems indifferent to him

---

[3]A more detailed description of Ricardo's political career can be found e.g.: Cannan (1894), Milgate and Stimson (1991), Gordon (1976).

whether you find the truth, or whether he finds it, provided it be found. (Vol. X, pp. 168–169)

And in his brother's *Memoir* there is a warm acknowledgment of Ricardo's integrity that expressed itself in his strong advocacy for general principles that often even harmed his own interests. Moses gives some examples:

When a Bank (of England) proprietor, he argued strenuously and warmly against the inordinate gains of that body; he defended the cause of the fund-holders when he had ceased to be one; he was accused of an attempt to ruin the landed interest after he became a large landed proprietor; and while a member of parliament, he advocated the cause of reform, which, if adopted, would have deprived him of his seat. (Vol. X, p. 13)

David Ricardo died in consequence of an ear infection at Gatcombe in 1823. He was only 51 years old.

2.2   Ricardo's Time and His Early Contributions

Ricardo's first contribution to the emerging science of political economy came to the public unknowingly. He wrote an anonymous letter to the *Morning Chronicle* in 1809, in which he discussed the depreciation of notes issued by the Bank of England (and private banks). Two letters followed after the topic had gained the attention of other writers; this time he signed his contributions simply with the letter *R*. His pamphlet in 1810, however, *The High Price of Bullion, a Proof of the Depreciation of Bank Notes* carried his name and brought him instant fame. The discussion's origins lay in the increasing threat to financial stability in Britain.

The war against Napoleon's France resulted in vast expenditure and substantially increased the national debt. When France declared war against England in 1793 the total national debt was around 234,035,716 pounds; 22 years later the debt had quadrupled to 834,252,726 pounds (Henderson & Davis, 1997, p. 196). This debt had to be financed. And after rumors of a French invasion of Britain led to a bank run, the government abolished the convertibility of bank notes to bullion (cash). The risk of the Bank of England going bankrupt was too high. The abolition of convertibility was later made permanent by the Bank Restriction Act of 1797. The debt could thus be financed by a rising money supply through issuing new bank notes. Indeed, the note circulation in England expanded from 10–11 million in 1795 to around 20 million in 1808 (Inglis Palgrave, 1901, p. 191). Furthermore, inflation and the disruption in foreign exchange rates were pressing on the British economy (Henderson & Davis, 1997, p. 197). Ricardo suspected the Bank of England of exploiting the Act and thus of being harmful to the economy. Ricardo's writings in these years, as Weatherall (1976) suggests, were one of the reasons that led finally to the appointment of a Select Committee in the House of Commons.

This Committee had the task of further examining the matter and proposing suitable policy measures. They soon published their *Bullion Report* and Ricardo his second pamphlet *A Reply to Mr. Bosanquet's Practical Observations of the Report of the Bullion Committee.* For the first time, the young businessman, provocatively called "a philosopher who writes in the Chronicle" (Weatherall, 1976, p. 58), showed early hints of his future status and influence. The Bank Restriction Act was finally repealed by parliament in 1819. The plan to do so originated from the appendix of the fourth edition of Ricardo's first pamphlet, and was given the name "Mr. Ricardo's Plan".

Ricardo's strength in theorizing and in abstract reasoning can already be seen in these first publications. Although he was familiar with currency and monetary issues through his daily work—"he knew the facts" (Mitchell, 1967, p. 269)—he broached the topic in his pamphlet with a far-fetched generalization, namely with "what he (Ricardo) calls the laws that regulate the distribution of precious metals throughout the world." (ibid.) But Ricardo was not, as the quote above suggests, "a philosopher" in an ivory tower, but a man who used generalizations in order to overcome "temporary" and non-lasting effects and circumstances. Attention to facts alone, as Ricardo wrote programmatically in his second pamphlet, does not suffice, when no theory is attached to it. Men without theory "can hardly ever sift their facts. They are credulous, and necessarily so, because they have no standard of reference." (Vol. III, p. 181). For some, Ricardo went too far in his abstract thinking. Some fame can be linked with the term "Ricardian Vice", attributed to Ricardo's method by Joseph Schumpeter. Schumpeter described Ricardo's theoretical approach critically:

> (...) he cut that general system to pieces, bundled up as large parts of it as possible, and put them in cold storage-so that as many things as possible should be frozen and 'given'. He then piled one simplifying assumption upon another until, having really settled everything by these assumption, (...) he set up simple one-way relations so that, in the end, the desired results emerged almost as tautologies. (Schumpeter, 1955, pp. 472–473)

After the Bullion Controversy, David Ricardo's attention shifted to another topic that was no less acute in England. Again the "theorist" attached his thoughts to a genuinely practical question. As Hollander (1910, p. 58) put it in a broader perspective, Ricardo's writings and correspondence were "in no small degree a reflex of the stirring economic events of the period". Or as Hartwell (1971, p. 7) said, "Ricardo's writing is a good chronological guide to Britain's economic problems".

2.2.1 Agriculture as the Source of National Wealth and Eighteenth Century Rule

Agriculture and foreign trade was an issue in England in the early years of the eighteenth century, even before the famous Corn Law debate evolved. Ricardo was occupied with his financial matters when a highly controversial pamphlet circulated in England. After Napoleon enforced the Continental Blockade in order to restrict and even cut off English trade, the British intelligentsia must certainly have felt the appeal of theories developed by a group of French economists around Mirabeau, Quesnay or Turgot. But in the end it was William Spence, an entomologist, who was tempted to adopt their theory and popularize their teachings in England. In his pamphlet *Britain Independent of Commerce* Spence tried to establish the physiocratic view that agriculture is the only source of wealth to a nation. A convenient theory for a truncated island! According to its claims, all other economic activities, e.g. manufacture or commerce (trade), cannot increase national wealth.

The reason lies in a particular idea attributed to agricultural production. Only there does *nature* add a surplus product to the work of men, which farmers pay to the landowner in the form of a rent. This product creates value and thus enriches the country. All other professions and industries alter given values, but do not create them. A carpenter, for example, needs raw material for production, as well as a sufficient level of food, etc. for him to produce a table. The value of this table corresponds in the end to the first two ingredients and thus no value has been created. William Spence also saw in foreign trade only a transformation but not a creation of value. It is mostly a zero-sum game and a transaction of equalities. Furthermore he even sees in the recourse to old mercantile ideas a disadvantage in foreign trade for England. Whereas British exports are mostly durable and solid goods (machines, clothes, etc.), imports comprise mostly luxury goods (tobacco, wine, sugar) and are widely used and thus do not have much value for the future from a "national point of view" (Spence, 1807, p. 50).

Although he adjusts the theory slightly to British circumstances, he sticks with the main assumptions of the French economists. It is agriculture alone that contributes to the wealth of a nation. The surplus, paid as rent, is the source of value creation. These few terms; *agriculture*, *value*, *rent* or *trade* will become the major theme of Ricardo's second appearance as a political economist. Yet some other theorists had first to reply to Spence's publication. There were about 30 responses in all, whereby two particular pamphlets were relevant for Ricardo's future. One was by James Mill (*Commerce Defended*) and the other one by Robert Torrens (*The Economists Refuted*). The former almost certainly fell into the hands of Ricardo, who, as an interested reader, soon tried to meet with the author. That meeting is assumed to have led to the closeness and lifelong friendship between James Mill and David Ricardo (Mitchell, 1949, p. 132). Of course both authors reject Spence's and the French economists' doctrine of agricultural superiority and their obscure perspectives on value.

However, and most importantly, they tried to defend the true value of foreign trade. Both authors argue in a setting which was later named by Viner the "eighteenth-century rule", a name given after the discovery of the concept in an anonymous work from 1701 (Viner, 1937, p. 104). Viner described the rule in these words:

> (. . .) the rule, namely, that it pays to import commodities from abroad whenever they can be obtained in exchange for exports at a smaller real cost than their production at home would entail. (Viner, 1937, p. 440)

In recourse to Adam Smith, James Mill understands commerce to be "an extension of that division of labour" that ultimately brings "so many benefits (...) upon the human race." (Mill, 1808, p. 38). Because of that process labor in different countries will move to its most productive areas. In Mill's fundamental statement, he says:

> (...) the sole question is, whether a particular description of wants can be most cheaply supplied at home or abroad. If a certain number of manufacturers employed at home can, while they are consuming 100 quarters of corn, fabricate a quantity of goods, which goods will purchase abroad a portion of supply to some of the luxurious wants to the community which it would have required the consumption of 150 quarters at home to produce; in this case too the country is 50 quarters the richer for the importation. It has the same supply of luxuries for 50 quarters of corn less, than if that supply had been prepared at home. (Mill, 1808, p. 38)

Torrens argues also in line with the division of labor argument. He differentiates the idea into territorial and geographical divisions and introduces the term of a "territorial division of labour" (Torrens, 1808, p. 14). In Torrens' main statement he points out the possible gains from trade:

> Thus, if I wish to know the extent of the advantage which arises to England, from her giving France a hundred pounds' worth of broad cloth in exchange for a hundred pounds' worth of lace, I take the quantity of lace which England has acquired by this transaction, and compare it with the quantity which she might, at the same expense of labour and capital, have acquired by manufacturing it at home. The lace that remains, beyond what the labour and capital employed on the cloth might have fabricated at home, is the amount of the advantage which England derives from the exchange. (Torrens, 1808, p. 53)

Both authors tried to defend trade by showing how the possible gains of trade arise from it. Their main statement might be summarized thus: it is advantageous for a country to shift its resources to a productive industry. These goods will then be shipped and sold in foreign countries. In return for them, England can import a good formerly produced at home, at lower costs than the domestic production costs. Clearly, they recognize the notion of "indirect production" from which the gains from trade arise. This is not yet the famous principle of comparative advantage, but the reader may well guess why there is, according to Viner (1937, p. 441), only "a sole addition of consequence" necessary to arrive at Ricardo's ingenious principle (See Chaps. 3 and 9 in this book).

2.2.2 Increasing Prices and Distress

The war and the blockade against England not only shook the foundations of the importance of trade in its entirety; it also led to a much more influential discussion of the required restrictions of trade. This time David Ricardo was one of the central figures in the discussion. The political economists of that day had to pay attention to the dramatic price increase of corn. The burden of a high price was felt first and foremost by the working class, who had difficulty paying for a sufficient amount of bread, wheat and so on. This led ultimately to a rising tension in society, which expressed itself in violent clashes and riots.[4]

Society and the economy in England were in a time of upheaval, facing new problems and challenges. The growing amount of manufactured goods, slowly heralding the coming period of industrialization, and the migration from more rural areas to the cities (especially London) or the ongoing urbanization, increasingly undermined the long-lasting dominance of landowners and landlords. England was—as we would say 200 years later—on the verge of becoming a modern industrialized state in the beginning of the nineteenth century. But the most dramatic change was recognized in population growth. The population growth rates were at a very low and constant annual level of around 0.46% for almost half a century before 1780. After 1780, the rate went up to nearly 10% per decade and ultimately reached a peak in Ricardo's most active period as a political scientist, between 1811 and 1821. The population growth rate in these 10 years lay at around 17% (Mathias, 1983, pp. 166–167).

Thomas Robert Malthus, who became one of Ricardo's dearest friends and stimulating conversation partners, had published *An Essay on the Principle of Population* in 1798. In that pamphlet, Malthus, alarmed by the increasing population growth, expressed a gloomy perspective on the future development of society. He depicted a future of epidemics, wars and famine, so-called "positive checks" triggered by uncontrolled population growth. This growth rate of the population would "when unchecked increase in a geometrical ratio." The level of subsistence would rise, however, only in "an arithmetical ratio." (Malthus 1798 (1909), p. 7). The cultivation of new land or the technological improvements to increase agricultural production thus would not suffice. This hypothesis cast a shadow over a previously optimistic view of the natural progress of society and brought with it the notion of economics as a dismal science. Ricardo would later share this pessimistic view.

Indeed one might have been able to recognize in the early decades of the nineteenth century some evidence for these assumptions. The population grew fast and the price of grain rose year after year and thus brought the poorer classes to the absolute limits of their own subsistence (Table 2.1).

The rising demand due to an increasing population was however not the only rationale for high prices. The high costs caused by the restriction of trade due to the blockade and the distortion of the currency also played a role. To make matters even worse, England was hit by a few very bad harvests that in the early years of the nineteenth century reduced the supply and increased the prices as well. All of these elements, including "the improved knowledge of agriculture" and "the enclosure of common-fields" further magnified another important economic factor: rent (Thompson, 1907, p. 589).

---

[4]See for example or Stevenson (1974) or Booth (1977).

Years	Average prices of a quarter of wheat
1711–1794	45s. (price never above 60s and 5¼ d.)
1780–1789	45s. 9d.
1790–1799	55s. 11d.
1800–1809	82s. 2d.
1810–1813	106s. 2d.

Table 2.1 Average price of a quarter of wheat (Cannan, 1903, p. 149)

2.2.3   Corn Law Debate

Political economists at that time were mostly engaged with economic theory, when there was some policy measure or some legislative action involved, an element of additional current importance. This additional ingredient was the Corn Law debate. England became, as the negative trade balance of corn suggests, a regular importer of corn or other grains from foreign countries from 1770 onward (Turner, 1986, p. 113). Since 1791, and driven by the interests of the land-owning class, England had introduced a duty on the importation of foreign wheat. Whenever the domestic price of corn fell below a certain threshold, an additional tariff was slapped on foreign producers' prices. Due to the price increase of corn, this threshold was raised in 1804 and another attempt was made in 1813 (when due to unusually good harvest the price of corn temporarily fell) to increase it to an even higher level.

In 1813 Parliament decided to instruct a committee with the objective of suggesting an appropriate policy measure (i.e., the appropriate price level). Their findings were—and it should not be surprising, when the composition of parliament is considered—indeed in favor of more restrictive terms in foreign trade, that is, of an increment in the threshold.[5] The discussions in political and intellectual circles in London must have been greatly affected by the discussions and thoughts of the committee. Evidence for this is the series of pamphlets (once again) that were published at the beginning of 1815. Malthus published *An Inquiry into the Nature and Progress of Rent* and *Grounds of an Opinion*. West's *An Essay on the Application of Capital* together with Torrens' *An Essay on the External Corn Trade* followed.

Although David Ricardo had been occupied by a slightly different topic, he was able to publish his *An Essay on the Influence of a Low Price of Corn on the Profits of Stock* (Essay on Profit) after he had read Malthus' pamphlet within just a few days. The issue at stake was a topic that had originated with Smith, who stated that capital accumulation was accompanied by a fall in the rate of profit. Evidently this was not the case; both numbers had been rising since 1793 (Meek, 1976, p. 89). But as Sraffa noted, these topics all had for Ricardo an inner relation to each other or as Sraffa expressed it:

---

[5]Behind this imposition was also the idea that it would stimulate agricultural production and thus lead to more cultivation and a greater domestic supply. The idea of self-sufficiency does not, in the light of the long war and blockade, seem entirely unreasonable.

> (...) by using his already developed theory of profits, incorporating Malthus's theory of
> rent, and adding a refutation of the protectionists' arguments put forward by Malthus in his
> *Grounds of Opinion*. (Vol. IV, p. 4)

All of these pamphlets had some striking similarities,[6] despite the fact that they
were mostly independent of each other. It is probably one of the rare occasions
where a "multiple discovery" is so much in evidence.[7] All of these pamphlets
entailed, among other ideas, a conception of rent and all of them pushed the notion
of diminishing returns into a prominent light. Concerning rent, Ricardo took his
general ideas from Malthus, to whom he referred prominently in his essay. He also
follows Malthus' premise of different rates in the population and in subsistence;
indeed, diminishing returns is an expression of the slow(er) rate of the amount of
agricultural produce.

2.2.4   Ricardian Rent Theory

Ricardo exemplifies the theory—which is generically called "Ricardian Rent Theory"—with settlers who arrive on new land. The first settlers will settle on rich and
fertile land. They will receive, after they subtract the outgoings connected with
cultivation, an amount that belongs fully to the owner of the capital and thus
consists in its entirety of profits of capital. The settler or farmer in this example is
thus also the capitalist. The population might increase and the demand for agricultural produce rise. New settlers will arrive to produce more corn. But, they either
have to go to land of inferior quality or to land that is far away from the market-
place. In both cases the farmer needs more capital to yield the same amount of
produce. This leads ultimately to a decreasing rate of profit. The farmer on the last
productive field needing the highest amount of capital to produce determines the
general profit of capital; in the words of Ricardo: "(the rate of profit is) regulated by
the profits made on the least profitable employment of capital on agriculture"
(Vol. IV, p. 13).

Rent is now most importantly not a "new creation of revenue, but always part of
a revenue already created." (Vol. IV, p. 18). Between rent and profit there is an
inverse relationship. Whereas the rate of profit decreases, the rent increases.
Ricardo shows this theory by the "clearest model that he ever produced" (King,
2013, p. 61) and by a sophisticated tabular expression of his idea (an excerpt of the
original depiction is shown in table 2.2).

For simplicity we shall just look at the case of two different qualities of land to
show this relationship: In the second line 210 quarters of wheat are used as
advanced capital for agricultural production (10 more than in the best suited
land). The net produce, or in other words the output minus the outgoings

---

[6]See for example (Blaug, 1958, pp. 6–7).

[7]In the words of Mitchell: "(...) is an interesting example of how, when times are ripe, intellectual
discovery seems to occur to different minds at about the same time." (Mitchell, 1967, p. 283).

Table 2.2 Excerpt of Ricardo's original table (Vol. IV, p. 17)

Capital estimated in quarters of wheat	Profit per cent	Neat produce in quarters of wheat after paying the cost of production on each capital	Profit of the 1st portion of land in quarters of wheat	Rent of the 1st portion of land in quarters of wheat	Profit of the 2d portion of land in quarters of wheat	Rent of the 2d portion of land in quarters of wheat	Profit of the 3d portion of land in quarters of wheat	Rent of the 3d portion of land in quarters of wheat	Profit of the 4d portion of land in quarters of wheat	Rent of the 4d portion of land in quarters of wheat
200	50	100	100	None						
210	43	90	86	14	90	None				
220	36	80	72	28	76	14	80	None		
230	30	70	60	40	63	27	66	14	70	None

(wages, etc.) is 90 measured in quarters of wheat (whole produce is still 300 (300−210 = 90)). The rate of profit is thus:

$$\frac{90}{210} = 43\% \tag{2.1}$$

Before this second section of land was cultivated the rate of profit on the first was 50%. Because the last productive land determines the general rate of profit at 43%, the difference now has to lie in the appearance of a rent. Therefore, the new situation for the farmer on the first section of land is: instead of a profit of 100 quarters of wheat, he will only get 86 quarters; 14 quarters will have to be paid as rent. Table 2.2 is dynamic, in so far as every cultivation of new land adds a new column to the right. The division between profit and rent appears natural or as Ricardo puts it as evident:

> And that such a division must take place is evident, when we consider that the owner of the capital of the value of two hundred and ten quarters of wheat would obtain precisely the same profit, whether he cultivated the distant land, or paid the first settler fourteen quarters for rent. (Vol. IV, p. 13)

Ricardo showed by the tabular expression and his corresponding explanation that at least in agricultural production Smith was right with his hypothesis of a decreasing rate of profit with an increasing capital accumulation. Ricardo was, as it seems, almost astonished himself by this discovery. He says:

> This is a view of the effects of accumulation which is exceedingly curious, and has, I believe, never before been noticed. (Vol. IV, p. 16)

And so, according to Ricardo, "there are hardly no limits to the rise of rent, and the fall of profit." (Vol. IV, p. 14).

Ricardo then turns his attention to the price of corn and sees its rise as something that can "naturally be expected under such circumstances." (Vol. IV, p. 19). As we have seen, the high price of corn was a clear fact at that time and led to much distress and even riots in England. The price or in the terms of Ricardo, the exchangeable value of a good, here of corn, is determined by the "difficulties in the production". It is obvious that more intensive or more extended agriculture increases the cost of obtaining food and thus leads to the high price of corn and to a high rent. Note here again that it is not the high rent that leads to a high price, but a high price that consists of a high rent.

2.2.5   Classes, Distribution and Trade

The next step for Ricardo is to think about the distributional effects of the high price of corn. And quite clearly, a high price of corn and high rent is in the greatest interest of the landlords. The famous dictum, thus, is:

> It follows then, that the interest of the landlord is always opposed to the interest of every
> other class in the community. (Vol. IV, p. 21)

The other classes are harmed by the high prices. The capitalist is punished two-fold by the rise of the rent: firstly, his rate of profit decreases as a consequence of the increased rent and, secondly, due to the common assumption of the time that the cost of corn determines the wage of the laborers. The wage of the working class had to meet their subsistence level. If the price of corn rose, the capitalist consequently had higher expenses and again his profits suffered. Especially the rising numbers of manufacturers were frightened by the prospect of higher production costs and a competitive disadvantage against foreign competitors.

With Ricardo's view of society as divisible into distinct classes, the conceptual framework in economic theory changed. There is a struggle between these classes, there are strong interests opposing each other and there are current problems of distributional matters that slow economic development in England. It is thus pro-grammatic when Ricardo expresses his fundamental approach to economics in the first lines of the *Principles of Political Economy and Taxation (Principles)*:

> The produce of the earth—all that is derived from its surface by the united application of
> labour, machinery, and capital, is divided among three classes of the community; namely,
> the proprietor of the land, the owner of the stock or capital necessary for its cultivation, and
> the labourers by whose industry it is cultivated. But in different stages of society, the
> proportions of the whole produce of the earth which will be allotted to each of these classes,
> will be essentially different; (...) To determine the laws which regulate this distribution is
> the principal problem in Political Economy. (Vol. I, p. 5)

In the world of Adam Smith economic growth was regarded as something uni-vocally good for all; now, with Ricardo, the classes are seen to conflict in their interests and in constant competition.

The economy is in a state of distress due to the high price of corn. Ricardo sees in his *Essay on Profit* three possible solutions to reducing the price. Apart from a general fall in real wages, they are "improvements in agriculture or implements in husbandry" or "the discovery of new markets, from whence corn may be imported at a cheaper price than it can be grown at home." (Vol. IV, p. 22) With the latter the possible role of foreign trade in the issue is set; the importation of corn—as long as the foreign corn is cheaper—sets a new level of domestic production. Cultivated land on inferior soil will therefore be relinquished and the least productive farmers will no longer have an economic basis to sustain production. A more productive farmer, compared with the previous situation, will now be at the margin and deter-mine the rate of profits. Undoubtedly, with the lower price of corn, the rate of profit will increase, whereas rent will decrease.

In view of the political debate surrounding the Corn Law controversy it is thus only consistent when Ricardo writes as his policy recommendation:

> If we were left to ourselves, unfettered by legislative enactments, we should gradually
> withdraw our capital from the cultivation of such lands, and import the produce which is at
> present raised upon them. The capital withdrawn would be employed in the manufacture of
> such commodities as would be exported in return for corn. (Vol. IV, p. 32)

Unrestricted trade in corn is absolutely necessary in Ricardo's system. Due to an increased rate of profit, capitalists have incentives to put their money into more productive areas and hence contribute to the progress of the economy. Restricting trade in corn is for Ricardo the same as not using the steam-engine or a perfected cotton-machine. He asks therefore: "Would it be wise at a great expense to use some of the worst machines, when at a less expense we could hire the very best from our neighbours?" (Vol. IV, p. 34).

In an atmosphere of war and trade blockades, Ricardo argued for stronger economic relationships with other countries. The often-used argument of England's strong dependence on other countries through importing corn was opposed by Ricardo along simple theoretical lines. Once England was established as an importing country, the other countries would invest their capital in agriculture and thus be liable partners. The slowness of adjustment in the different branches of an economy would leave time for England to adjust as well. These dynamics play a role in the earlier conception of Ricardo's system. He would even give farmers of the least productive fields, who would be the losers if tariff abolition occurred, some time (3 or 4 years) before they would have to adjust. But in the end the most important thing is that the losses of the losers will be replaced by a gain "many times the amount of their losses" (Vol. IV, p. 33) in order to justify that kind of policy. The few important ones at that time—the landed class—have in Ricardo's system no longer the right to rule against the interests of others—even if Ricardo himself belonged to it. Malthus noted:

> It is somewhat singular that Mr. Ricardo, a considerable receiver of rents, should have so much underrated their national importance; while I, who never received, nor expect to receive any; should probably be accused of overrating their importance. Our different opinions, under these circumstances, may serve at least to show our mutual sincerity, and afford a strong presumption, that to whatever bias our minds may have been subjected in the doctrines we have laid down, it has not been that, against which perhaps it is most difficult to guard, the insensible bias of situation and interest. (Malthus 1820 (1922), pp. 216–217)

2.3 Ricardo's Principles

Great thinkers sometimes seem not only to have incredible talent but are also endowed with an exorbitant amount of self-confidence. This was definitely not true for David Ricardo. He was successful in almost every branch in which he was active. He made a fortune as a businessman, achieved with his first pamphlets wide recognition and acclaim, lived in Gatcombe, one of the most beautiful spots in England, and was on friendly terms with the other great political economists. Yet he reacted reluctantly, when James Mill, his loyal friend, asked him to write a prolonged and elaborated version of the *Essay on Profits*. "I fear", Ricardo wrote in a letter, "the undertaking exceeds my powers." (Vol. VI, p. 249).

Jeremy Bentham once wrote: "I was the spiritual father of Mill, and Mill the spiritual father of Ricardo" (Bain, 1882, p. 74), and indeed James Mill was in the 2 years between the publication of the *Essay on Profits* and the *Principles* a constant and enduring friend at Ricardo's side. Ricardo, himself, was full of doubt and reluctance to write the *Principles*. In one letter, he almost shouts out in despair: "Oh that I were capable of writing a book." (Vol. VI, p. 314).

2.3.1 Malthus and the Labor Theory of Value

It was an inner desire, due presumably to the everlasting differences in opinion with Malthus, that led Ricardo to finally overcome his doubts (rather than possible fame and glory). In the same letter Ricardo wrote about how much he differed with Malthus and described an "astonishing mixture of truth and error" in Malthus' opinions "on the subject of rent profit and wages" (ibid). For Ricardo, who never doubted his logical reasoning and aimed to find the correct principles, this seems to have been incentive enough.

Whereas the correspondence between Ricardo and Mill was mostly about personal matters and, as we shall see, matters of encouragement and support, the letters between Ricardo and Malthus were almost fully dedicated to the discussion of political economy. The one time when Ricardo expressed his problems in writing, Malthus replied to Ricardo:

> I cannot help thinking that the reason why with your clear head, you find a difficulty in your progress is that you are got a little into a wrong track. On the subject of determining all prices by labour, and excluding capital from the operation of the great principle of supply and demand, I think you must have swerved a little from the right course. But on this point of course you differ from me. (Vol. VII, p. 7)

Malthus' critique touches the core of Ricardo's thoughts in the years before the *Principles*. And it also anticipates one major line of attack and critique from subsequent writers of political economy. Concerning a theory of value, the *Essay on Profits* already entailed some aspects of the emergence of one of Ricardo's most disputed theories. Yet, he needed some further thoughts to develop it fully for the *Principles*. Piero Sraffa, the editor of the monumental edition *The Works and Correspondence of David Ricardo* provided especially for the Essay an interpretation that is not undisputed but surely a point of reference. In the introduction to the edition he tries to give the "rational foundation" (Vol. I, xxxi) of Ricardo's dictum "it is the profits of the farmer that regulate the profits of all other trades." As we have seen, the importance of a free trade in corn lies in its effects on all other trades and industries. But why is that the case after all?

To Sraffa this is given by the corn model. In agricultural production "corn" works as the input factor (capital in the agricultural production is thus fully given by the wages of the laborers) and as the output factor. There is thus no problem of valuation in this production; the quantities that were put into production and the quantities that come out of the production matter and can thus directly determine the ratio of profit. Sraffa now concludes that because this production consists of the same commodity "no value change can alter the ratio of product to capital". It is thus the case, that rate of profit in the production of other commodities, in which there is not identity between input and output, have to adjust. In Sraffa's interpretation the rate of profit is therefore of high importance. Others, for example, Peach, have criticized this interpretation. He simply sees in the output of agricultural production the wage good. By an increased exchangeable value of corn, the production cost (the capital) rises, and hence leads to a smaller rate of profit (Peach, 1998, p. 599).

In writing the *Principles,* Ricardo needed a more profound theory that did not determine the rate of profit only "through the microcosm of one special branch of production." (Vol. I, xxxii). He found in his more general approach to the problem of value in labor the ultimate solution. Ricardo substituted "Labour for Corn as the quantity in terms of which product, wages and surplus were alike expressed." (Dobb, 1973, p. 74). Not corn, but labor could be found now on either side of the production process. Ricardo managed therefore to distance himself from the simplifying assumption that corn is the only good entailed in the wages. Thus, as Sraffa wrote:

> (...) the rate of profits was no longer determined by the ratio of the corn produced to the corn used up in production, but instead, by the ratio of the total labour of the country to the labour required to produce the necessaries for that labour. (Vol. I, p. xxxii)

Thus the labor theory of value emerged and its explanation was the first and longest chapter in the *Principles.* The object of inquiry is the exchangeable value of a commodity that entails as a prerequisite usefulness and can be fabricated and replicated by labor. The value-in-exchange of a commodity—the question thus how much of a good shall be given for another—depends "almost exclusively on the comparative quantity of labour expended on each." (Vol. I, p. 12). Ricardo describes this principle as "a doctrine of the utmost importance in political economy." (Vol. I, p. 13). It follows that if a commodity can be produced more efficiently due to an innovation, its relative amount of labor falls comparatively to the other goods and it thus becomes less expensive. The same is true when the difficulties of production increase; then, the commodity becomes more expensive and will cost relatively more compared to the other commodities.

Starting from a rural society—as Smith does—the hunter example with the deer and the beaver and their different difficulties in hunting resulting in their relative exchangeable value seems straightforward. But the economy changed and the reality in English industry showed that labor in its purest form cannot suffice. There is thus also an idea of capital involved, which is, in Ricardo's conception, bestowed labor. He distinguishes this further in circulating and fixed capital. The circulating capital is used in fixed proportions to labor. Whenever the amount of labor used in production is known, the amount of circulating capital is given as well. Fixed capital is not proportional to labor; more importantly it can be substituted for by labor. A rising wage now has different effects. Whenever there is only circulating capital in the production of a good, the price of the commodity will increase. With fixed capital the effect can—through substitution—even fall. The factor land, however, is excluded in Ricardo's labor theory of value.

2.3.2   Mill and His Encouragement

Whereas the labor theory of value completed Ricardo's "system" and therefore made it possible to write the *Principles,* it was James Mill who remains a central figure in the development of the *Principles.* But unlike Malthus, he could not sharpen Ricardo's theory through objections or stimulating ideas. It was his encouragement, his inexhaustible persuasion and his faith in Ricardo's strengths that were so important. He therefore wrote to Ricardo with almost pathetic encouragements:

> When I am satisfied, however, that you can not only acquire that reputation, but that you can very greatly improve a science on which the progress of human happiness to a singular degree depends; in fact that you can improve so important a science far more than any other man who is devoting his attention to it, or likely to do so, for Lord knows how many years— my friendship for you, for mankind, and for science, all prompt me to give you no rest, till you are plunged over head and ears in political economy. (Vol. VI, p. 252)

Or at the end, when Ricardo sent him the first chapters of the book, still unsure whether it should be published at all, Mill wrote to him:

> Your doctrines are original, and profound, for it was by no means an easy matter to get down to them; and I have no hesitation whatsoever in saying that they are fully and completely made out. I embrace them against all the world. (Vol. VII, p. 106)

The relationship between Mill and Ricardo is probably best described by his son. John Stuart Mill would become one of the last great economists in the classical era. Interestingly he, could have learned his craft from the masters. He describes Ricardo as "very attractive to young persons" and talks about the invitation to Ricardo's house and the walks with him in order "to converse on the subject (of political economy)." (J. S. Mill 1873 (2009), p. 54). Concerning the relationship between his father and Ricardo and the emergence of the book, he said:

> His loved and intimate friend, Ricardo, had shortly before published the book which formed so great an epoch in political economy; a book which would never have been published or written, but for the entreaty and strong encouragement of my father; for Ricardo, the most modest of men, though firmly convinced of the truth of his doctrines deemed himself so little capable of doing them justice in exposition and expression, that he shrank from the idea of publicity. (J. S. Mill 1873 (2009) pp. 29–30)

On the 19th of April 1817 *The Principles of Political Economy and Taxation* was published in London by John Murray. "The success which followed amply compensated him;" writes Moses Ricardo in the *Memoir.* "And this book" he continues "upon a subject which had heretofore not been popular, in a very short time passed through three editions [1819, 1821], and placed the author in the highest rank as a philosophical writer." (Vol. X, pp. 10–11).

References

Bain, A. (1882). *James Mill a biography*. London: Longmans, Green and Co.

Blaug, M. (1958). *Ricardian economics*. New Haven: Yale University Press.

Booth, A. (1977). Food riots in the North-West of England 1790–1801. *Past Present, 77*(1), 84–107.

Cannan, E. (1894). Ricardo in parliament. *The Economic Journal, 4*(14), 249–261.

Cannan, E. (1903). *A history of the theories of production and distribution*. London: P. S. King & Son.

Colvin, C. (Ed.). (1971). *Maria Edgeworth: Letters from England 1813–1844*. Oxford: Oxford University Press.

Dobb, M. (1973). *Theories of value and distribution since Adam Smith*. Cambridge: Cambridge University Press.

Gordon, B. (1976). *Political economy in parliament 1819–1823*. London: The MacMillan Press.

Hartwell, R. M. (1971). Introduction. In *David Ricardo principles of political economy and taxation*. Harmondsworth: Penguin.

Henderson J. P., & Davis, J. B. (1997). *The life and economics of David Ricardo* (W. J. Samuels & G. B. Davis, Eds.). New York: Springer Science + Business Media.

Higgs, H. (1921). *Political economy club; minutes of proceedings, 1899–1920*. London: MacMillan.

Hollander, J. H. (1910). *David Ricardo a centenery estimate*. Baltimore: The Johns Hopkings Press.

Hollander, J. H. (1911). The work and influence of Ricardo. *The American Economic Review, 1*(2), 71–84.

Inglis Palgrave, R. H. (1901). *Dictionary of political economy* (Vol. I). London: MacMillan.

King, J. E. (2013). *David Ricardo* (Great thinkers in economics. Series Ed. A. P. Thirlwall). Houndmills, Basingstoke: Palgrave Macmillan.

Malthus, T. R. (1909). *An essay on the principle of population*. London: MacMillan.

Malthus, T. R. (1922). *Principles of political economy*. New York: Augustus M. Kelley.

Mathias, P. (1983). *The first industrial nation. An economic history of Britain 1700–1914*. London: Methuen.

McCulloch, J. R. (1825). *Memoir of the life and writings of David Ricardo*. London: Richard Taylor.

Meek, R. L. (1976). *Studies in the labor theory of value*. New York: Monthly Review Press.

Milgate, M., & Stimson, S. C. (1991). *Ricardian politics*. Princeton, NJ: Princeton University Press.

Mill, J. (1808). *Commerce defended*. London: C and R. Baldwin.

Mill, J. S. (2009). *Autobiography of John Stuart Mill*. Auckland: The Floating Press.

Mitchell, W. C. (1949). *Lecture notes on types of economic theory* (J. M. Gould & A. M. Kelley, Eds.). New York: Augustus M. Kelley.

Mitchell, W. C. (1967). *Types of economic theory from mercantilism to institutionalism* (J. Dorfman, Ed.). New York: Augustus M. Kelley.

Peach, T. (1998). On interpreting Ricardo: A reply to Sraffians. *Cambridge Journal of Economics, 22*, 597–616.

Schumpeter, J. A. (1955). *History of economic analysis*. New York: Oxford University Press.

Spence, W. (1807). *Britain independent of commerce*. W. Savage: London.

Stevenson, J. (1974). Food riots in England 1792–1818. In J. Stevenson & R. E. Quinault (Eds.), *Popular portest and public order: Six studies in British history, 1790–1920*. London: Allen & Unwin.

Sraffa, Piero (Ed.). (2005). *The works and correspondence of David Ricardo* (11 Vols.) (in collaboration with M. H. Dobb, Ed.). Indianapolis: Liberty Press.

Thompson, R. J. (1907). An inquiry into the rent of agricultural land in England and Wales during the nineteenth century. *Journal of the Royal Statistical Society, 70*(4), 587–624.

Torrens, R. (1808). The economist refuted. In *Principles and practical observations of Sir Robert Peel's Act of 1844*. (1857). London: Longman, Brown, Green, Longmans, and Roberts.

Turner, M. (1986). Corn crises in Britain in the age of Malthus. In *Malthus and his time* (pp. 112–128). New York: Palgrave Macmillan.

Viner, J. (1937). *Studies in the theory of international trade*. London: George Allen & Unwin.

Weatherall, D. (1976). *David Ricardo a biography*. The Hague: Martinus Nijhoff.

Chapter 3
David Ricardo's "On Foreign Trade": The Original Idea

Thomas Gerber and Rolf Weder

Abstract In this chapter we lead the reader through some of the important passages written by David Ricardo in the famous chapter "On Foreign Trade" in his book *On the Principles of Political Economy and Taxation*. We have a detailed look into Ricardo's *three paragraphs* in which he developed the basis for international trade theory, using the numerical example of Portugal and England exchanging wine and cloth. Further aspects of his theory, his way of thinking and his methodology are also discussed. We follow closely Ricardo's own words and interpret different parts of his brilliant contribution.

David Ricardo's *On the Principles of Political Economy and Taxation* was published on the 19th April of 1817 (Ricardo, 1817). Note that the book includes a long list of totally 24 chapters most of which have general titles and thus signal that they aim at a discussion of fundamental issues. The first chapter is "On Value", the second one "On Rent", the fifth chapter "On Wages", the sixth "On Profits". Chapter VII then has the title "On Foreign Trade", the original version of which is found in Chap. 20 of this book *200 Years of Ricardian Trade Theory*.

The title appears rather modest—which might be interpreted as "my preliminary thoughts on foreign trade"—and, with 30 pages in length, the chapter could be considered as mediocre. However, with respect to its contents, the chapter turns out to be grand—extraordinary. It is even more astonishing that Ricardo's central argument is almost entirely entailed in *three paragraphs*.

Readers who are familiar with the Ricardian model of the "gains from trade", typically encountered in introductory courses to (international) economics,[1] will be surprised that the buzzword "comparative advantage" is not even used one time in Ricardo's Chapter VII. But, of course, the concept of comparative advantage is presented in an unequivocal manner. His presentation differs in some respect to

---

[1]See, e.g., Caves, Frankel, and Jones (2007), Mankiw and Taylor (2014), Krugman, Obstfeld, and Melitz (2015).

T. Gerber (✉) • R. Weder (✉)
Faculty of Business and Economics, University of Basel, Basel, Switzerland
e-mail: thomas.gerber@unibas.ch; rolf.weder@unibas.ch

© Springer International Publishing AG 2017
R.W. Jones, R. Weder (eds.), *200 Years of Ricardian Trade Theory*,
https://doi.org/10.1007/978-3-319-60606-4_3

what we would generally state as the Ricardian trade model today (see also Chap. 4 in this book).

A theory develops over the course of time, and so does the methodology and the discipline as a whole. As a consequence, different and altered layers of understanding add to the original thought. The reconstruction of this thought is not the aim of this chapter. In order to do that, our understanding of Ricardo and of his whole economical system, including the labour theory of value, would have to be more comprehensive. Readers who may be more familiar than we with the history of economic thoughts, in general, or with certain aspects of Chapter VII may find our presentation unsophisticated. On the other hand, they may lack the understanding of international trade theory and emphasize elements which, from a trade theory perspective, may be irrelevant. What is right or wrong may generally be difficult to prove from today's perspective. Interpretations remain thus what they are: Interpretations.

Thus, our target is to show to the reader some ingenious statements made by Ricardo 200 years ago which definitely were crucial for the development of the (Ricardian) trade theory. We want to guide the reader through David Ricardo's original words and motivate his thoughts. We hope to intrigue the readers with the words of a man who developed a remarkable theory. Or, to quote Paul Krugman (1996, p. 10) in his essay "Ricardo's Difficult Idea": "Ricardo's idea is truly, madly, deeply difficult. But it is also utterly true, immensely sophisticated—and extremely relevant to the modern world."

In the first section we present some of the preliminary thoughts of Ricardo. The second section then concentrates on Ricardo's famous example of Portugal and England exchanging cloth and wine. The third section alludes to important assumptions of the model regarding the immobility of factors of production. In the fourth section, we emphasize quotes which show the modern methodology David Ricardo introduced 200 years ago. Conclusions follow in the fifth section.

3.1   Ricardo's Opening Statement: The Sum of Enjoyments

David Ricardo begins the chapter with a reservation:

> No extension of foreign trade will immediately increase the amount of value in a country, although it will very powerfully contribute to increase the mass of commodities, and therefore the sum of enjoyments. (p. 131)[2]

A country that opens its harbors and its ports for international trade will at least not immediately increase its wealth. A simple and straightforward interpretation would be that an increase in foreign trade through—what many business men would emphasize—exports is not by itself (e.g., in terms of the collected currency)

---

[2]All quotes from David Ricardo's chapter "On Foreign Trade" are from the original third edition, reprinted in Chap. 20 of this book.

beneficial for a country, but rather what can be acquired with it in terms of the larger quantity or number ("mass") of foreign commodities.

In light of Ricardo's general conception of the economic system this reservation can also be understood as an opposition to a proposition brought forward by Adam Smith. Smith writes in his "Wealth of Nations" that new beneficial trades tend to attract capital to the (booming) export industries. Capital thus leaves the other industries and has, according to Smith, the effect of a rising profitability of capital. The rate of profitability depends in Smith's view on the amount of capital that is competing with each other. As the export industries have a high(er) rate of profit, the rate increases in the other industries as well (due to, according to Smith, less capital competing in the other industries). Hence the general rate of profit increases (see Smith 1776 (1975), book IV, p. 110).

Ricardo in contrast sees no reason for a capital outflow from these industries, unless the demand for domestic goods diminishes. Obtaining cheaper goods from abroad implies for the consumers simply that they can buy more domestic goods. And even if the import-competing industries lose, the rate of profit will not be affected. Capital which is released by one industry will be employed by another. Note that the rate of profit or, in other words, the rate of return to capital is central in Ricardo's economic system. If the rate is high, so goes the argument, capitalists have incentives to invest their money in new production facilities and thus contribute to the progress (amount of value) of the society. From this reasoning, Ricardo follows that trade will at least not immediately affect this rate of profit.[3]

Ricardo emphasizes here that trade is important because of the access to a larger quantity or number ("mass") of commodities. The consumption basket for each individual will increase and thus contribute to his or her "sum of enjoyments." The second sentence in the chapter deepens this thought:

> As the value of all foreign goods is measured by the quantity of the produce of our land and labour, which is given in exchange for them, we should have no greater value, if by the discovery of new markets, we obtained double the quantity of foreign goods in exchange for a given quantity of ours. (p. 131)

International trade is beneficial not because it creates new jobs or allows for a collection of money, but rather because it allows for a better use of a country's resources and thus for a better exchange (transformation) of a country's exports for (into) imports. So, this constitutes already a summary of an important ingredient to Ricardo's idea: International trade ("the discovery of new markets") serves as an indirect production method as it raises the quantity of certain (foreign) goods obtained in exchange for other (domestic) goods.

This conception stands in a rather strong opposition to the mercantile thought, which was the prevailing idea of trade from the sixteenth to the eighteenth century. Mercantilists declared the accumulation of gold and silver to a country's most important task. This goal was for most countries only achievable through an excess

---

[3]Foreign trade will indeed affect the rate of profit whenever the imported good lowers the real wage in a country (see Chap. 2 in this book).

of exports over imports and the corresponding inflow of the metals. The economic policy was thus strongly oriented around this maxim. Import restrictions could be seen as the less harmful policy measures at the time. The politics had in general a rather nationalistic characteristic or, as Viner (1968, p. 438) stated, the ultimate aim through the accumulation of gold was a "superiority of power" in order to "give the law to other countries".

Ricardo's conception of trade was not entirely new. It was in the late eighteenth century, when the "mercantile system" led by Adam Smith's "very violent attack" (Smith 1785 (1987), p. 251) was seriously questioned. He and his ultimate successors allowed for a more sophisticated and scholarly perspective on the implications of foreign trade. But it was surely Ricardo who "nailed it down" with his chapter.

The following sentence takes up this important point from above, now introducing a country (England) and an imported good (wine):

> If one increases, the other must diminish. If the quantity of wine, imported in exchange for the same quantity of English commodities, be doubled, the people of England can either consume double the quantity of wine that they did before, or the same quantity of wine and a greater quantity of English commodities. (p. 134)

Importantly, the increased efficiency in the use of resources can also be transformed in a smaller amount of inputs used in the export industry which, in turn, frees up resources for the production of other—possibly non-traded—"English commodities". In other words, it is not necessarily the quantity of imports that may rise because of specialization. A country may instead use the smaller amount of resources necessary to "indirectly produce the imports" for alternative productive objectives—or simply save these resources.

In the following paragraph, Ricardo further differentiates his idea from other possible benefits of international trade and summarizes the essence:

> It is not, therefore, in consequence of the extension of the market that the rate of profit is raised, although such extension may be equally efficacious in increasing the mass of commodities, and may thereby enable us to augment the funds destined for the maintenance of labour, and the materials on which labour may be employed. It is quite as important to the happiness of mankind, that our enjoyments should be increased by the better distribution of labour, by each country producing those commodities for which by its situation, its climate, and its other natural or artificial advantages, it is adapted, and by their exchanging them for the commodities of other countries, as that they should be augmented by a rise in the rate of profits. (pp. 136–137)

The first sentence could, in our view, be interpreted as an alternative advantage of international trade which apparently has already been mentioned by Adam Smith and emphasizes the possibility of exploiting increasing returns to scale: Extending the market size could lead to a reduction of average costs, raise efficiency and thus increase the "mass of commodities". However, Ricardo seems to stress the fact that his idea of reallocating labor to those commodities in which a country "by its situation, its climate, and its other natural or artificial advantages" has a productive advantage, is also very important to raise profitability and thus consumption or, as he calls it, "enjoyments". Note that Ricardo already uses the expression "happiness of mankind" which he believes his positively related to consumption.

It is worthwhile to recall the eighteenth-century-rule, which was from Smith onward a predominant idea. Clearly the traces of this idea, applied among others by James Mill and by Robert Torrens, are apparent. Trade in the above description has the function to allow for an efficient division of labour among different countries. It is as Torrens (1808) called it a "territorial division of labor".

From the perspective of the new trade theory it is also interesting that Ricardo stresses throughout the chapter not only the increase in the mass, but also in the "variety" (p. 137) of goods as a consequence of international trade—a topic that has been occupying trade economists during the last 50 years based on the work by Grubel and Lloyd (1975) and Krugman (1979, 1980).

3.2 Ricardo's Famous Example of Portugal and England Exchanging Wine and Cloth

John Ramsey McCulloch wrote in the Edinburgh Chronicle a mostly appreciative review of Ricardo's *Principle* in 1818. It was the first widely recognized comment on the book and is likely to have led to an increased amount of sold books (Sraffa, 2005, Vol. I, l). McCulloch experienced a particular pleasure in reading chapter VII:

> This is one of the most valuable and original parts of the work before us; and affords a striking example of Ricardo's uncommon sagacity in investigating and tracing the operation of fixed and general principles, and in disentangling and separating them from those of a secondary and accidental nature. (McCulloch, 1818, p. 83)

McCulloch had in mind Ricardo's example of Portugal and England, exchanging cloth and wine. There hardly is any more famous example in the history of economics than the one Ricardo developed in only a few paragraphs.

3.2.1 Comparative Advantage

In the first paragraph of the chapter (p. 131), David Ricardo introduces England and wine. Then, only a little later, he uses cloth in an enumeration of manufactured goods, together with hats and shoes and referring to Adam Smith (p. 132). Finally, when Ricardo stresses once more that "each country naturally devotes its capital and labour to such employments as are most beneficial to each" (p. 139), he introduces Portugal (besides France) where "wine shall be made" along with other examples ("corn shall be grown in America and Poland") (p. 139).

Before the central *three paragraphs* (pp. 140–141) begin, Ricardo writes:

> If Portugal had no commercial connection with other countries, instead of employing a great part of her capital and industry in the production of wines, with which she purchases for her own use the cloth and hardware of other countries, she would be obliged to devote a

part of that capital to the manufacture of those commodities, which she would thus obtain probably inferior in quality as well as quantity. (p. 140)

The argument is that in autarky Portugal would have to use some of its resources for the production of cloth ("and hardware") which she cannot produce as well as wine. In using some of her resources in the clothing industry she has to take into account an inferior "quantity as well as quality".

In the next step, Ricardo defines the fundamental difference between the international and domestic exchange of goods:

The quantity of wine which she shall give in exchange for the cloth of England, is not determined by the respective quantities of labour devoted to the production of each, as it would be, if both commodities were manufactured in England, or both in Portugal. (p. 140)

Ricardo thus states that the relative price of the two goods is determined differently in international trade than domestically. Whereas the relative price in autarky is simply given "by the respective quantities of labour" (if labour is the only factor of production), this rule cannot be applied with respect to internationally traded goods. Ricardo diverges thus from his classical conception of the labour theory of value (it is not "the same rule", p. 138). As soon as wages are different between the two countries, the relative costs of internationally exchanged goods not only depend on the relative amount labour used, but also on the wage rate.

He continues:

England may be so circumstanced, that to produce the cloth may require the labour of 100 men for one year; and if she attempted to make the wine, it might require the labour of 120 men for the same time. England would therefore find it her interest to import wine, and to purchase it by the exportation of cloth. (p. 140)

Some readers have long been puzzled by this opening paragraph of Ricardo's most famous example. The problem is rather obvious: How can Ricardo, by just mentioning the two different production costs of England, conclude what the efficient pattern of trade should be—since we do not know anything about Portugal up to this point? Chipman (1965) assessed this paragraph (and the following one) as rather "unsatisfactory" if read by itself and as "non sequitur" (pp. 479–480). By that he meant that the conclusion ["England (...) find it her interest (...)"] is not supported by the preceding premise.

The problem resolves itself if we continue to read and realize that Ricardo implicitly assumes that, in the trade equilibrium, the relative price of the described cloth and wine is 1. Given this assumption the relative cost of producing wine is larger than the relative price of wine on the "world" market. This implies that England would want to specialize in cloth. This would allow England to use 100 men in the clothing industry and exchange the output against wine that would, if produced in England, require 120 men. Whether we interpret the 100 (120) men as an input per one unit of cloth (wine) or per X (Y) units of cloth (wine) does not matter in our view as long as we take into account that Ricardo assumed that the generated output by 100 and 120 men, respectively, has the same price in the trade equilibrium.

We may note that, in the last years, there has been some discussion whether Ricardo assumed that the 100 and 120 men are unit labour coefficients or not. Whereas the textbook version of the model usually works with unit labour coefficients (e.g., 100 men per unit of cloth), Ruffin (2002) correctly emphasized that the numbers given by Ricardo can also be interpreted as the input per any quantity of output—X and Y—as mentioned above.[4] This does not affect the conclusion. Note that Ricardo's argument is in line with the so-called "eighteenth-century rule" that emphasized before the possible gains through an indirect production method (see Chap. 2 in this book).

Ricardo then introduces the situation in Portugal to pursue his argument:

> To produce the wine in Portugal might require only the labour of 80 men for one year, and to produce the cloth in the same country might require the labour of 90 men for the same time. It would therefore be advantageous for her to export wine in exchange for cloth. (p. 141)

The same argument is now applied to Portugal. Ricardo continuously assumes a relative price of 1 of the respective quantities of the two goods exchanged in the trade equilibrium. For Portugal, the costs of producing cloth in terms of labour (90) are thus higher than the price it would have to pay "indirectly" by exchanging it against wine (80 in terms of labour). This indeed implies that it would be "advantageous for her to export wine in exchange for cloth". Again, it does not matter how much output is produced with 80 or 90 men as long as the quantities are comparable to those mentioned for England. In assuming that the value of *"the wine"* and *"the cloth"* is equal on the world market; the gains from trade in the above described reallocation is, in terms of units of labour, 20 for England and 10 for Portugal.

Having now established the gains from trade for both countries, Ricardo emphasizes that this kind of exchange takes place even though Portugal could produce the imported good (cloth) with less labour than England (with 90 men instead of 100 men). For many observers—200 years ago and even today—this may be surprising: Why would and why should a country import a good from another country even though it is "more competitive" in producing this good? Ricardo's answer follows right in the next sentence:

> This exchange might even take place, notwithstanding that the commodity imported by Portugal could be produced there with less labour than in England. Though she could make the cloth with the labour of 90 men, she would import it from a country where it required the labour of 100 men to produce it, because it would be advantageous to her rather to employ her capital in the production of wine, for which she would obtain more cloth from England, than she could produce by diverting a portion of her capital from the cultivation of vines to the manufacture of cloth. (p. 141)

If Portugal shifted, for example, 80 men from the production of cloth to the production of wine, she "would obtain more cloth from England" through trade

---

[4]Since Ruffin (2002) published his paper, subsequent writers such as Maneschi (2004, 2008) or Morales Meoqui (2011, 2013) have elaborated on this point that might be of interest to some readers.

than she had to give up. Let us put the theorem in modern terms. Even though Portugal has an absolute advantage in producing either good, it nevertheless can benefit from trade if it specializes in that good (wine) in which it has a relative or comparative advantage (i.e., where her relative labour costs (80/90) are smaller than those in England (120/100)).

In the last of the three paragraphs, Ricardo explains that this pattern of specialization not only benefits the two countries (as shown above), but that it is also economically feasible—i.e., that markets will adjust such that the pattern of specialization happens:

> Thus England would give the produce of the labour of 100 men, for the produce of the labour of 80. Such an exchange could not take place between the individuals of the same country. The labour of 100 Englishmen cannot be given for that of 80 Englishmen, but the produce of the labour of 100 Englishmen may be given for the produce of the labour of 80 Portuguese, 60 Russians, or 120 East Indians. (p. 141)

The reason why "the produce of the labour of 100 Englishmen" can be exchanged for the output of "the labour of 80 Portuguese" is that wages can be different in two countries. In fact, the wage rate will be 25% higher in Portugal than in England in Ricardo's numerical example.[5]

> The difference in this respect, between a single country and many, is easily accounted for, by considering the difficulty with which capital moves from one country to another, to seek a more profitable employment, and the activity with which it invariably passes from one province to another in the same country. (pp. 141–142)

Ricardo emphasizes that this situation is not possible within a country due to labor mobility which would make the industry with the lower wages uncompetitive and lose its labor. He thus stresses the point that his concept relies on the assumption of the immobility of factors of production between countries which he considers to be realistic ("by considering the difficulty with which capital moves from one country to another, to seek a more profitable employment").

In Footnote 1, Ricardo relates his conclusion to Adam Smith's argumentation about the advantages of specialization among individuals (that is at least our interpretation). Remember the famous argument by Adam Smith (1776):[6] "The tailor does not attempt to make his own shoes, but buys them of the shoemaker. The shoemaker does not attempt to make his own clothes but employs a tailor. (. . .). All of them find it for their interest to employ their whole industry in a way in which they have some advantage over their neighbours, (. . .)." Ricardo emphasizes his findings that are based on relative rather than absolute advantages as a reason for international trade:

> It will appear, then, that a country possessing very considerable advantages in machinery and skill, and which may therefore be enabled to manufacture commodities with much less labour than her neighbours, may, in return for such commodities, import a portion of the

---

[5]As the prices of the two exchanged quantities of goods are equal, the costs of production have to be equal. This implies a higher wage rate in Portugal: its relative wage rate has to equal 100/80.

[6]See also Chap. 2 in Helpman (2011) with some quotes from Smith.

corn required for its consumption, even if its land were more fertile and corn could be grown with less labour than in the country from which it was imported. Two men can both make shoes and hats, one is superior to the other in both employments; but in making hats he can only exceed his competitor by one-fifth or 20 per cent., and in making shoes he can excel him by one-third or 33 per cent.;—will it not be for the interest of both that the superior man should employ himself exclusively in making shoes, and the inferior man in making hats? (p. 142)

Thus, David Ricardo seems to argue that his idea is also applicable to the division of labor within a country and thus between individuals. An individual does not have to be better at doing something in order to benefit from specialization and exchange. This challenges Adam Smith who appears to have argued on the basis of absolute advantages.[7]

3.2.2   Ricardo's Choice of the Countries, Goods and Productivities

David Ricardo's example with the involved theoretical principle had a strong impact on the theory of international trade. Many use it as a foundation for unrestricted trade, in general. Ricardo, indeed, begins—before he comes to the example—with a strong claim. "Under a system of perfectly free commerce", he says, "each country naturally devotes its capital and labour to such employments as are most beneficial to each." (p. 139). He then concludes that free trade "diffuses general benefit, and binds together, by one common tie of interest and intercourse, the universal society of nations throughout the civilised world" (p. 139).

One may discuss Ricardo's motivation for choosing the concrete examples of goods, wine and cloth, the two countries, Portugal and England, as well as the assumed inferiority in England's capability of producing both goods. If one reads a deeper meaning into his choices, there is, for various reasons, at least a difficulty in understanding his motivation:

- Political economists in the early nineteenth century were occupied with an important political issue: The import restriction on agricultural products (the so-called Corn Laws). Ricardo was in fierce opposition against these restrictions. Surprisingly, he uses under the above claim for free trade, not corn as an example (and as an implicit political message) to show the benefits of an unrestricted trade.
- Portugal is assumed more productive in the production of both goods. In the case of wine, this seems justified. In the case of cloth, however, there are some reasonable doubts. England was on the verge of industrialization and thus must have had a technological advance in the manufacturing of commodities.

---

[7]See also Ruffin's (2005) interpretation of Adam Smith's view on absolute versus comparative advantage and Chap. 9 in this book.

– England and Portugal agreed on the Methuen treaty in 1703 (called after the British ambassador Paul Methuen). Friedrich List who wrote on the advantage of restricting international trade, discussed this treaty years later (in 1841). Part of this treaty included the abolishment of taxes on British cloths in Portugal and a reduction of duties on Portuguese wines, relative to those on wines from other countries, in England. Portugal, as List (1909) wrote in 1841, became the "vineyard of England" (p. 20) and "sank into complete political dependence upon England" (p. 34). On the other hand, "Portugal was deluged with English manufactures, and the first result of this inundation was the sudden and complete ruin of the Portuguese manufactories." (p. 50).

These abbreviated considerations may suffice to show some adversities with Ricardo's choice of example. Some argued that Ricardo "was simply rather careless in his choice of examples" (King, 2013, p. 88). Others concluded that he "set the example up this way in order to make it as striking as possible in order to short-circuit the popular argument in favour of protection home industry against low-cost imports" (Robinson, 1974, p. 4).

Even though it is difficult to judge, we are inclined to argue that these examples were not more than examples which Ricardo used to make his point. He mentions a lot of countries in Chapter VII and could also have chosen them as a basis for the numerical example. But he had to choose at least two countries, two goods and one factor of production to make his point.

3.3   International Immobility of Factors of Production

The significance of comparative advantage hinges on the immobility of the factors of production. Ricardo spends therefore some time in elaborating on this assumption. He first asks whether it would be desirable to allow for international mobility of factors of production:

> It would undoubtedly be advantageous to the capitalists of England, and to the consumers in both countries, that under such circumstances, the wine and the cloth should both be made in Portugal, and therefore that the capital and labour of England employed in making cloth, should be removed to Portugal for that purpose. (p. 142)

Thus he recognizes that given the superior technology in Portugal it would be an advantage for consumption (or the efficiency of production) if the resources were shifted to Portugal. The following is one way to see this in the example: In autarky, Portugal and England need 390 laborers to produce the four goods (and the assumed quantities), with trade and specialization only 360 laborers and with factor mobility only 340 laborers. But this would imply that absolute advantage determines where goods are produced.[8] In order to exclude or at least reduce the likelihood of this

---

[8]See Jones (1980) and Chap. 19 of this book for an extension of the Ricardian model in this direction.

possibility—which would challenge his main argument—Ricardo defends his assumption based on real-world examples:

> Experience, however, shows that the fancied or real insecurity of capital, when not under the immediate control of its owner, together with the natural disinclination which every man has to quit the country of his birth and connections, and intrust himself, with all his habits fixed, to a strange government and new laws, check the emigration of capital. These feelings, which I should be sorry to see weakened, induce most men of property to be satisfied with a low rate of profits in their own country, rather than seek a more advantageous employment for their wealth in foreign nations. (p. 143)

It may be interesting to state that Ricardo explained the immobility of factors with people's "feelings" that affects their behavior. Good other reasons would have been possible, especially at the time: For example, geographical distance, differences in the institutions (Ricardo hints on that in the quote above) or differences in language and social customs (see Cairnes, 1878, p. 305). McCulloch (1818) wrote in his review at the time:

> The love of country,—the thousand ties of society and friendship,—the ignorance of foreign languages, and the desire of having one's fund employed under their own inspection, will no doubt, in very many cases induce capitalists to put up with a less rate of profit in their own, than they might realize by investing their funds in other countries. But this love has its limits. (McCulloch, 1818, p. 82)

3.4   Modern Style and Methodology of Argumentation

It is striking how modern Ricardo's argumentation is in his Chapter VII. It is very close to today's argumentation in economics. Here are a few examples:

> Thus, suppose before the improvement in making wine in England the price of wine here were £50 per pipe, and the price of a certain quantity of cloth were £45, whilst in Portugal the price of the same quantity of wine was £45, and that ... (p. 145)

Ricardo uses concrete numerical examples to start with. "Thus, suppose" is exactly the way economists (at least trade economists) would even today describe a situation the reader should imagine. After a careful description of the situation the reader has to imagine, Ricardo then goes on and determines the envisioned change of one thing:

> Suppose that, after the improvement, wine falls to £45 in England, the cloth continuing at the same price. (...) (p. 145)

He thus expresses himself very clearly and almost in a mathematical way. This allows him to make his arguments precise and to differentiate them from those of others. Also, he simplifies the real world and explains it carefully:

> To simplify the question, I have been supposing the trade between two countries to be confined to two commodities—to wine and cloth; but it is well known that many and various articles enter into the list of exports and imports. (pp. 149–150)

The following is another example of this: As can be seen in the quote below, he defends his way of abstracting from other changes in the economy. We could call this a "comparative statics" exercise where, in a general equilibrium model, we change only one variable at the time and see what happens. But Ricardo carefully explains this to the reader:

> Beside the improvements in arts and machinery, there are various other causes which are constantly operating on the natural course of trade, and which interfere with the equilibrium and the relative value of money. (p. 150)

This way of argumentation was very different from that of many other writers and scientists at the time. Thus, we argue that this modern style was crucial for Ricardo in, first, detecting his ingenious understanding of international trade and, second, in expressing clearly his idea to a broad audience in a lasting way.

As a comparison one may read a contemporary statement by James Mill about trade in 1814. Mill and Ricardo communicated a lot with each other (see Chaps. 2 and 9 in this book). Mill was probably involved in this new way of thinking about international trade:

> If we import, we must pay for what we import, with the produce of a portion of our labour exported. But why not employ that labour in raising the same portion at home? The answer is, because it will procure more corn by going in the shape of commodities to purchase corn abroad, than if it had been employed in raising it at home . . . .. A law, therefore, to prevent the importation of corn, can have only one effect,—to make a greater portion of the labour of the community necessary for the production of its food.[9]

3.5 Conclusions

David Ricardo's Chapter VII "On Foreign Trade" is ingenious—even more so if one compares it with the contemporary thinking of nonspecialists about international trade. Thus, by having read some of the extracts we have chosen, the reader can—we hope—better understand why Ricardo became such an important figure in the history of economic thoughts. His influence reaches beyond international trade and thus affected the development of economics and political economy, in general.

But to develop the basis for international trade theory just over a few pages is astounding. We have also tried to illustrate Ricardo's modern style and methodology. He uses an (abstract) example of which we may say it seems rather simple at first glance: two countries, two goods and one factor. But when we start to read it slowly and carefully, a truly and extremely ingenious and very complex idea develops itself in front of our eyes.

Even 200 years after its first appearance, Ricardo's idea is still highly relevant and affects, in principle, scientists, policy makers and businessmen all over the world (see Chap. 5 in this book). After having read selected extracts from the

---

[9]Quoted by Irwin (1996) p. 89.

original text, we hope that the reader understands the ingredients of this break-through at the time (Chap. 2 in this book tells more about Ricardo's life and per-sonality, whereas Chap. 9—and its discussion in Chap. 10—in this book focuses on the discovery of comparative advantage in 1816).

And we also hope to have been able to convey that Ricardo's idea was, in terms of what he was thinking about beyond "the three paragraphs", very broad. Thus the Ricardian trade theory as we know it today made many aspects of the idea more precise and also extended it (Chaps. 4 and 5 in this book develop the basis and show some applications, whereas Chaps. 6, 7 and 8 as well as Chaps. 12, 13 and 14 discuss recent and possibly future developments of the model and its empirical analyses).

References

Cairnes, J. E. (1878). *Some leading principles of political economy*. New York: Harper & Brothers.

Caves, R. E., Frankel, J. A., & Jones, R. W. (2007). *World trade and payments: An introduction*. London: Pearson Addison Wesley.

Chipman, J. S. (1965). A survey of the theory of international trade: Part 1, The classical theory. *Econometrica, 33*(3), 477–519.

Grubel, H. G., & Lloyd, P. (1975). *Intra-industry trade: The theory and measurement of international trade in differentiated products*. New York: Wiley, Halsted Press.

Helpman, E. (2011). *Understanding global trade*. Cambridge, MA: Harvard University Press.

Irwin, D. A. (1996). *Against the tide: An intellectual history of free trade*. Princeton, NJ: Princeton University Press.

Jones, R. W. (1980). Comparative and absolute advantage. *Swiss Journal of Economics and Statistics (SJES), 116*(III), 235–260.

King, J. E. (2013). *David Ricardo*. Basingstoke: Palgrave Macmillan.

Krugman, P. R. (1979). Increasing returns, monopolistic competition, and international trade. *Journal of International Economics, 9*, 469–480.

Krugman, P. R. (1980). Scale economics, product differentiation, and the pattern of trade. *American Economic Review, 70*(5), 950–959.

Krugman, P. R. (1996). *Ricardo's difficult idea*. Paper presented at the Manchester Conference on Free Trade (mimeo).

Krugman, P. R., Obstfeld, M., & Melitz, M. J. (2015). *International economics* (10th ed.). London: Pearson Education Limited.

List, F. (1909). *The national system of political economy*. London: Longmans, Greend, and Co.

Maneschi, A. (2004). The true meaning of David Ricardo's four magic numbers. *Journal of International Economics, 62*(2), 433–443.

Maneschi, A. (2008). How would David Ricardo have taught the principle of comparative advantage? *Southern Economic Journal, 74*(August), 1167–1177.

Mankiw, N. G., & Taylor, M. P. (2014). *Economics*. Boston: Cengage Learning.

McCulloch, J. R. (1818). Article on Ricardo's political economy. *The Edinburgh Review, XXX*(59), 59–88.

Morales Meoqui, J. (2011). Comparative advantage and the labor theory of value. *History of Political Economy, 43*(4), 743–763.

Morales Meoqui, J. (2013). *Essence and merits of David Ricardo's proof of comparative advantage*. Working Paper.

Ricardo, D. (1817). *On the principles of political economy and taxation*. London: John Murray.

Robinson, J. (1974). *Reflections on the theory of international trade: Lectures given in the University of Manchester*. Manchester: Manchester University Press.

Ruffin, R. J. (2002). David Ricardo's discovery of comparative advantage. *History of Political Economy, 34*(4), 727–748.

Ruffin, R. J. (2005). Debunking a myth: Torrens on comparative advantage. *History of Political Economy, 37*(4), 711–722.

Smith, A. (1975). *The Glasgow Edition of the works and correspondence of Adam Smith: An inquiry into the nature and causes of the wealth of nations* (Vol. 1). Oxford: Oxford University Press.

Smith, A. (1987). *Correspondence of Adam Smith* (I. Mossner, & E. C. Simpson Ross, Eds.). Oxford: Oxford University Press.

Sraffa, P. (Ed.). (2005). *The works and correspondence of David Ricardo* (11 Vols.). Indianapolis: Liberty Fund.

Torrens, R. (1808). The economists refuted. In *Principles and practical operation of Sir Robert Peeel's Act of 18*. London: Longman, Brown, Green, Longmans, and Roberts.

Viner, J. (1968). Mercantilist thought. In *International encyclopedia of social science* (pp. 435–443). New York: Macmillan.

Chapter 4
The Standard Ricardian Trade Model

Rolf Weder

Abstract This chapter presents the standard Ricardian trade theory. It introduces the reader to the 2 × 2 model (two countries, two goods, one factor of production) and shows the effects of trade liberalization on the pattern of trade, production and wages. The extension from two to many goods (2 × N model) allows for an introduction of transportation costs as a basis to study the co-existence of internationally traded and nontraded goods as well as so-called Dutch-Disease effects. With, finally, the extension from many to very many goods (i.e., to a continuum of goods), the reader is introduced to the Dornbusch-Fischer-Samuelson (1977) model that is widely used in international trade theory.

In this chapter, I present the standard Ricardian trade model. The model focuses on the key insight David Ricardo came up with in 1817: Countries gain from trade if they are *relatively* different in their productivities. If a country specializes in those goods in which it is relatively more productive, it obtains more of the other goods through imports than if it would produce those other goods by itself. A country does not have to be "better" than other countries in producing something in order to gain from trade. And a country which is better in producing all the goods, can still benefit by specializing in the production of those in which it is *relatively* better. This is the principle or law of *comparative advantage*.

Note that it is not enough for a trade model to show that gains from trade are possible if countries specialize according to their comparative advantage. The model also should demonstrate that such a pattern of trade will be the result in decentralized (market) economies in which private agents pursue their own goals. Thus, it will be particularly important to show that a country which is inferior in its ability to produce all goods can nevertheless "compete" with the other countries in the world market. This is the second important insight Ricardo came up with. He emphasized the limited international mobility of factors of production which implies an adjustment of factor prices (e.g., wages) to the countries' productivities. This assures that all countries are *able to trade*.

R. Weder (✉)
Faculty of Business and Economics, University of Basel, Basel, Switzerland
e-mail: rolf.weder@unibas.ch

© Springer International Publishing AG 2017
R.W. Jones, R. Weder (eds.), *200 Years of Ricardian Trade Theory*,
https://doi.org/10.1007/978-3-319-60606-4_4

The Ricardian trade model assumes that countries have different technologies to produce goods and services. The technology is captured by the amount of labour (a_{Li})—the so-called labour coefficients—necessary to produce one unit of the output i: Clothing, wine, computers, software, hotel or banking services, for example. Note that the reciprocal of the labour coefficients ($1/a_{Li}$) equals labour's productivity in producing good i: It denotes the quantity of output that can be produced with one unit of labour. These labour productivities can be broadly interpreted as the outcome of a combination of technology, skills, climate, institutions and other factors of production. Importantly, however, the coefficients are assumed to be constant, i.e., they are not affected by the amount of labour used in a certain industry or the quantity of the good produced in a country. The marginal product of labour is thus constant which, in turn, implies constant opportunity costs. Moreover, the labour productivity is considered to be exogenously given.

Countries are assumed to be endowed with a fixed amount of labour, L and L^*, for the home and foreign country, respectively.[1] Within a country, labour is homogeneous and perfectly mobile between the different industries. All occupations thus pay the same wage rate, w and w^*, within the home and foreign country, respectively. The wage rates are a result of supply and demand, the latter of which is determined by the production of the goods in each country. Labour is assumed to be immobile between the two countries (and so are the technologies and all the characteristics affecting the labour productivities). The prices and the quantities of the goods (and services) produced in a country are determined in the general equilibrium that requires that in all markets supply equals demand.

This chapter is structured as follows. The first section develops the simplest version of the Ricardian model with two countries and two goods (the 2×2 model). Section 4.2 then introduces many goods which also allows for the discussion of the effects of small transportation costs on the international tradability of goods. Section 4.3 then goes to the extreme and allows for a continuum of goods as introduced by Dornbusch, Fischer, and Samuelson (1977). Section 4.4 introduces nontraded goods and services (e.g., haircuts or local transportation) and their relevance in an open economy. Concluding remarks are found in Sect. 4.5.

4.1   Two Countries and Two Goods

Suppose two countries, Home and Foreign, of which each is endowed with a fixed amount of labour, L (L^*). Labour can be used in the production of good 1 and 2. It is assumed to be perfectly mobile between the two industries. However, the model assumes that labour is immobile between the two countries. Given the labour coefficients for Home (Foreign), a_{Li} (a_{Li}^*), the autarky situation can be reflected by the

---

[1]All variables for the foreign country are denoted by an asterisk (*) throughout the chapter.

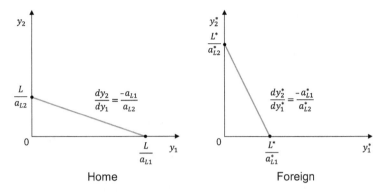

Fig. 4.1 The Ricardian production possibilities setting

full employment condition for the home country (analogously for the foreign country) with the quantities of output, y_i, to be produced in the economy:

$$a_{L1}y_1 + a_{L2}y_2 = L \tag{4.1}$$

The production possibility frontiers (PPF) are drawn in Fig. 4.1. Note that they are linear which is due to the constant labour coefficients. Equation 4.1 implies the maximum quantities of good 1 (good 2) producible in case of complete specialization: L/a_{L1} (L/a_{L2}). The slope of the PPF equals (minus) the ratio of the two labour coefficients (a_{L1}/a_{L2}) and shows how much of good 2 must be given up in order to release enough labour to produce another unit of good 1 (dy_2/dy_1). In other words, it equals the opportunity costs of good 1: To produce one unit more of good 1, we need a_{L1} units of labour which reduces the output of good 2 by a_{L1}/a_{L2} units.[2] The PPF of the foreign country is determined analogously.

In autarky, an economy must rely on its own production to satisfy consumption needs. Any point on the PPF can, however, be chosen. Which point this will be, depends on the precise preferences of the consumers.[3] In any case, relative prices in autarky are equal to the opportunity costs and reflected by the constant slope of the PPF: $-p_1/p_2 = -a_{L1}/a_{L2}$. Note that, in Fig. 4.1, they differ between the two countries: The opportunity costs of producing good 1—and thus the price of good 1—are assumed to be lower in the home country. Home has to give up less of good 2 than Foreign to produce more of good 1. In other words, the home country is able to

---

[2]The slope can also be found by solving Eq. (4.1) for y_2 and differentiating y_2 with respect to y_1. Or, as a special case, we simply divide L/a_{L2} (dy_2) by L/a_{L1} (dy_1).

[3]Thus, the optimal production point on the PPF in autarky could be determined by introducing preferences of the consumers in a country. The representative consumer would choose a consumption bundle where an indifference curve is tangent to the PPF: The opportunity costs of producing the two goods equal the willingness of consumers to marginally substitute the two goods (i.e., the marginal rate of substitution). See, e.g., Caves, Frankel, and Jones (2007, Chaps. 2 and 4).

produce good 1 with *relatively* less resources than the foreign country—it has a *comparative advantage* in the production of good 1:

$$\frac{a_{L1}}{a_{L2}} < \frac{a_{L1}^*}{a_{L2}^*} \tag{4.2}$$

Inequality (4.2), however, implies that the foreign country has a comparative advantage in good 2! It uses relatively less labour than the home country in the production of good 2 as $a_{L2}/a_{L1} > a_{L2}^*/a_{L1}^*$. The autarky situation can thus be summarized: Both countries are producing both goods somewhere on their PPF. Because of the assumed differences in the relative productivities and thus in relative costs of producing the two goods, the relative price of good 1 (good 2) will be lower in the home (foreign) country in autarky.

The question now arises what will happen if the two countries open up trade. The presumption is that consumers will find it beneficial to buy the relatively cheaper good abroad: Foreign consumers buying good 1 in the home country and Home's consumer buying good 2 in the foreign country. This, in turn, implies that p_1/p_2 tends to rise in Home (and p_2/p_1 in Foreign). If there are no international transaction costs, this process would last until the two relative prices become equalized, i.e., $p_1/p_2 = p_1^*/p_2^*$. In Fig. 4.1, this would imply that the slope of the relative price in the trade situation is steeper (flatter) than the opportunity costs in the home (foreign) country.

In order to understand the implications for production, it is helpful to introduce the so-called *competitive profit conditions*—again for Home (with analogous conditions for Foreign):

$$a_{L1}w \geq p_1 \tag{4.3}$$

$$a_{L2}w \geq p_2 \tag{4.4}$$

A competitive equilibrium must be characterized by equality between unit cost and price if production of a good takes place. If unit cost would be less than the price in the industry producing good 1, for example, firms would hire more labour in order to expand production which would raise wages (and possibly lower p_1) until an equilibrium is reached where unit cost equals price. Unit costs may, however, exceed the price implying that all producers leave the industry. This implies that there is equality between unit cost and price in (4.3) and (4.4) if we are in the autarky equilibrium in which both goods are produced.

Suppose we now open up trade. As mentioned above, opening up trade implies a greater demand for good 1 produced in the home country, shifting Home's production point down along the PPF and raising (decreasing) y_1 (y_2). The opposite happens in the foreign country. If the additional demand for good 1 is large enough, p_1 rises which, according to (4.3), raises w in the home country: Firms in industry 1 bid up the wage rate in order to get the required labour to increase production. This, however, squeezes firms in industry 2 which become uncompetitive to pay the higher wage rate—$a_{L2}w > p_2$ in (4.4)—and exit the industry. The home country thus becomes completely specialized in industry 1. The analogous adjustment happens in Foreign: It shifts its resources from industry 1 to industry 2 and may eventually become completely specialized in good 2.

4.1.1   Gains from Trade

The gains from trade can easily be imagined with the help of Fig. 4.1. The relative price of the two goods, p_1/p_2, will—as discussed above—lie in-between the two countries' or equal one country's opportunity cost in the free-trade equilibrium. Suppose the former is the case. This implies that the home country becomes completely specialized in good 1: It produces L/a_{L1} of good 1 (Foreign: L^*/a_{L2}^* of good 2). This, however, allows each country to reach a higher consumption point on the new relative price line in free trade, the so-called terms of trade. Home exports good 1 against good 2 and vice versa the foreign country. The gains from trade then capture the additional quantity of good 1 and good 2 each country is able to consume compared to the autarky situation.[4]

The gains from trade can nicely be illustrated with the World Production Possibility Frontier (see Fig. 4.2) which captures the efficient world output possibilities in free trade—the world being composed of the two countries as also used in Caves, Frankel, and Jones (2007, p. 63). Point C (E) equals the maximum possible output of good 2 (1) if both countries use all of their resources in one industry. Suppose we are in point C with both countries only producing good 2 (this situation would arise

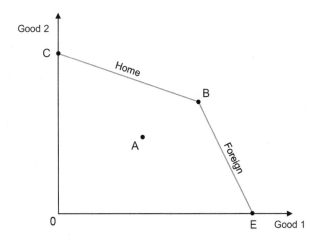

Fig. 4.2 The world production possibility frontier

---

[4]Suppose the demand side of the economy is specified and thus determined in form of indifference curves. We would easily find out that a higher indifference curve can be reached in each country with international trade if relative prices differ from the countries' opportunity costs.

if p_1/p_2 were very low). Which country would be first to start production of good 1? The answer: The home country, as it has a comparative advantage of good 1. Thus, CD shows a situation in which Foreign only produces good 2 and Home produces both goods. In point B, both countries are completely specialized in that good in which they have a comparative advantage. If demand for good 1 (and its relative price p_1/p_2) rises further, also Foreign starts to produce it (line BE).

If the two countries thus specialize in that good in which they have a comparative advantage (though not necessarily both of them completely), a point on the World Production Possibility Frontier will be reached. Which point that is, depends on the preferences in the two countries and the countries' relative size. Compare this with the autarky situation (where both countries produce both goods). Such a point in which each country produces and consumes somewhere on its PPF (see Fig. 4.1) according to its preferences is reflected by A (i.e., the countries' individual productions of both goods are summed up). There is a whole set of autarky points which could be traced out and which would typically lie below the World Production Possibility Frontier (except for points C and E).[5] We conclude that free trade generally raises the world output compared to autarky, given the countries' limited resources. Or, in other words, the consumption level in autarky could be reached by a lower amount of resources devoted to its production.

4.1.2   Free-Trade Equilibria

Figure 4.3 captures the relationship between the relative price, p_1/p_2, and relative world production and consumption, $(y_1 + y_1^*)/(y_2 + y_2^*)$, of the two goods in free trade.[6] Note that world relative supply (RS) is a step-function due to the linear PPFs of the two countries. Only if the relative price of good 1, p_1/p_2, rises to Home's opportunity cost, a_{L1}/a_{L2}, can good 1 be produced. If $p_1/p_2 = a_{L1}/a_{L2}$, rising relative demand for good 1 is satisfied by a move along and down Home's PPF—Home producing both goods, but substituting y_1 for y_2—with Foreign remaining completely specialized in good 2. When p_1/p_2 lies above Home's opportunity cost to produce good 1, but still remains below the foreign country's relative productivities, the two countries are completely specialized in that good in which they have a comparative advantage (Home produces L/a_{L1} of good 1, Foreign L^*/a_{L2}^* of good 2). When the relative price reaches Foreign's opportunity cost, this country also starts to produce good 1. If the relative price were to rise even further, both countries would be completely specialized in good 1 with RS converging to infinity.

As can be seen from Fig. 4.3, there are three different free-trade equilibria possible, depending on relative demand (RD) of the world economy, composed of

---

[5]See also Chap. 6 in this book.

[6]Similar figures are used by Caves, Frankel, and Jones (2007, p. 64), Krugman, Obstfeld and Melitz (2015, p. 63) or Feenstra (2016, p. 3).

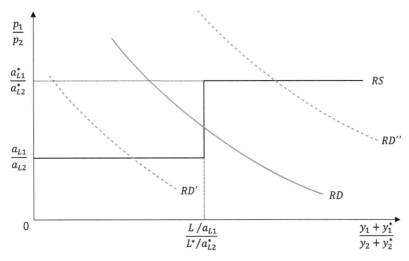

Fig. 4.3 World relative supply (RS) and demand (RD) in free trade

the two countries. If aggregate relative demand for good 1 is characterized by *RD*, the equilibrium relative price of the two goods lies between the opportunity costs of the two countries. There is complete specialization: Each country produces and exports that good in which it has a comparative advantage (this would correspond to Point *B* in Fig. 4.2). If aggregate relative demand for good 1 is relatively small (and for good 2 relatively large) as depicted by *RD'*, Home produces both goods (i.e., also good 2 in which it has a comparative disadvantage) and Foreign produces only good 2 (this equals an equilibrium on *CB* in Fig. 4.2). Note that Home exports some of good 1 for imports of good 2. Finally, *RD"* describes a free-trade equilibrium in which aggregate relative demand for good 1 is large and thus in which both countries produce good 1—Home being completely specialized in good 1 and Foreign producing both goods (this equals a point on *BE* in Fig. 4.2).

We conclude that incomplete specialization of one country (not both countries) is possible in free trade. The pattern of trade, however, is always determined by comparative advantage. If there is trade, each country exports that good in which it has a comparative advantage.

4.1.3   International Wage Comparison

Query: "Does absolute productivity matter?" The answer: "not for the pattern of trade". As shown above, the pattern of trade is completely determined by *relative* differences in productivity, i.e., by *comparative advantage*. However, absolute differences in productivity between the countries are important determinants of the wage rate residents earn in the countries. The more productive a country is on average, the higher the wage rate and thus the greater the average income in a country. We now derive the range of the relative wage rate in the two countries, w/w^*, more carefully.

Let us start again by supposing that the relative price of good 1 is very low such that even the home country puts some or all of its labour into the production of good 2. In Fig. 4.3, the equilibrium would be characterized by $p_1/p_2 \leq a_{L1}/a_{L2}$ (in Fig. 4.2 by a point on CB). As both countries are producing good 2 (Home possibly also good 1), the wage rate in each country will be pinned down by the price of good 2 and the productivities in industry 2 in the two countries, which in turn determines the relative wage rate:

$$w a_{L2} = p_2 = w^* a_{L2}^* \tag{4.5}$$

$$\frac{w}{w^*} = \frac{a_{L2}^*}{a_{L2}} \tag{4.6}$$

Thus, the concept of *absolute advantage* comes into the picture: If the home country is twice as productive in producing good 2, its workers will earn twice as much as those in the foreign country (remember that there is no global market for labour). Note that Eq. (4.6) establishes the lower bound of relative wages, w/w^*, where a relatively high price of good 2 even makes Home produce that good (2) in which it has a comparative disadvantage. A very high price of good 1, in contrast, implies that both countries are producing (some of) good 1. If this is the case, relative wages reflect the two countries' productivities in industry 1:

$$w a_{L1} = p_1 = w^* a_{L1}^* \tag{4.7}$$

$$\frac{w}{w^*} = \frac{a_{L1}^*}{a_{L1}} \tag{4.8}$$

This establishes the upper bound of relative wages. Equations (4.6) and (4.8) imply that Home for sure has a higher wage ($w > w^*$) in the trade equilibrium if it has an absolute productivity advantage in both goods ($a_{L2} < a_{L2}^*$, $a_{L1} < a_{L1}^*$). If this is not the case for good 2 (and thus for the lower bound), but for good 1, Home could still have a higher wage, depending on the relative price of the two goods. In the case of complete specialization, the competitive profit conditions apply for good 1 (Home) and good 2 (Foreign), respectively. The relative wage rate thus equals:

$$\frac{w}{w^*} = \frac{p_1/a_{L1}}{p_2^*/a_{L2}^*} = \frac{a_{L2}^* p_1}{a_{L1} p_2}. \tag{4.9}$$

Therefore, if the countries are completely specialized, their relative wage rate reflects not only a comparison of the productivities of the goods they produce, but also of the relative price of the two goods in free trade. The higher the price of good 1, the higher Home's relative wage. An increase of the relative price of good 1 thus tends to benefit the home country. Home gets more for its export good and thus is

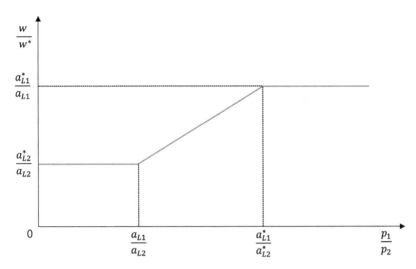

Fig. 4.4 Relative wages in free trade

able to buy a greater quantity of imports. All of this is captured by Fig. 4.4 which shows the range of possible equilibria of wages in free trade, depending on the countries' productivities and the relative price of the two goods.[7] Note that a 10% increase in good 1's price would raise Home's wages by 10% relative to the foreign country's wage if the countries are completely specialized.

We can conclude that, if there is trade between the two countries, the pattern of trade is determined by comparative advantage. The production pattern, however, is not completely determined and depends on demand characteristics. It may incorporate complete specialization of each country (according to comparative advantages), but can also include a situation with one country producing both goods. Also note that wages are determined by productivities and the relative price of the two goods. If, however, one country is more productive in both goods (i.e., if it has an absolute advantage in both goods) it will always enjoy a higher wage rate in the free trade equilibrium.

Finally, we should note that countries benefit from international trade. This can be nicely illustrated with Fig. 4.2 above: If the relative free-trade price lies in-between the two countries' opportunity costs, then point B can be attained. A small country tends to benefit relatively more from trade compared to a large country due to the fact that the relative free-trade price is closer to the opportunity cost of the large country. In other words, the small country's consumption point lies farther from the PPF and thus per-capita consumption increases by more in the smaller country (see Fig. 4.1). For a very small home country, the free-trade equilibrium may be characterized by a relative price that equals Foreign's

---

[7]The figure is adapted from Caves, Frankel, and Jones (2007, p. 67).

opportunity costs ($p_1/p_2 = a_{L1}{}^*/a_{L2}{}^*$). As shown by Fig. 4.4, the wage ratio takes on its upper bound and all the gains from trade accrue to the home country.

Note that there are no distributional effects within the two countries: the gains from trade are equally distributed among all individuals. Individuals who lose their job because of specialization move from the import-competing to the export-oriented industry in which they find a better-paid job. The assumed perfect mobility of labour between industries implies that nobody loses within a country.

4.2 Two Countries and Many Goods

One of the attractive features of the Ricardian model is that it can easily incorporate more than two goods. We thus extend the 2×2 case to a model with many goods, still assuming two countries (Home and Foreign) and one factor of production (Labour). We assign each of the goods a number from 1 to N. We make use of the findings regarding the pattern of trade and the equilibrium wage ratio for the 2×2 model as implied by Fig. 4.4:

$$\frac{a_{L1}^*}{a_{L1}} \geq \frac{w}{w^*} \geq \frac{a_{L2}^*}{a_{L2}} \tag{4.10}$$

Remember that whereas the lower and upper bounds of the wage ratio is exogenous, the equilibrium wage ratio depends on the relative price of the two goods and thus on demand conditions. Ranking the goods or industries by comparative costs in a "chain" of decreasing Home relative productivities and including the equilibrium relative wage rate, leads to a natural expansion of the expression (4.10) to (4.11):

$$\frac{a_{L1}^*}{a_{L1}} > \frac{a_{L2}^*}{a_{L2}} > \frac{a_{L3}^*}{a_{L3}} = \frac{w}{w^*} > \frac{a_{L4}^*}{a_{L4}} > \ldots > \frac{a_{LN-2}^*}{a_{N-2}} > \frac{a_{LN-1}^*}{a_{N-1}} > \frac{a_{LN}^*}{a_N} \tag{4.11}$$

Note that we arbitrarily assumed an equilibrium wage ratio ($w/w^*=a_{L3}^*/a_{L3}$), determined by demand and supply in the labour market of each country. The demand for labour, in turn, is derived from the demand for all the goods produced with each country's labour and thus depends on demand conditions reflecting the two countries' size and preferences. Suppose the result of this process is depicted by the situation reflected in expression (4.11). What is the implication regarding the pattern of trade and production?

First, the home country exports all goods to the left of where the chain is broken (i.e., goods 1 to 2, whereas the foreign country exports those to the right of the break (i.e., goods 4 to N). This is in analogy to the two-goods case and can easily be confirmed by multiplication of terms that are unequal in (4.11): $a_{L1}^*w^*>a_{L1}w$ or $a_{LN}w > a_{LN}^*w^*$, for example. Second, there is complete specialization in all goods with the exception of one good, good 3, for which production costs happen to be equal in the two countries: $a_{L3}*w*=a_{L3}w$. Thus, the Ricardian $2 \times N$ model leads to extreme specialization which however would be reduced if international trade required small international transaction costs. As will be shown in Sect. 4.4, this would give rise to nontraded goods with relative productivities in the neighbourhood of the equilibrium wage ratio.

4.3   Two Countries and Very Many Goods

We now push the assumption of many goods to the limit by assuming that the two countries are producing "very many goods", i.e., an extremely large number of goods whose ratio of labour requirements reflected in (4.11) varies continuously. This Ricardian model with a continuum of goods has been established by Dornbusch et al. (1977) and, in some ways, simplifies the discussion of the equilibrium and possible applications of the Ricardian trade theory. We thus suppose that goods are indexed by z on an interval of $[0,1]$ according to the home country's diminishing comparative advantage:

$$A(z) = \frac{a^*(z)}{a(z)} \quad \text{with } A'(z) < 0. \tag{4.12}$$

Thus, $A(z)$ is a continuous and monotonically decreasing function of z as shown in Fig. 4.5. It is downward sloping by construction as the goods are indexed based on their ranking regarding Home's comparative advantage: The goods with the lowest "number" (z) are (again) those in which the home country has its greatest comparative advantage. We now suppose that there is an endogenous equilibrium relative wage rate, $\left(\dfrac{\tilde{w}}{w*}\right)$, associated with a marginal good $(\tilde{z})$ for

Fig. 4.5 The Ricardian model with a continuum of goods. Source: Adapted from Dornbusch et al. (1977, p. 825)

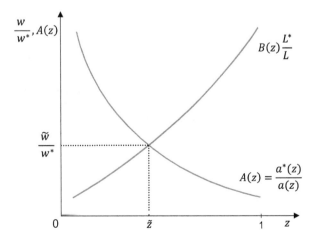

which the unit costs of production are identical, $wa(\tilde{z}) = w^*a^*(\tilde{z})$, and which therefore is produced in both countries. Efficient specialization implies that those goods are exported by the home country, for which $\left(\dfrac{\tilde{w}}{w^*}\right) < \dfrac{a^*(z)}{a(z)}$. In other words, Fig. 4.5 implies that all goods z in the interval $[0, \tilde{z}]$ are produced by the home country, whereas those in the interval $[\tilde{z}, 1]$ are produced by the foreign country. There is complete specialization in all goods except for $\tilde{z}$.

In order to determine the labour market equilibrium and thus the relative wage, w/w^*, we specify the demand conditions. Dornbusch et al. (1977) assume identical Cobb-Douglas preferences in the two countries, i.e., the consumers spend the constant share $b(z)$ of their income on good z (note that $b(z)$ may differ between each good, but is assumed to be identical in the two countries and independent of income). Let us hypothetically assume that $\tilde{z}$ is the borderline good produced in both countries. As the home country produces all the goods with the index in the interval $[0, \tilde{z}]$, the share of income spent on goods produced by the home country equals $\theta(\tilde{z}) = \displaystyle\int_0^{\tilde{z}} b(z)dz$. Thus, $\theta(\tilde{z})$ is the fraction of each consumer's income on Home's produced goods—and $(1 - \theta(\tilde{z}))$ equals the fraction of each country's income spent on goods produced by Foreign. Equilibrium in the product and labour markets requires that the labour income, for example, in the home country is equal to the expenditures of consumers in the home and the foreign country for home-produced goods.[8] Thus,

$$wL = \theta(\tilde{z})wL + \theta(\tilde{z})w^*L^* \tag{4.13}$$

Solving for the relative wage, w/w^*, implies the following relationship:

$$\frac{w}{w^*} = \frac{\theta(\tilde{z})}{1 - \theta(\tilde{z})} \frac{L^*}{L} \tag{4.14}$$

With Eq. (4.14), each $\tilde{z}$ is associated with a relative wage rate, w/w^*. If $\tilde{z}$ increases, the relative wage rate rises. The right-hand side of Eq. (4.14) is simplified to $B(z)L^*/L$, with $B'(z) > 0$ and drawn as an upward-sloping curve in Fig. 4.5: If the range of domestically produced goods were increased, the fraction of world income spent on the home country's goods rises which, in turn, implies a relatively higher wage rate in the home country. The general equilibrium is also captured by Fig. 4.5. It requires that the world (i.e., the two countries) is efficiently specialized and that there is full employment (and balanced trade).

---

[8]An alternative condition would be to require balanced trade.

$$A(z) = \frac{w}{w^*} = B(z)\frac{L^*}{L} \tag{4.15}$$

The gains from trade can easily be demonstrated. The home country gains from trade if it imports those goods for which production costs abroad are lower than at home, given the equilibrium relative wage rate. Producing goods at home implies a unit price and thus production costs of $p(z) = wa(z)$. Importing them from the foreign country implies a price to pay of $p(z) = w^*a^*(z)$. Home should thus import those goods for which $[wa(z)/w^*a^*(z)] > 1$ or $w/w^* > a^*(z)/a(z)$. Note that this is exactly what happens in the efficient equilibrium in Fig. 4.5 for goods on the right of $\tilde{z}$.

As in the two-goods case, the home country's wage rate (and thus real income per capita) in the free-trade equilibrium tends to be relatively higher the smaller the home country is: The upward-sloping schedule becomes steeper if L is small. This also implies that a small home country tends to produce a smaller number of goods ($\tilde{z}$ falls with rising L), specializing on those goods with the greatest relative advantage.

4.4   Nontraded Goods

So far we neglected the costs involved in transporting goods and services from one location to another. Also, we did not explicitly consider artificial impediments to trade such as tariffs, quotas or administrative barriers at the border. In reality, no good or service can be made available in another country without additional costs. To some extent, however, we took into account transportation costs by comparing two extreme cases: Autarky with prohibitively high costs of international trade for all goods and services and free trade with no transportation costs at all for all exports and imports. For some purposes, however, it is useful to consider—in free trade—a situation in which some goods and services are internationally traded and some are not. The Ricardian model is receptive to incorporate nontraded goods, i.e., to explain their existence and to discuss different adjustments of an economy in the traded and nontraded sector.

Real examples abound. Goods have to be packaged and transported from the producer to the buyer. If they cross borders, additional paper work is usually necessary. Shipping a good abroad typically requires additional costs because of, for example, a longer distance, a different currency, another language, special insurances, different liability laws and assuring payment. This is often also the case if a good or service, such as a piece of software, a video, an instruction or a piece of music is transmitted through the internet. The export of a service may, in contrast, require consumers from one country to move to the location of the producer of another country. This is, for example, the case for tourism, auto repairs, or haircuts. If the transportation costs are, compared to the price of the service, too high the service may de facto become an internationally nontraded service (e.g., for haircuts). The share of nontraded services and goods remains relatively large in a country's GDP which is another reason why we may want to consider them in a trade model.

The existence of nontraded goods (and services) can easily be taken into account in the 2 × N Ricardian model by incorporating small (international) transportation costs into the chain of decreasing (Home) comparative advantage. Suppose small transportation costs, T, per unit of output and that they are identical for all goods. We assume the following situation:

$$\frac{a_{L1}^*}{a_{L1}} > \frac{a_{L2}^*}{a_{L2}} > \frac{a_{L3}^*}{a_{L3}} > \frac{w}{w^*} > \frac{a_{L4}^*}{a_{L4}} > \frac{a_{L5}^*}{a_{L5}} > \dots > \frac{a_{LN}^*}{a_N}, \tag{4.16}$$

and

$$wa_{L3} + T > w^* a_{L3}^*, wa_{L2} + T < w^* a_{L2}^*, \tag{4.17}$$

$$w^* a_{L4}^* + T > wa_{L4}, w^* a_{L5}^* + T < wa_{L5}. \tag{4.18}$$

Question: "Which goods will be traded and what is the pattern of trade?" The answer is straight forward. Without trade costs, the home country exports good 1, 2 and 3 and it imports all the other goods, given the equilibrium relative wage rate in (4.16). The existence of small trade costs now implies that despite the home country's smaller production costs of good 3, its total cost of making good 3 available to foreign consumers are higher than the foreign production costs. Thus, good 3 becomes nontraded as home producers are not able to compete with the foreign country's producers of good 3, given their higher total costs. The analogous situation applies to good 4 in which foreign firms are not able to compete with home's firms despite their lower production costs. It therefore also becomes nontraded.

As can be seen from (4.16) to (4.18), the goods of the marginally more competitive industries 2 and 5 in the home and foreign country, respectively, are internationally traded as the difference in production costs in the two countries outweigh the transportation costs. Therefore, (4.16) and (4.17, 4.18) imply that the goods on the left (right) of the chain in which the home (foreign) country has it greatest comparative advantage are exported by home (foreign), i.e., good 1 and 2 (goods 5 to N). The goods in the middle, i.e., good 3 and 4, are nontraded and thus only produced for the domestic market in each country. Thus, it is those goods in which countries do not have large differences in production costs that turn out to be nontraded. An analogous result applies to the Ricardian model with a continuum of goods. As shown by Dornbusch et al. (1977, p. 830) the $A(z)$ schedule in Fig. 4.5 would be replaced by two schedules which include Home's and Foreign's transportation costs (see Fig. 4.7 in the Appendix).[9]

Let us now go one step further to answer questions about the effects of technology or price shocks on traded and nontraded goods. Suppose the home country is extremely small. In this case it may only produce good 1, with a relative wage rate (w/w^*) being greater than the relative labour coefficient in industry 2. As the country is small, the price of good 1 remains exogenous. Thus, the wage rate in the home country is pinned down by $w = p_1/a_{L1}$. We also assume that there is some nontraded good (*NT*)—for example, restaurant or other personal services—for which there is local demand. The price of this nontraded good must equal the unit cost of its domestic production, i.e., $p_{NT} = a_{LNT}w$. In other words, the price of the nontraded good is determined by the domestic technology (a_{LNT}) and the domestic wage rate (w) which, in turn, is determined by the world market price of the traded good (p_1) and the technology with which it is produced in the home country (a_{L1}).

We assume that the country produces a certain mix of the export good 1 and the nontraded good *NT*. Given the resource constraint, the allocation will have to fulfill the full-employment constraint: $L_1 + L_{NT} = L$. We should note that the value of the exported quantity of good 1 $(L_1/a_{L1})p_1$ has to be equal to the value of all imported goods if there is balanced trade as assumed in this model. This situation is depicted by Fig. 4.6, adapted from Caves, Frankel, and Jones (2007, p. 73). We assume the trade-equilibrium is in point *A* due to the preferences of all consumers in the country. Note that this implies the production and consumption of a certain quantity of the nontraded good (L_{NT}/a_{LNT}) and the consumption of goods 1 to *N* (of which 2 to *N* are imported), the value of which equals the value of production of $(L_1/a_{L1})p_1$ of good 1.

Suppose now that world prices do not change, but that the conditions of producing good 2 considerably improve in the home country such that it is able to offer a higher wage than producers in industry 1 can. In other words, a_{L2} decreases such that $\dfrac{p_1}{a_{L1}} < \dfrac{p_2}{a_{L2}}$. As the prices are given on the world market and as the labour coefficients are constant (there is no diminishing marginal product), the effect is drastic: Local production of industry 1 is wiped out. There is a so-called Dutch Disease effect on industry 1 due to the technological improvement in industry 2.[10] Note the implication of this in Fig. 4.6: The value of the traded goods

---

[9]If transportation costs are, however, good-specific and possibly large, the ranking of the goods in (4.16) may not be relevant anymore regarding the distinction between traded and nontraded goods. In this case we would have to re-order the goods in the chain of decreasing relative costs, taking into account the different transportation costs. Also note that Sanyal and Jones (1982), in their paper "Trade in Middle Products" present a model, in which all goods which are "consumed" are nontraded. These goods differ, however, regarding the share of the domestic added value.

[10]An analogous effect would arise if, alternatively, the price of good 2 increased accordingly. The notion of the "Dutch Disease" goes back to the rapid development of the natural gas sector in the Netherlands which squeezed other traditional export sectors of the Dutch economy. Other examples are the (sometimes) booming oil industries in Norway, Great Britain or in the Canadian Province of Alberta which typically results in a burden on other export industries. The "Dutch Disease effect" has thus become a generic effect in (Ricardian) trade theory that emphasizes the fact that industries in a country do compete for domestic factors of production such as labor.

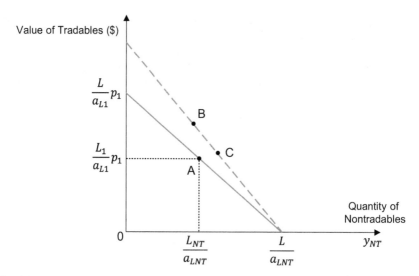

Fig. 4.6 Nontraded and traded goods

based on the new best industry 2 rises, letting the PPF turn clockwise as shown by the dotted line. Depending on the precise preferences of the consumers in the home country the new equilibrium could be in point C or B. In other words, the local production of the nontraded good could fall or rise. The economy as a whole clearly gains from this replacement of industry 1 by industry 2.

The result is interesting. On the one hand, the price of the nontraded good, p_{NT}, rises which tends to reduce the demand for the nontraded good (the increase in p_{NT} is due to the increase of the wage rate as labour is now employed in the more productive industry 2). On the other hand, the real wage in terms of the traded goods increases, which increases demand also for the nontraded good. Depending on the relative size of these two effects (i.e., the substitution and the income effect), the equilibrium can be found in B or C. In other words, the impact of the productivity increase in one industry on other industries may be rather different, depending on whether these industries produce nontraded goods or have to compete on the world market.

This example also has interesting implications for a country's price level. Query: "What is the effect of this technological change on the average price level, e.g., the consumer price index (CPI), in the home country?" The answer is: It rises because of the price increase of the nontraded good. Note, however, that the price increase is entirely due to the technological improvement in industry 2, and it is associated with an overall increase in the wellbeing of the home country's residents.[11]

---

[11]This is the so-called Balassa-Samuelson effect and may partly explain why in some countries as Switzerland or the Scandinavian countries prices are considered to be pretty high.

4.5   Conclusions

In his graduate textbook, Robert Feenstra (2016) argues that in order to explain "historical or modern trade patterns" it is necessary to "allow for technological differences across countries". He then adds: "For this reason, the Ricardian model is as relevant today as it has always been." (p. 1) Even though this is certainly true, the model's relevance goes deeper. It is the emphasis on international trade that allows imports to be produced "indirectly" through exports. And it is the explanation that the resulting gains from trade depend on the existence of *relative* differences in the countries capabilities. The model also simplifies complex real-world situations by using one factor of production, perfect competition and constant factor coefficients which allow many differences among countries (including technological differences) to be captured by one parameter per country and industry. This makes the model irreplaceable to study complex relationships in the real world.

The implication of the model that all countries, in principle, are able to trade and gain from trade is very basic and important. The model, however, also shows the determinants of these gains (countries have to be *relatively* different in their abilities to produce goods and services) and of the ability to trade (countries have to allow for flexible wage rates). The fact that nobody loses from trade *within* a country is closely related to the assumption that there is perfect labour mobility between the industries. The model thus also implies that with limited labour mobility within a country, some individuals are likely to lose in those industries that are wiped out by opening up trade. As the marginal labour productivities are assumed to be constant in the model, the degree of specialization becomes extreme in the standard Ricardian model (without international transaction costs).

The inclusion of many or even a continuum of goods as well as of the so-called nontraded goods makes the model more realistic and receptive to the study of many interesting real word issues. A number of implications and applications of the standard Ricardian trade model are presented and discussed in Chap. 5 of this book. Chapters 6, 7 and 12 show how the model can be extended to many countries, how it relates to other trade models and how it can be empirically analyzed in a rigorous way.

Appendix

Please note that, in the following Fig. 4.7, $g < 1$ reflects iceberg transportation costs due to Samuelson (1954): For each unit of a good, z, only the fraction g arrives. This implies that $A(z)>w/w^*$ is not a sufficient condition for a good to be exported by the home country as $1/g > 1$ of transportation costs have to be taken into account in Home's "total" unit costs: $wa(z)1/g$. This implies the new adjusted $A(z)g$ and $A(z)/g$ curves, respectively. For a given equilibrium relative wage rate $\left(\frac{\tilde{w}}{w^*}\right)$, the home

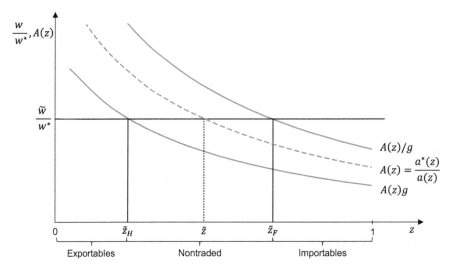

Fig. 4.7 The Ricardian model with a continuum of goods and transportation costs. Source: Own figure in analogy to Dornbusch, Fischer, and Samuelson (1977, p. 830)

country will export those goods for which $A(z)g > \left(\dfrac{\tilde{w}}{w^*}\right)$ and the foreign country those for which $A(z)/g < \left(\dfrac{\tilde{w}}{w^*}\right)$. Therefore, the goods "in the middle", i.e. goods $z \in \left[\tilde{z}_H, \tilde{z}_F\right]$, remain nontraded.

References

Caves, R. E., Frankel, J. A., & Jones, R. W. (2007). *World trade and payments. An introduction* (10th ed.). Boston: Pearson.

Dornbusch, R., Fischer, S., & Samuelson, P. A. (1977). Comparative advantage, trade, and payments in a Ricardian model with a continuum of goods. *The American Economic Review, 67*(5), 823–839.

Feenstra, R. C. (2016). *Advanced international trade* (2nd ed.). Princeton, NJ: Princeton University Press.

Krugman, P., Obstfeld, M., & Melitz, M. J. (2015). *International economics. Theory and policy* (10th ed.). Boston: Pearson.

Samuelson, P. A. (1954). The transfer problem and the transport costs, II: Analysis of effects of trade impediments. *The Economic Journal, 64*(254), 264–289.

Sanyal, K. K., & Jones, R. W. (1982). The theory of trade in middle products. *American Economic Review, 72*(1), 16–31.

Chapter 5
The Ricardian Trade Model: Implications and Applications

Rolf Weder

Abstract This chapter argues that the Ricardian trade theory's small-scale general equilibrium characteristics are helpful in understanding the complex world economy and in uncovering some of the misconceptions of the globalization debate. First, it is shown that the main predictions of the model seem roughly in line with empirical observations regarding the pattern of trade and relative wages. Second, it is explained why countries do not compete in the way companies do and that wage comparisons between the North and the South that focus on export industries are misguided. Third, the model is applied to the topical question of how an improvement in productivity abroad affects the home country.

There is, and has always been, a lively debate about the effects of globalization. The idea of this chapter is to show what can be learned from the Ricardian trade model to the benefit of the quality of this debate. As a trade economist, observing the discussion among citizens, politicians, entrepreneurs and even academics, one is often surprised about the arguments made by, in principle, intelligent people—arguments that are based on prejudice, on generalizations of individual experience or on a vague intuition about the functioning of the world economy.

Paul Krugman once gave this widely observable practice the name "Pop Internationalism": Seemingly impressive and sophisticated talk about international trade while ignoring basic economic concepts—such as the Ricardian trade theory.

Here are some examples of the associated misconceptions. It starts with the common belief that countries compete in the world economy the way companies do: *If you want to survive in and benefit from the world economy as a country, you have to remain internationally competitive and thus constantly raise your productivity.* This view neglects the fact that wages adjust to a country's (low or high) productivity. The correct perspective implies a much less dramatic nature of the world economy: A country cannot become uncompetitive. A related fallacy is the fear that a country's standard of living is threatened by a general (i.e., uniform) technological progress abroad. As will be shown below, such a scenario should,

R. Weder (✉)
Faculty of Business and Economics, University of Basel, Basel, Switzerland
e-mail: rolf.weder@unibas.ch

© Springer International Publishing AG 2017   73
R.W. Jones, R. Weder (eds.), *200 Years of Ricardian Trade Theory*,
https://doi.org/10.1007/978-3-319-60606-4_5

instead, largely be welcomed. Others, again, believe that poor countries' wages are too low compared to their productivities (exploitation by rich countries comes to their mind). Their comparison, however, is often based on wrong productivities.

Krugman (1996) does a fine job in making a broad audience aware of *some* misconceptions in his book "Pop Internationalism". In contrast to his analysis, I plan to tighten the relationship between misconceptions and the Ricardian trade theory. The target is to relate these points of views as closely as possible to the Ricardian model and, thereby, to show in which way Ricardian trade theory is most helpful in answering the associated questions about the real world economy—particularly for those readers, who are willing to take the effort to study the model and apply it. In other words, the discussion in this chapter builds on the basic understanding and framework of the Ricardian trade theory developed in Chap. 4, with two countries and two goods and, for some applications, extended to N or a continuum of goods.

The remainder of this chapter is structured as follows. In Sect. 5.1, we have a look at how the Ricardian trade model matches with some real world observations. Section 5.2 takes on the international competitiveness debate and shows implications of the Ricardian theory for wages and prices in the North and South. In Sect. 5.3, we apply the model to the question of how an improvement in productivity abroad or, more generally, in the rest of the world is likely to affect the home country. Section 5.4 concludes.

5.1   Empirical Analysis of the Model

What should be empirically analyzed? The answer is clear if one takes the majority of existing studies of the Ricardian trade model as an indication: It is the pattern of trade. Krugman, Obstfeld, and Melitz (2015, p. 77) confirm and conclude regarding the model's quality in this respect: "[T]he basic prediction of the Ricardian model—that countries should tend to export those goods in which their productivity is relatively high—has been strongly confirmed by a number of studies over the years." The authors illustrate the evidence by referring to the empirical analysis in the classical paper by Bela Balassa (1963) who analyzed the trade pattern for the U.S. and the U.K., using data of 1951.

In his article in the *Handbook of International Economics (Vol. 1)* on "Testing Trade Theories and Predicting Trade Flows", Alain Deardorff (1984, p. 469) decomposed his fundamental question "How do you test a trade theory?" into three sub-questions. A trade theory "might be expected to answer": (1) what goods, (2) with whom and (3) how much do countries trade? He then adds that "the fundamental theories of international trade deal only with the first" (p. 470). The reason why the second question has not received much interest is that most trade models, including the Ricardian model, are based on the assumption of two countries. Thus, the question with whom a country trades is pretty obvious: With the other one—or the rest of the world. Regarding the third question (volume of trade), one might also debate how interesting and important it is from a pure trade-theory perspective.[1]

In a more recent article in the *Handbook of International Economics (Vol. 2)* on "International Trade Theory: The Evidence" Edward Leamer and James Levinsohn (1995) also provide fundamental thoughts on these questions. "Don't take trade theory too seriously" is their first message which, according to them, means in practice: "Estimate, don't test" (p. 1341). This implies, in my view, that—when empirically analyzing a trade theory—we should realize that the theory is always wrong in some respect. We know that. This is why it is called a theory. It tries to abstract from certain aspects of reality in order to better capture the essential relationship the model intends to focus on. In the Ricardian model, for example, the relationship between relative exports and relative productivities is an essential prediction of the model and it, therefore, should be empirically analyzed. The extreme degree of specialization between the countries implied by the model, is, however, a consequence of the assumed constant labour productivities (i.e., the constant marginal product) and would be refuted in an attempt to literally "test" the theory. But the purpose of this unrealistic assumption, including the one that there is only one production factor, is strategic simplification. It is a simplification which opens up the door to focus on the main idea of the theory, as it was so ingeniously set up by David Ricardo 200 years ago.

Edward Leamer and James Levinsohn (1995, p. 1341) are, however, right to caution about taking the advice too far and complement their first message with a second one: "Don't treat the theory too casually" which, in practice, means "Work hard to make a clear and close link between the theory and the data". And finally: "High partial correlations by themselves are not enough. We need a good story." Motivated by this expressed challenge by the experts which implies a fine line between success and failure, I will point to two, in my view, important empirical implications of the Ricardian model, i.e., regarding the pattern of trade (Sect. 5.1.1) and relative wages (Sect. 5.1.2).

5.1.1 Pattern of Trade

What should be analyzed when estimating (and not testing) the Ricardian trade model? Let us recall from Chap. 4 the chain of the home country's decreasing comparative advantage with N industries and some equilibrium relative wage rate

---

[1]This does not mean that an inquiry into the discriminatory effects of a preferential trade agreement on a third country may not be interesting. Note that this is typically done using the so-called Gravity Model in order to explain and estimate (changes in) bilateral trade volumes.

of Home and Foreign, w/w^*, in free trade.[2] Thus, suppose for example the following relationship:

$$\frac{a_{L1}^*}{a_{L1}} > \frac{a_{L2}^*}{a_{L2}} > \frac{a_{L3}^*}{a_{L3}} > \ldots > \frac{a_{LI}^*}{a_{LI}} > \frac{w}{w^*} > \frac{a_{LK}^*}{a_{LK}} > \ldots > \frac{a_{LN-1}^*}{a_{LN-1}} > \frac{a_{LN}^*}{a_N}. \qquad (5.1)$$

The Ricardian model implies that the home country will be exporting goods 1 to I, whereas the foreign country exports goods K to N. In other words, each country is an exporter in those industries in which its labour productivity is relatively high or, in other words, in which it has the greatest comparative advantage.[3] The equilibrium relative wage rate determines where the chain of decreasing relative costs is broken. Note that the model implies an extreme degree of specialization: Home will be the only producer of goods 1 to I and Foreign of goods K to N. With no transportation costs, there is a maximum of one good for which the relative productivity happens to equal the relative wage rate and which is thus produced by both countries.[4] This extreme degree of specialization is not realistic and would, in fact, prevent us from empirically analyzing the predicted pattern of trade: Labour coefficients of non-existing industries in a country would not be observable. But this predicted extreme degree of specialization is a result of the simplifying assumption of constant labour coefficients and should not be regarded an essential characteristic when estimating—and not testing—the model.

Suppose we computed relative exports (EX_i/EX_i^*) as well as relative productivities (a_{Li}^*/a_{Li}) for two countries, Home and Foreign, for several industries (i) based on observable exports and labour productivities. Imagine we found a scatter plot such as the one shown in Fig. 5.1. How would we interpret these observations from the perspective of the Ricardian model? First, the evidence illustrated in Fig. 5.1 seems to confirm the Ricardian principle of comparative advantage as the determinant of the pattern of trade (see inequality 5.1): The higher the relative productivity in the home country's industry, the more likely it is that Home's rather than Foreign's firms export in that industry and thus the greater would we expect relative exports of Home to Foreign.

Second, Fig. 5.1 implies that the home country is more productive in all industries: Foreign's labour coefficients are larger than Home's in all industries. Nevertheless, Foreign is able to "compete" with Home and to participate in the world market. It even exports more than the home country in a number of industries (i.e., in those where $EX_i/EX_i^* < 1$). These are the ones in which the home country has a relatively low productivity—thus, a further confirmation of the Ricardian

---

[2]Note that the variables which refer to the foreign country are denoted with an asterisk (*).

[3]Note that $a_{LI}^*/a_{LI} > a_{LK}^*/a_{LK}$ also implies $a_{LI}^*/a_{LK}^* > a_{LI}/a_{LK}$ and thus that Home has a comparative advantage in I relative to good K. This is a fortiori true for good 3 relative to good K and for good 2 or 1 relative to K. This is why we can call inequality (5.1) as the chain of decreasing comparative advantage.

[4]If there would be small international transaction costs, those goods in the middle of the chain would be produced by both countries and remain nontraded (see Chap. 4).

Relative Exports

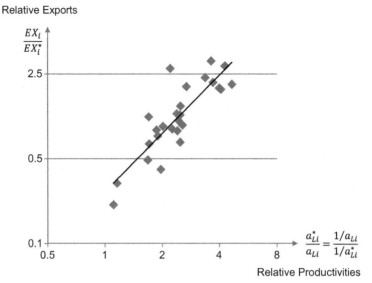

Fig. 5.1 Relative exports and relative productivities of the home and foreign country

trade model's implication that comparative and not absolute advantage is the crucial determinant of the pattern of trade.

Some of the readers may have recognized that the example illustrated in Fig. 5.1 is not a hypothetical case. It rather represents the findings by Balassa (1963, p. 235) in his Chart 2, in which the author of this classical article calculated relative exports to third countries of the U.S. (home country) and the U.K. (foreign country) as well as their relative labour productivities for a number of industries in 1951.[5] Each dot thus reflects one industry i. Note that, as in Balassa (1963), both axes are in logarithmic scale which reduces the typically larger deviations of higher values of observations from the regression line. Thus, Fig. 5.1 is broadly in line with the Ricardian trade theory. It confirms the important message of the model that a country (like the U.K.), which has an absolute disadvantage in all industries can nevertheless participate in the world economy as its wage rate endogenously adjusts to the lower productivity. As inequality (5.1) shows and Fig. 5.1 confirms, countries tend export relatively more of those goods for which their unit production costs are lower, given the equilibrium wage rate.

Krugman et al. (2015, p. 78)—referring to Balassa (1963) when discussing the usefulness of the Ricardian trade theory—argue that it is more difficult to find a confirmation with recent data as "we do not get a chance to see what countries do

---

[5]Note that the first study that aimed at an empirical estimation of the Ricardian model and that was quite successful in this regard was the study by MacDougall (1951). See Chap. 12 in this book.

badly! In the world economy of the 21st century, countries do not produce goods for which they are at a comparative disadvantage, so there is no way to measure their productivity in those sectors". However, a recent econometric study by Golub and Hsieh (2000) of bilateral trade patterns between pairs of countries, one of which remains to be the U.S., finds "fairly strong support for the Ricardian model" (p. 231). The authors conclude: "In the vast majority of cases, relative productivity and unit labor cost help to explain US bilateral trade patterns, particularly when sector-specific purchasing-power-parity exchange rates are used." (p. 231). Golub and Hsieh (2000) caution: "In most cases only a small part of the variation of trade patterns is explained by the model". In other words, the scatterplots shown in Fig. 5.1 are likely not to be as close to the regression line if we use more recent data.

In Fig. 5.2, I show a scatter plot with more recent data (2014) for relative exports of the U.S. and the U.K. (to third countries) and relative productivities (value added per hour worked) for a number of manufacturing industries. We also used a logarithmic scale as Balassa (1963).[6] We see, again, a positive relationship between relative exports and relative productivities which is—as expected from the statements by Krugman et al. (2015) and Golub and Hsieh (2000)—not as smooth as the one with the data of 1951. Note, however, that we used all industries of the data set for which we had numbers and applied the same Purchasing Power Adjusted exchange rate for all industries to transform British pounds into U.S. Dollars.[7]

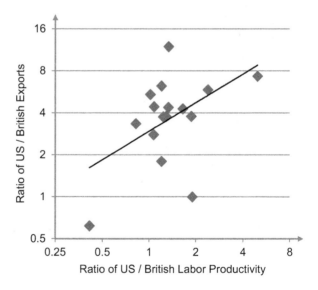

Fig. 5.2 Relative exports and productivities for the U.S. and the U.K. (2014). Source: Based on own calculations using data from OECD Structural Analysis (STAN) database (ISIC Rev. 4). The PPP-adjusted exchange rate is from the ICP database of the World Bank

---

[6]I thank Till Schmidlin for excellent research assistance in putting together Figs. 5.2 and 5.3.

[7]These are the industries for which data was available for the most recent year (2014): Textiles (D13), Wearing Apparels (D14), Wood Products (D16), Paper Products (D17), Printing Products (D18), Coke and Refined Petroleum (D19), Rubber and Plastic Products (D22), Non-Metallic Mineral Products (D23), Basic Metals (D24), Fabricated Metal Products (D25), Computer,

Even with this rather straight-forward approach, we see some support of the Ricardian trade theory's prediction, now using the most recent data available.

Note that Alain Deardorff (1984, p. 477), in his analysis of this type of empirical literature, was principally willing "to accept an analysis of third-country trade performance as relevant for the Ricardian model, if suitably modified to be compatible with incomplete specialization." Edward Leamer and James Levinsohn (1995) appear more critical as they describe this literature as "theoretically fuzzy" and conclude: "(...) the Ricardian one-factor model is a very poor setting in which to study the impacts of technologies on trade flows, because the one-factor model is just too simple." (p. 1344).

Interestingly, the main extension of the Ricardian model from the perspective of its empirical analysis came about in terms of an increase of the number of countries (and not of factors of production). This very important contribution is due to Eaton and Kortum (2002) and extends the Ricardian model from two to a continuum of countries, using a fundamental insight from Jones (1961).[8] Eaton and Kortum (2002) "employ a probabilistic formulation of technological heterogeneity under which the model extends naturally to a world with many countries separated by geographic barriers" (p. 1742) and estimate the model, including bilateral trade patterns, using data of 19 OECD countries in 1990.

The recent contributions by Eaton and Kortum (2002), Costinot, Donaldson, and Komunjer (2012), Costinot and Donaldson (2012) and Eaton and Kortum (2012) thus opened up a new area of empirical analyses of the Ricardian trade model. Costinot et al. (2012) analyze a multi-country multi-industry Ricardian model with trade and productivity data of 1997 and claim to "offer the first theoretically consistent Ricardian test" (p. 582). They find considerable support for the Ricardian model. Costinot and Donaldson (2012) use the fact that agronomists know the (hypothetical) productivity of different pieces of land to grow different crops and apply the Ricardian model to the explanation of the relative output "across 17 agricultural crops and 55 major agriculture-producing countries in 1989" (p. 458). They also conclude: "Ricardo's theory of comparative advantage (...) has significant explanatory power in the data, at least within the scope of our analysis." (p. 458). Finally, Eaton and Kortum (2012) infer from their updated estimation of the Ricardian model: "In short, the framework we present in this paper is tractable, versatile, and amenable to empirical analysis. It is keeping Ricardo busy." (p. 88). In Chap. 12 of this book, Jonathan Eaton nicely shows why and how this can be done.

Electronic and Optical Products (D26), Electrical Equipment (D27), Machinery and Equipment (D28), Motor Vehicles and Trailers (D29), Other Transport Equipment (D30), Furniture and Other Manufacturing Products (D31).

[8]See also Chaps. 6 and 12 in this book.

5.1.2 Relative Wages

Another fundamental empirical implication of the model is that, in the free-trade equilibrium, wages adjust to a country's (average) productivity. This adjustment is central to the Ricardian principle of comparative advantage. Let us assume a standard 2×2 Ricardian trade model. Suppose for a moment that wages would be identical in the home and the foreign country and assume that the home country is more productive in both goods, i.e., that the home country has an absolute advantage in both goods. In this case, the foreign country would not be able to compete with the home country in producing either of the two goods. Thus, there would be unemployment. As labour is assumed to be internationally immobile, the wage rate would, therefore, adjust downwards in the foreign country—and vice versa in the home country. The endogeneity of wages allows each country to export that good in which it has a comparative productivity advantage (and thus an absolute cost advantage, given the equilibrium wage rate) and to gain from international trade.

As discussed in Chap. 4, the equilibrium wage rate in the 2×2 case is bounded by the following range, assuming that Home has a comparative advantage in good 1:

$$\frac{a_{L1}^*}{a_{L1}} \geq \frac{w}{w^*} \geq \frac{a_{L2}^*}{a_{L2}}. \tag{5.2}$$

Thus, if the home country is absolutely more productive in both goods, its wage rate has to be larger than abroad: Both ratios of the two countries' labour coefficients are greater than one. Note, however, that home's wage rate may be larger *or* smaller than abroad if each country has an absolute advantage in only one of the two industries. In this case, the relative price of the two goods becomes an important determinant of whether Home's or Foreign's wage rate is higher. Also note that, in this latter case, each country has an absolute advantage in the good it exports to the other country. But this is obviously not—see Eq. (5.2)—a sufficient condition to enjoy a higher wage rate. We will come back to this point in Sect. 5.2.

The same is true in the N-goods case as can be seen from the inequality (5.1) above. If the home country has an absolute advantage in all goods, its wage rate must be larger than abroad. If, however, there are some industries in which the foreign country is more productive, it depends on the location of w/w^* in the chain of decreasing comparative advantage and thus on the goods each country is producing—and thus on the average productivity in each country. If the foreign country had an absolute productivity disadvantage in all the goods except for good N and good $N-1$, it would have a lower wage rate in the equilibrium described by (5.1). If, instead, it were a rather small country and only produced good N (its best good) its wage rate would be higher ($w^*/w > 1$). Thus, a country's wage rate depends on the productivity of all the goods it produces (including the nontraded goods). This is exactly what we typically find in reality.

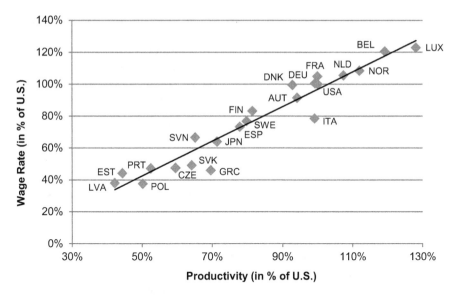

Fig. 5.3 Relative productivity and relative wage rate of the OECD Countries (2015). Source: Based on own calculations using data from OECD Structural Analysis (STAN) database (ISIC Rev. 4). Productivities are calculated as value added at current prices divided by hours worked. Wage rates are determined as compensation of employees divided by hours worked. The PPP-adjusted exchange rate is from the ICP database of the World Bank

Figure 5.3 shows a scatter plot of the OECD countries' relative productivity (value added per hour worked) and relative wage rate (compensation per hour worked) for the most recent year available (2015).[9] Note that all numbers are indexed and compared with the U.S. (index = 100). Figure 5.3 confirms that wages depend on productivities or, in other words, on absolute advantage as proposed by Ricardian trade theory.

We conclude Sect. 5.1 by emphasizing that there is considerable empirical support for the Ricardian trade model's main prediction: Explaining (1) the pattern of international trade based on comparative advantage (measured by differences in relative labour productivities) and (2) relative wages based on absolute advantages (measured by differences in absolute labour productivities). Other empirical analyses have determined the size of the gains from trade due to the Ricardian specialization along comparative advantage.[10] A further analysis could include an explanation of differences in the real price level among countries, taking into account nontraded goods (see Sect. 4.4). So-called Dutch-Disease effects—caused

---

[9]We have chosen these variables in units per hour as this measure is close to the Ricardian model and also because countries typically differ in the number of hours worked per week by a full-time employee.

[10]See Costinot et al. 2012, p. 582) who estimate these gains of about 5% of the total gains from trade in their cross-country analysis based on 1997 data.

by terms-of-trade improvements or productivity increases in a country's export industries—may explain why prices in some countries (such as Switzerland) are felt to be much higher than in other countries.[11] As specialization is the main driving force of the gains from trade in the Ricardian trade model, one could also study the associated trade-offs between the degree of specialization and the standard of living, possibly including some volatility measure.

5.2   Competitiveness and the North-South Debate

Misconceptions about the world economy often neglect the interaction between "markets with overlapping domains" (Jones, 1995, p. 273) and assume prices (e.g., wages) as given. In particular, observers use their daily experience of working in firms, associations or non-governmental agencies as the basis for their judgement. Krugman (1994, p. 39) complains: "Tell a group of businessmen that a country is like a corporation writ large, and you give them the comfort of feeling that they already understand the basics. Try to tell them about economic concepts like comparative advantage, and you are asking them to learn something new."

Why is a country not like a big corporation? One major difference is that, for an individual company, the wage level it faces when hiring employees is largely given exogenously, whereas the countries' wage level is set in a so-called general equilibrium process: It is a result of the interactions between the primarily local labour markets and the international markets for goods and services. In the words of Krugman (1993, pp. 23–24): "(...) a national economy bears very little resemblance to a corporation. And the ground-level view of businessmen is deeply uninformative about the inherently general-equilibrium issues of international economics." We first apply the Ricardian trade theory to the discussion of the "international competitiveness" of countries and firms in Sect. 5.2.1. Section 5.2.2 looks at the North-South debate with respect to wage levels and productivities.

5.2.1   Competiveness Debate

It starts on the firm level in the regularly performed analyses of the international competitiveness of a firm. As many companies compete with foreign competitors on the market for their products and services, they usually closely watch what their competitors do and how they progress. Take the example of the U.S. automobile industry. Companies like Ford or General Motors will, for example, compute indicators such as the companies' productivities and carefully compare them over time. A crude measure would be the number of cars produced per unit of input

---

[11]See, e.g., Sax and Weder (2009) for an empirical analysis of the Swiss case.

(labour and/or capital) as proposed by Womack, Jones, and Roos (1990). As long as Ford's or GM's productivity develops more favourably than that of Japanese Honda's or Toyota's, the managers might conclude that things go well and there is nothing to fear. But, in fact, they may wake up on a morning and find out that their company is getting into trouble. What happened?

One answer is related to the insight provided by the Ricardian trade theory. Whether a whole industry or a firm within an industry of a country remains internationally competitive, not only depends on the productivities of this industry or firm in the home and the foreign country. At least as important is also the development of the productivity in those industries with which the firms compete for labour in the local labour market. In other words, whether an industry—and thus a firm within the industry—remains competitive depends on comparative and not on absolute advantage. Thus, the U.S. automobile firms not only have to watch carefully their foreign competitors, but also the local U.S. firms with which they are competing on the local labour market—firms that hire similarly skilled employees as Ford or GM. If these domestic competitors become more productive, the U.S. automobile producers have to pay a higher wage rate and may, therefore, not be able to compete anymore against their foreign rivals in car manufacturing.

Note that the situation is even more complex. As known from the Ricardian trade theory, the determination of a comparative advantage requires to compare the (magic) *four* parameters. Let us assume that, in both countries, the automobile producers compete with a number of other industries (e.g. electronics, steel, textiles) for labour. We call them "others". Whether the U.S. has a comparative advantage in the automobile industry, depends on the following inequality:

$$\frac{a_{Auto}^{US}}{a_{Others}^{US}} < \frac{a_{Auto}^{Jap}}{a_{Others}^{Jap}}. \tag{5.3}$$

The U.S. firms have to be *relatively* more productive (i.e., to use relatively less labour in the model) in car manufacturing than the Japanese competitors. Thus, the U.S. firms may experience a reduction in their ability to compete against their car manufacturing rivals, even though their productivities develop in accordance with that of (1) the Japanese car manufacturers and (2) the U.S. firms in the other industries with which they compete on the labour market. The reason of the trouble could, however, be a change in the fourth parameter in Eq. (5.3): If the firms in the other Japanese industries experience a reduction in their productivities (i.e., if there is an increase in their labour coefficient), the U.S. could lose its comparative advantage in car manufacturing. The reason is that the Japanese car manufacturers become *relatively* more productive or, in other words, they benefit from the induced reduction in the wage level in Japan. This allows them to out-compete the U.S. car producers.

We conclude that a careful analysis of the competitors of a firm always involves an analysis not only of those companies with which it competes on the market for its product or service, but also of those corporations with which it and its competitors compete locally regarding inputs such as labour. The analysis requires that businessmen eventually realize the importance of the Ricardian trade model, in particular, and of general-equilibrium theory, in general. An analysis of only the development of the productivities of the foreign competitors neglects that wages are endogenous in the firms' home markets. Of course, one could alternatively say that an analysis of foreign competitors should also incorporate the development of the foreign wage level, among others. But this is exactly what the Ricardian trade theory proposes, taking into account that wages are endogenous.

A related perception is the common belief that *countries* have to be strong and competitive to stand up against competition from foreign countries. The perception is that if foreign countries improve their institutions and thus increase their productivity, it will become difficult to trade with and compete against these countries. The metaphor of this point of view is the corporation: *A country is like a big corporation competing on the global market*. This leads to the opinion that "(...) the United States and Japan are competitors in the same sense that Coca-Cola competes with Pepsi." (Krugman, 1994, p. 29). If Coca-Cola becomes more successful, this tends to be to Pepsi's detriment. The same is, so the argument, true for countries. Also, many people worry that if foreign countries pay low wages for their labour, this makes it difficult for "us" to compete with "them" on global markets. Some may even argue that it is not only *difficult* for us to compete, but it is also *unfair* that they compete against us by paying those unfairly low wages. What is the answer to these worries and stressful point of views about the world economy?

These perspectives are inconsistent with the Ricardian trade theory. Both of them disregard the fact that wages—and factor prices more generally—are endogenous and thus reflect the average productivities of countries. If the foreign country raises its productivity, this does not imply that its firms become internationally more competitive. Wages will rise accordingly, maybe not immediately, but they will. And this is not only a theoretical implication. As shown in Fig. 5.3 above, it is reasonable to assume that this happens in practice. Thereby, the unit costs of foreign production may not change at all. Of course, foreigners will be happy about the productivity increase as it raises their wages. But it does generally not increase their firms' international competitiveness.

The analogous argument applies to the opposite, i.e., the fear that we may not be able to compete against foreign firms because of the low wage rate they enjoy there. Again, the low wages are related to the low average productivities in these countries. Thus, paying low wages in these countries is not unfair, because the low wage reflects the (marginal) productivity of labour—at least, if labour markets work to some extent. Thus, labour gets a wage rate in these countries that reflects its marginal value in production. And the latter is usually low because of institutional, political and technological deficiencies. It would, indeed, be unfair to require that these countries pay a higher wage rate (above productivity) as this would undermine their capability to participate in the world market and gain from trade. If these countries become more productive, their wage rates will rise.[12]

5.2.2 North-South Debate

Some people argue that the low wage rate in developing countries (South) is a result of exploitation by the industrial countries (North) and that it is typically below the labour productivity in these countries. I acknowledge that wages are extremely low and working conditions very bad in many countries of the South. Thus, this reality is not satisfying. The question, however, is why these wages are so low? The answer from the perspective of Ricardian trade theory is clear. It is the low labour productivity which is responsible for this fact. It is not only the inferior technology, but also the limited quality of infrastructure, the lack of security, the uncertainty, the political instability and also the lower amount of human and physical capital. They all together translate into a lower labour productivity, captured by the labour coefficients in the Ricardian model.

Thus, again, the lower productivity in the South is reflected in the—partly extremely—low wage rate. The low wage rate, however, allows the countries to participate in the world economy and gain from international trade. They specialize in those industries in which they have a comparative advantage (despite their absolute disadvantage in all industries) and gain from trade by reaching a higher level of consumption with their limited resources. In other words, their *real wage rate*—i.e., what they can buy with the nominal wage—is higher in the trade equilibrium than it would be in autarky. Thus, if the countries did not take part in international trade, their wages would even be lower. This is the typical Ricardian result we described and developed in Chap. 4 and for which we found some evidence in Sect. 5.1 above. There may be a number of potential problems associated with the participation in international trade such as possibly (temporary) negative effects on the environment which tend, however, to become smaller as the countries become richer.[13]

But how about the critique that wages in the South are typically below their productivity? Aside from temporary disequilibria in the labour market or in the

---

[12]Some commentators have argued that wages of the industrial country, Germany, were too low during the aftermath of the Euro crisis of 2008. The low wages would be responsible for the large German trade surplus and for the difficulties of other countries within the Euro zone to export to Germany or compete with German exports on other markets. They required that German wages should be raised (by government order). The counter-arguments from the perspective of the Ricardian model are that, first, wages will rise in Germany in the long term if they are indeed below productivity. Second, the other members of the Euro zone have to ensure that nominal wages can fall after having eliminated the natural adjustment through exchange rate realignments.

[13]See Antweiler, Copeland, and Taylor (2001) in their thought-provoking and fundamental paper with the title "Is Free Trade Good for the Environment? ".

exchange rate, wages should reflect countries' productivity. The question, however, arises: What productivities? The answer: The *average* productivity, as mentioned in Sect. 5.1. Thus, we cannot only compare the productivities of the North and South in those industries in which each of them exports, but rather have to include also the productivities in the other industries to explain the relative wage rate. This is important and may be the reason why some people believe that wage rates are too low in the South.[14]

Let us illustrate this point based on a numerical example using the 2×2 Ricardian model. Suppose the labour productivities are given by the labour coefficients in Table 5.1 for two goods, good 1 and good 2, in the North and the South (*). Looking at the numbers, we can see that the North has a comparative advantage in good 1: It uses twice as much labour per unit of output as in good 2, whereas the South needs 4 times as much. Thus, North uses relatively less labour in the production of good 1. This, however, implies that the South needs relatively less labour in good 2: It has to give up ¼ of a unit of good 1 to produce one additional unit of good 2, whereas the North would have to give up ½ of a unit of good 1. South has a comparative advantage in good 2. In a free-trade situation, the North would therefore export good 1 and the South good 2. We could show that both countries gain from trade—i.e., increase their real wage rate—if the free-trade relative price lies somewhere in-between the two countries' opportunity costs ($2 < p_1/p_2 < 4$).

We now want to focus on the relative wage rate in the free-trade equilibrium. As discussed above and in detail in Chap. 4, relative wages depend on absolute advantage. As can be seen from Table 5.1, the North has an absolute advantage in producing both goods: It requires less labour per unit of output in both industries (2 instead of 24 units of labour per unit of output in industry 1 and 1 compared to 6 in industry 2). With a higher productivity in the North, the North will therefore have a higher wage rate. It will be between 12 times and 6 times as high as in the South, depending on whether both are producing (some of) good 1 (12 times higher) or (some of) good 2 (6 times higher). Remember the range of the relative wage rate equals $a_{L1}^{*}/a_{L1} \geq w/w^{*} \geq a_{L2}^{*}/a_{L2}$.[15]

Let us now suppose that the relative price of the two goods (p_1/p_2) lies in-between the two autarky prices which equal the opportunity cost (2 for the

Table 5.1 Productivities and wages in the North and the South: An example

	Labour coefficients	
	Good 1	Good 2
North	$a_{L1} = 2$	$a_{L2} = 1$
South (*)	$a_{L1}^{*} = 24$	$a_{L2}^{*} = 6$

Productivities equal the inverse of the labour coefficients. The North's productivity in industry 1 thus equals ½ unit of good 1 per unit of labour

[14]This point has also been emphasized by Krugman et al. (2015, pp. 300 ff.).
[15]See Eq. (4.10) in Chap. 4.

North and 4 for the South). To be concrete, assume $p_1/p_2 = 3$. Question: What is the relative wage rate in this situation? Answer: $w/w^* = 9$. The explanation is straightforward. With $p_1/p_2 = 3$, there is complete specialization. The North (South) produces good 1 (good 2) in which it has a comparative advantage. Using the zero-profit conditions (unit cost equals the price in each country), the relative wage rate can easily be computed (see Chap. 4 for details):

$$\frac{w}{w^*} = \frac{p_1}{p_2} \times \frac{a^*_{L2}}{a_{L1}} = 3\frac{6}{2} = 9. \tag{5.4}$$

An increase of the relative price of good 1 would raise the relative wage rate of the North (note it is the good which the North exports) to a maximum of 12. An increase in the relative price of good 2 would raise the wage rate of the South, reducing w/w^* to a minimum of 6 (which is determined by the relative productivities in good 2). Let us now come back to the allegation that wages are too low in the South. Note that the wage rate in the South is only 1/9 of that in the North in the discussed free-trade equilibrium. This is lower than what one would expect by comparing the labour coefficients or productivities in the South and the North for good 2: Based on this comparison the wage rate in the South should only be 1/6 (and not 1/9) of that in the North.

Thus, is there indeed some kind of exploitation, because a comparison of the South's productivity in its export industry with the productivity in the same industry of the North obviously suggests that wages should be higher in the South? The answer is that this comparison is not suitable. As discussed above and developed more precisely in Chap. 4, relative wages reflect the overall or average productivity of a country, and not only of the productivity of a country's export industry. For the South, industry 2 is the industry in which the country has a comparative advantage. Thus, it is the country's best industry. Specializing in the production of this industry, allows the South to increase its real wage rate and thus to gain from trade. But it is not the right basis for an explanation of the relative wage rate in equilibrium. Suppose it were. This would imply that, from the North's perspective, the South's relative wage rate would be too high: The North is 12 times as productive in its export industry (good 1) as the South, but only achieves a wage rate that is 9 times as high as the South's.

We conclude Sect. 5.2 by emphasizing that wages adjust to differences in productivities between countries. It is the productivities over all industries that determine the relative wage rate and not just the productivities of the countries' (most productive) export industries. The adjustment of wages—downwards and upwards—is very important in the world economy as it basically takes away a lot of pressure from the countries that may be felt from the world economy. Whereas firms are in a constant competition against foreign and domestic competitors on the product and input markets and, indeed, have to upgrade their capabilities and productivities in order to survive, countries and their residents and politicians can be much more relaxed regarding pressures from the world markets. If countries fall back in aggregate productivity, they do not have a problem of "competitiveness" against other countries or of being "thrown out of work". They only have to accept a lower nominal (and real) wage. Productivity is thus important to keep and possibly increase the standard of living, but it is not important to export and remain "competitive" on the world market.[16]

5.3 Productivity Improvement Abroad

We now want to elaborate on a related question which produces a lot of heat in political debates: "What happens if foreign countries become better at what they are doing?" In other words, what happens if foreign countries improve their "business environment"—increase the stability of their political system, invest in their infrastructure and in education and give firms more incentives to invest in new technologies? In short, what are the effects of a productivity improvement abroad?

We may agree rather quickly that this should be good for the foreign countries as their standard of living, for example measured in terms of the real wage rate, rises. The countries will be able to use their scarce resources in a more efficient way and reduce the waste of time, money and natural resources. If properly measured, this will increase the level of foreign wellbeing. But how about the home country, will it lose or also benefit? Remembering the discussion above, we notice that it is probably misleading to interpret the rise in foreign productivity as an increase in competitiveness which will make life in the home country more difficult. One reason discussed above, is the fact that nominal wages will increase abroad along with the increase in foreign productivity.

Another reason is that, in contrast to companies, countries buy some of each other's goods. Let us come back to the Pepsi and Coca-Cola example emphasized by Paul Krugman (1994, p. 34) in his publication "Competitiveness: A Dangerous Obsession":

> Coke and Pepsi are almost purely rivals: only a negligible fraction of Coca-Cola's sales go to Pepsi workers, only a negligible fraction of the goods Coca-Cola workers buy are Pepsi products. So if Pepsi is successful, it tends to be at Coke's expense. But the major industrial countries, while they sell products that compete with each other, are also each other's main export markets and each other's main suppliers of useful imports. If the European economy does well, it need not be at U.S. expense; indeed, if anything a successful European economy is likely to help the U.S. economy by providing it with larger markets and selling it goods of superior quality at lower prices.

The Ricardian trade model is, again, most suitable to think about these issues. In the following, we start with a uniform productivity improvement in all industries of the foreign country and determine how this affects the home country, using the

---

[16]Krugman (1994) writes: „One can, of course, take the position that words mean what we want them to mean, that all are free, if they wish, to use the term "competitiveness" as a poetic way of saying productivity, without actually implying that international competition has anything to do with it." (p. 35).

Ricardian model—first based on the 2×2 case and then extended to the continuum of goods case due to Dornbusch, Fischer, and Samuelson (1977). We then discuss the effects of biased—import-biased or export-biased—productivity improvements abroad, taking into account the recent contributions by Samuelson (2004) and Jones and Ruffin (2008). The following discussion is based on the framework developed in Chap. 4 of this book.

5.3.1 Effects of a Uniform Productivity Increase Abroad

In the 2×2 Ricardian model, a uniform increase of productivity in the foreign country leads to a proportional shift of the foreign linear production possibility curve (PPF) to the right. With a limited amount of resources the foreign country can produce more of both goods. This should, as mentioned above, be good for the foreign country. If it is a very large country and thus it produces both goods in the free-trade equilibrium it will reach a higher production and consumption point on the new PPF. If it is completely specialized in free trade and if the relative price of the two goods does not change, it also benefits from the increase in consumption. The foreign benefit may, however, be smaller if the completely specialized foreign country faces a reduction of the relative price of its export good, due to the increase in the quantity of production in its export industry. If the foreign productivity increase (and thus the shift to the right of the foreign PPF) is big enough, the foreign country should always benefit from its productivity increase.

But how about the home country—how will a uniform improvement of foreign productivities affect the home country? The answer from the reasoning above is straightforward: The home country will either not be affected (if the relative price of the two goods does not change) or it will benefit from the improvement abroad because of the reduction of the relative price of its imported good. Imagine the home country's PPF which remains unaffected by the productivity improvement abroad and assume that the home country has a comparative advantage in good 1 and is completely specialized. If the relative price of good 1 rises (because the price of good 2 falls), the home country will be able to reach a higher level of consumption or real wage rate. If the relative price does not change, the home country will not be affected by the foreign productivity increase.

To be more precise, note that Home's real wage in terms of good 1 remains constant ($w/p_1 = 1/a_{L1}$) as it is completely determined by its productivity in industry 1. The real wage rate in terms of good 2 (w/p_2) may or may not increase depending on whether (p_2) falls or remains constant. As good 2 is produced by the foreign country we can make use of the zero-profit condition abroad and derive the following relationship for Home's real wage rate in terms of good 2:

$$\frac{w}{p_2} = \frac{w}{w^* a_{L2}^*} = \frac{p_1}{p_2} \times \frac{1}{a_{L1}}. \tag{5.5}$$

Note that we have made use of the fact that w/w^* equals $(p_1/p_2)(a_{L2}^*/a_{L1})$—easily determined from the zero-profit conditions in the case of complete specialization. Substituting this expression into Eq. (5.5) yields the result that home will only gain if the relative price of its export good (i.e., its terms of trade) increases. If both countries are completely specialized, this is in fact the case. Thus, the home country will either gain or remain unaffected by a uniform technological improvement abroad. One may argue that the 2×2 case hides an important adjustment we would expect to happen in the real world. Shouldn't some export industries of the home country get under pressure from the productivity improvement abroad—particularly those in which the home country has only a marginal comparative advantage? In order to address this issue, we should introduce more than two industries.

Instead of moving to N goods and discussing the effects based on the chain of comparative advantage mentioned above, it may however be convenient to move to a very large number of goods, i.e., the continuum-goods case introduced by Dornbusch et al. (1977) and presented in Chap. 4.[17] Suppose we are in the free-trade equilibrium described by Fig. 5.4 with the equilibrium relative wage rate, $\left(\dfrac{\tilde{w}}{w^*}\right)$, and thus the goods z in the interval $[0, \tilde{z}]$ being produced by the home country and those in the interval $[\tilde{z},1]$ by the foreign country. Note that the upward-sloping function $B(z)L^*/L$ reflects the demand side of the economy: The greater the number of goods produced by the home country, the larger the demand for its labour and thus the higher Home's relative wage rate. The downward-sloping function $A(z)$ describes efficient specialization: The lower Home's relative wage rate, the larger the number of goods produced by the home country. Thus, the general equilibrium is a result of tastes, population sizes and productivities in both countries.

Suppose that there is a uniform increase in productivity in the foreign country (e.g., by 10%). This implies that all foreign labour coefficients, $a^*(z)$, are proportionally reduced which shifts $A(z)$ down to $A'(z)$ as shown in Fig. 5.4. This implies that Home's relative wage rate falls and that Foreign takes over the production of the goods in the interval $[z', \tilde{z}]$. One might conclude from this observation that the home country is worse off because of its "loss of international competitiveness". The correct answer is, however: The home country clearly benefits from this productivity improvement abroad! Remember, it is not the (relative) change in the nominal wage that counts. The question is what happens to the *real wage* of the home country, i.e., the wage in terms of what you can buy. Let us differentiate between the three identified groups of goods—A, B and C—in Fig. 5.4.

---

[17]Krugman and Obstfeld (1994) performed a similar analysis in the third edition of their textbook in international economics. See also Chaps. 7 and 12 in this book for applications of the Dornbusch-Fischer-Samuelson model.

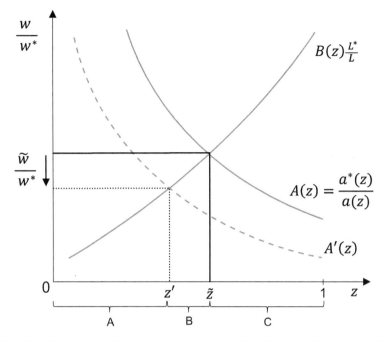

Fig. 5.4 The effects of a uniform productivity increase abroad. Source: Own extended figure based on Dornbusch et al. (1977, pp. 827)

Group A describes the goods in which the home country has its greatest comparative advantages. These are the goods which Home continues to produce after Foreign's productivity increase. Thus, Home's real wage rate in terms of the price of these goods ($p^A(z)$) does not change: $w/p^A(z)$ equals $1/a(z)$ and thus remains constant. How about the goods in group C? These are the goods which are produced and exported by the foreign country before and after the productivity increase. For all of these goods, Home's real wage rate equals

$$\frac{w}{p^C(z)} = \frac{w}{w^*} \times \frac{1}{a^*(z)}. \tag{5.6}$$

The second right-hand term increases due to the productivity improvement abroad (e.g., by 10%). As shown in Fig. 5.4, Home's relative wage rate falls. This is due to the fact that Foreign's nominal wage, w^*, rises as a consequence of the productivity increase. Note, however, that w/w^* falls by less than $A(z)$ and thus by less than $a^*(z)$. In other words, foreign wages rise by less than productivity implying that foreign goods become cheaper. Thus, Home's real wage in terms of goods in group C increases.

Finally, let us consider the goods in group B. These are the goods in which the home country is not competitive anymore after the productivity increase abroad. When the home country still produced them, the price equalled Home's unit costs: $p^B(z)=wa(z)$. In the new equilibrium, these goods are produced by Foreign at lower costs: $w^*a^*(z) < wa(z)$.[18] But this implies that

$$\frac{w}{p^B} > \frac{1}{a(z)}. \tag{5.7}$$

We conclude that the home country enjoys an increased real wage rate and thus purchasing power in two groups of goods (group B and C) and has the same real wage rate for the goods in group (A). This analysis implies that the world economy is not a zero-sum game. If a country gains from trade in a Ricardian trade model, this does not come at the expense of the other country; it is likely to benefit, too. Similarly, if there is a productivity improvement in one country, the other country should welcome this as it tends to be positively affected. These findings can also be interpreted as further support of the argument that countries to not compete with each other as firms do.

5.3.2   Effects of a Biased Productivity Increase Abroad

In a widely read and often misunderstood recent article, Paul Samuelson (2004) emphasized that a technological change abroad (e.g. in China) may not necessarily be to the benefit of a home country (e.g. the U.S.). He thereby criticized the "economist proglobalization debaters" with their "oversimple complacencies about globalization" (pp. 136–137). Based on an extreme numerical example using the Ricardian trade model, he showed that a biased technological improvement in China (i.e., an improvement in the production of the export good of the *United States* or, in other words, in the Chinese import-competing industry) may hurt the U.S. economy—in fact, it may eliminate all the gains from trade enjoyed by the U.S. before the technological improvement took place. In the Professor Samuelson's words:

> The new winds of free trade have blown well for China. But in my overdramatic example, they have blown away *all* of the United States' previous enjoyments from free trade. (p. 141)

Even though some commentators used Samuelson's article as an argument in favour of protectionism and others as an opportunity to criticize the unreality of the

---

[18]Note, that this is in line with our argument above that w^* increases by proportionally less than $a^*(z)$ falls.

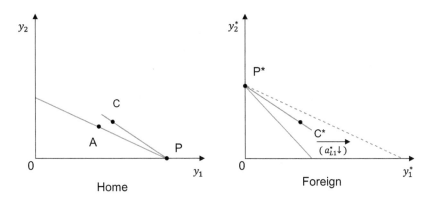

Fig. 5.5 The effects of a biased productivity increase abroad. Source: Own figure based on Samuelson's (2004) main argument

example, these conclusions seem farfetched given the author's own interpretation of his argument in the "Epilogue" of his paper:

> Acts I and II have demonstrated that sometimes free trade globalization can convert a technical change abroad into a benefit for both regions; but sometimes a productivity gain in one country can benefit that country alone, while permanently hurting the other country by reducing the gains from trade that are possible between the two countries. (...). It does not follow from my corrections and emendations that nations should or should not introduce selective protectionisms. (p. 142)

What is the implication of Samuelson's elaborations for our topic of interest, i.e., how an improvement in the productivity abroad affects the home country? The answer is that if this improvement is not uniform, a general verdict as the one derived in Sect. 5.3.1 is hard—may be impossible—to get. Figure 5.5 captures Samuelson's case. In the free-trade equilibrium, the two countries—Home and Foreign—are completely specialized: Home in good 1 (P) and Foreign in good 2 (P*). Both countries reach a consumption point (C, C*) outside of their PPF and thus enjoy the gains from trade. Imagine the foreign country experienced a technological improvement in industry 2 (i.e., in its export industry). The quantity of production and thus supply of good 2 would increase (P* moves upwards on the Y-axis). This, in turn, would tend to lower the price of good 2 and thus make both relative price lines (p_1/p_2) in free trade steeper. The home country would (again) benefit from the improvement of its terms of trade: It can buy more with its exports.[19]

Suppose, however, that Foreign's improvement in productivity takes place in that industry in which Home had a comparative advantage, i.e., in Home's export

---

[19]As mentioned by Samuelson (2004, p. 140) the foreign country could, in principle, lose if the price of its export good falls enough—a well-known phenomenon described as "Self-Immiseration" or "Self-Immiserizing Trade". This has, according to Samuelson (2005, p. 243), been "made cogently" by Johnson (1955) and Bhagwati (1958).

industry. This could arise, as Samuelson (2004) suggests, because of "imitation" or "ingenuity" (p. 141). In the Ricardian model, $a_{L1}*$ falls, as shown in Fig. 5.5. If Foreign's productivity in industry 1 improves such that Foreign's relative production costs equal Home's, the two countries stop trading and Home is back in its previous autarky situation. This is illustrated by point A on Home's PPF which reflects the new point of production *and* consumption. Foreign, of course, is better off due to its productivity improvement. It produces and consumes somewhere on the new dotted line in Fig. 5.5. Thus, the biased technological improvement abroad has, indeed, "blown away" all the gains from trade Home previously enjoyed.

This analysis seems to suggest that if the foreign country's productivity improvement is biased and if it takes place in the home country's export industry, Home tends to lose. Going back to our discussion of competitiveness, one could argue that this indeed negatively affects the international competitiveness of the firms in Home's export industry (the price of the exported good falls) without creating a benefit on the import side. Home's real wage falls. Note, however, that this effect only arises because the home country does not adjust its production structure: It remains completely specialized in industry 1 which faces the reduction in its price. Only when the price of good 1 falls to the autarky situation ($p_1/p_2 = a_{L1}/a_{L2}$), the home country just begins to produce good 2. This "overdramatic example" chosen by Paul Samuelson is, in a way, the "worst case" for the home country.

What would happen if the productivity in industry 1 abroad improved further? The answer: The home country would start to specialize in good 2 as it now has a comparative advantage in industry 2. The reduction of the relative price of good 1 due to the further productivity increase abroad now starts to work in favour of Home as it imports good 1 and exports good 2. If the improvement continues Home may eventually benefit from the improvement abroad, as the new consumption point could lie above and to the right of point C in Fig. 5.5.

This is where Jones and Ruffin (2008) come in with their paper on "The Technology Transfer Paradox". They discuss the effect of a technological improvement in the foreign country on Home based on a two-country, multi-good Ricardian model. This allows for richer adjustment possibilities of the home country in its export "sector" which is typically composed of many industries. They show that there always exists "a paradoxical possibility" (p. 321) where a country may in fact gain from an uncompensated transfer of the technology in one of its export industries to the foreign country. This is even the case if Home loses its "best technology", i.e., the good in whose production it has the greatest comparative advantage.

What is the intuition of the argument? Imagine the chain of Home's decreasing comparative advantage with goods 1 to N (see inequality 5.1). We suppose Home produces good 1 and 2 and "incipiently" produces good 3 (i.e., just begins to produce it), whereas Foreign produces goods 3 to N for the entire market. Note that, in this case, the relative wage rate ($w/w*$) equals the relative productivities in industry 3 ($a_{L3}*/a_{L3}$). If Foreign gets access to Home's best technology (i.e., the technology described by a_{L1}), Home loses industry 1 and shifts those resources to industry 3. Foreign, in turn, does the exact reverse, shifting those resources from the production of good 3 into that of good 1. As shown by Jones and Ruffin (2008, p. 324) such a shift may not affect the equilibrium relative wage rate (w/w^*). Home thus clearly benefits as its real wage rate in terms of good 1 rises and remains unaffected in terms of all the other goods. This result is referred to as the equilibrium at a "turning point".

The authors show, however, that Home could lose from this selective technology transfer. This happens if, after the technology transfer, the foreign wage rate rises enough because Foreign stops producing the common good that was produced by both countries before the transfer. Jones and Ruffin (2008): "(...) the greatest danger to Home real incomes comes from situations in which w^* is raised by the maximal amount, and this occurs when both before and after transfer Home and Foreign produce a commodity in common, a different commodity after the transfer." (p. 325). In the example above, just assume for a moment that the technology transfer would lead to a situation where, before the transfer, both countries produced good 3 and, after the transfer, they both produce good 4 in common. This implies that w^* rises (w/w^* falls). The home country now faces a trade-off. On the one hand, Home's real wage in terms of good 1 rises as, with the new technology, Foreign will be able to produce this good at a lower price. On the other hand, Home's real wage in terms of the goods 4 to N is now lower as Foreign produces them with the same technology, but at a higher wage rate.

We conclude from Sect. 5.3 that a biased productivity improvement abroad tends to be beneficial for the home country if it happens in Foreign's export industries. In this case, Home tends to benefit as an importer of these goods due to the reduction of the price of imports and thus an improvement in its terms of trade (note that the effect would, of course, be different if Home and Foreign competed in a third market in these export industries).

If the productivity increase abroad, however, occurs in the foreign import-competing industries or, in other words, in the export industries of the home country, Home may lose due to a deterioration of its terms of trade as emphasized by Samuelson (2004). As shown by Jones and Ruffin (2008) this is, however, not unavoidable. As the home country may adjust and shift its resources into other (export) industries, it can maintain full employment and possibly enjoy a higher real wage rate from importing the goods of the lost industries at a lower price. The important insight from Jones and Ruffin (2008):

> What is striking in our scenario is that it is precisely the complete loss of Home's original best industry that allows a reduction in its world price and thus works in favor of the increase in real wages at Home. (...). Without denying the importance of new technological developments in advanced countries (...), what we have argued is that even without such advances, pure improvements abroad, such as represented by stealth or uncompensated acquisition of some of our better technology, may serve to raise real wages and incomes in the advanced home country. Trade patterns are altered, and the subtle mechanisms of comparative advantage can yield net gains to the advanced country. (p. 328)

5.4   Conclusions

This chapter shows that the Ricardian trade model can be put to work—and it works. It has interesting implications regarding the pattern of trade and relative wages of countries which can be empirically analyzed and which turn out to be largely in line with observations. The model also leads to interesting insights regarding the often misguided public discussion about the international competitiveness of firms and countries. The same is true regarding the question of how improvements in productivity abroad affect the home country. In all these applications of the Ricardian trade model, its small-scale general equilibrium characteristics are crucial and helpful to understand the complex mechanisms in the world economy.

Our discussion of the implications and applications of the Ricardian trade model implies, in many ways, a more "relaxed view" about the world economy—from the perspective of an individual country. The real wage in a country depends to a large extent on its own effort. This requires self-responsibility, but also eliminates the often heard pressure that countries have to constantly become better to survive and cope with the "rough winds" of the world economy. Politics should, however, understand this. It implies that nominal wages in a country have to be flexible—not only upwards, but also downwards. This is particularly important if adjustments through changes of the exchange rate between countries have been abolished.

Further applications and extensions of the Ricardian model are, however, possible and also have been pursued. Jones (1980, 2000), for example, created the so-called "Augmented Ricardian model" that includes an internationally mobile input—in addition to internationally immobile labour—used in one of two international tradable goods. We will come back to this in Chap. 19 of this book. Eaton and Kortum (2002) have extended the model beyond two countries which opened up a whole new perspective of how the Ricardian trade theory can be empirically analyzed. This theme will be explored in Chap. 12 of this book. Others have started to make productivities endogenous and model the interactions within industries based on imperfectly competing heterogeneous firms. This could possibly create different effects of foreign technological improvements.[20]

References

Antweiler, W., Copeland, B. C., & Taylor, M. S. (2001). Is free trade good for the environment? *American Economic Review, 91*(4), 877–908.
Balassa, B. (1963). An empirical demonstration of classical comparative cost theory. *Review of Economics and Statistics, 45*(3), 231–238.

---

[20]See, for example, Demidova (2008) with negative effects on the partner country and Choudhri and Marasco (2017) who emphasize the reverse.

Bhagwati, J. (1958). Immiserizing growth: A geometric note. *Review of Economic Studies, 25,* 201–206.

Choudhri, E. U., & Marasco, A. (2017). Is foreign technological advance harmful in the Melitz model? *Open Economies Review, 28*(1), 149–166.

Costinot, A., & Donaldson, D. (2012). Ricardo's theory of comparative advantage: Old idea, new evidence. *The American Economic Review, 102*(3), 453–458.

Costinot, A., Donaldson, D., & Komunjer, I. (2012). What goods do countries trade? A quantitative exploration of Ricardo's ideas. *The Review of Economic Studies, 79*(2), 581–608.

Deardorff, A. V. (1984). Testing trade theories and predicting trade flows, Chap. 10. In R. W. Jones & P. B. Kenen (Eds.), *Handbook of international economics* (Vol. 1, pp. 467–517). Amsterdam: Elsevier.

Demidova, S. (2008). Productivity improvements and falling trade costs: Boon or bane? *International Economic Review, 49*(4), 1437–1462.

Dornbusch, R., Fischer, S., & Samuelson, P. A. (1977). Comparative advantage, trade, and payments in a Ricardian model with a continuum of goods. *The American Economic Review, 67*(5), 823–839.

Eaton, J., & Kortum, S. (2002). Technology, geography, and trade. *Econometrica, 70*(5), 1741–1779.

Eaton, J., & Kortum, S. (2012). Putting Ricardo to work. *The Journal of Economic Perspectives, 26*(2), 65–89.

Golub, S. S., & Hsieh, C. T. (2000). Classical Ricardian theory of comparative advantage revisited. *Review of International Economics, 8*(2), 221–234.

Johnson, H. G. (1955). Economic expansion and international trade. *The Manchester School of Economic and Social Studies, 23*(2), 95–112.

Jones, R. W. (1961). Comparative advantage and the theory of tariffs: A multi-country, multi-commodity model. *The Review of Economic Studies, 28*(3), 161–175.

Jones, R. W. (1980). Comparative and absolute advantage. *Swiss Journal of Economics and Statistics (SJES), 116*(2), 272–288.

Jones, R. W. (1995). The discipline of international trade. *Swiss Journal of Economics and Statistics (SJES), 131*(3), 273–288.

Jones, R. W. (2000). *Globalization and the theory of input trade*. Cambridge, MA: MIT Press.

Jones, R. W., & Ruffin, R. J. (2008). The technology transfer paradox. *Journal of International Economics, 75*(2), 321–328.

Krugman, P. R. (1993). What do undergrads need to know about trade? *The American Economic Review, 83*(2), 23–26.

Krugman, P. R. (1994). Competitiveness. A dangerous obsession. *Foreign Affairs, 73*(2), 28–44.

Krugman, P. R. (1996). *Pop internationalism*. Cambridge, MA: MIT Press.

Krugman, P. R., & Obstfeld, M. (1994). *International economics, theory and policy* (3rd ed.). Reading, MA: Addison-Wesley.

Krugman, P. R., Obstfeld, M., & Melitz, J. M. (2015). *International economics. Theory and policy* (10th ed.). Boston: Pearson.

Leamer, E. E., & Levinsohn, J. (1995). International trade theory: The evidence, Chap. 26. In G. M. Grossman & K. Rogoff (Eds.), *Handbook of international economics* (Vol. 3, pp. 1339–1394). Amsterdam: Elsevier.

MacDougall, G. D. (1951). British and American exports: A study suggested by the theory of comparative costs. Part I. *The Economic Journal, 61*(244), 697–724.

Samuelson, P. A. (2004). Where Ricardo and Mill rebut and confirm arguments of mainstream economists supporting globalization. *The Journal of Economic Perspectives, 18*(3), 135–146.

Samuelson, P. A. (2005). Response to the comments by Avinash Dixit and Gene Grossman. *Journal of Economic Perspectives, 19*(3), 242–244.

Sax, C., & Weder, R. (2009). How to explain the high prices in Switzerland? *Swiss Journal of Economics and Statistics, 145*(4), 463–483.

Womack, J. P., Jones, D. T., & Roos, D. (1990). *The machine that changed the world*. New York: Rawson Associates.

Part II
Scientific Conference "Celebrating 200 Years of Ricardian Trade Theory" on May 12, 2017 at the University of Basel in Switzerland

Part II offers 13 chapters in which the reader is led through issues that occupy trade economists: (1) What are the central features, what the limitations of Ricardian trade theory? (2) How was comparative advantage discovered? (3) How can and should the theory be tested? (4) What are the current challenges in trade policy and how do or should trade economists address them? Many chapters are based on transcriptions of the conference.

Active participants at the conference (*from left to right*). *Back*: Th. Gerber, A. Loprieno. N. Schmitt, C. Hefeker, W.J. Ethier, R. Ruffn, E. Rossi-Hansberg, S. Evenett, P. H. Egger. *Front*: J. Eaton, M.S. Taylor, H. Dellas, R.W. Jones, R. Weder

All authors in this book (*from left to right, top down*):
Harris Dellas, Jonathan Eaton, Carsten Hefeker, Simon Evenett
Ronald Jones, Roy Ruffin, Esteban Rossi-Hansberg, Nicolas Schmitt
Antonio Loprieno, Scott Taylor, Thomas Gerber, Wilfred Ethier
Andrew Lee, Peter Egger, Rolf Weder

Chapter 6
The Main Contribution of the Ricardian Trade Theory

Ronald W. Jones

Abstract In the Ricardian trade model, even a country with no absolute advantage in the production of any commodity can gain from international trade, specializing in the production of the good in which it is has a comparative advantage. A three-country, three-commodity setting with given numbers for each country's labor requirement is used to illustrate possible patterns of trade. More recent trade models, such as the Swedish contribution by Heckscher and Ohlin, enriched the basic form of the Ricardian model by allowing more factors of production and differences in the endowments between countries and capital/labor ratios between commodities. However, the basic importance of the power of *comparative advantage* as the key to possible international trade patterns is maintained. The Ricardian model, with its basic simplicities, remains a popular set of explanations for fundamental features of international trade.

In 1817 a business man working in London, David Ricardo, published a book, *On the Principles of Political Economy and Taxation,* a collection of his pamphlets (Ricardo, 1817). The many topics discussed by Ricardo are clearly worthy of a 200 year celebration. Chapter 7 of his book, *On Foreign Trade,* is the focus of what I wish to talk about in this paper.

The concept of *Comparative Advantage* that he described has since been thought of as *The Ricardian Trade Model.* My own view, shared by many, is that the Ricardian model still has an important place in International Trade Theory two centuries after the book's appearance.

6.1   The Ricardian Trade Model

Imagine a world in which initially there are two countries, each consuming and producing the same two commodities. If one country is better at producing one commodity, and the other country is better at producing the other, it seems obvious

R.W. Jones (✉)
Department of Economics, University of Rochester, Rochester, NY, USA
e-mail: ronald.jones@rochester.edu

© Springer International Publishing AG 2017
R.W. Jones, R. Weder (eds.), *200 Years of Ricardian Trade Theory,*
https://doi.org/10.1007/978-3-319-60606-4_6

that both countries could benefit if free trade between the countries becomes possible. By contrast, suppose one country is better at producing *both* commodities than is the other. It may seem that in such a setting there is no basis for mutual gains from international trade. Ricardo disagreed. He argued that both countries could benefit from free trade as long as the *pattern of trade* reflects each country exporting the commodity in which it has a *comparative* advantage in production, even if one country does not possess an *absolute* advantage in producing the commodity it is exporting compared with the other country. Ricardo emphasized that such a result rests on an important assumption: International trade takes place in these commodities, but labor, the assumed single factor of production, does not move from country to country.

Phrased differently, free trade takes place in commodities but not in the factors that produce the commodities. If a country's labor force is less productive in making either good than its trading partner, this country can nonetheless be competitive in production of the commodity in which it has a *comparative* advantage (i.e. compared with its costs of producing the *other* commodity) if the wage rate is sufficiently lower than the rate in the other country. The kind of international trade that is considered by economists typically is not assumed to be found in a world in which all markets are international. Countries are countries for a reason—they do not want all items (such as most factors of production) to be tradeable or mobile in world markets.

In working with economic models in international trade theory it is often the case that much can be learned by starting with a model that has a small number of commodities and countries. The smallest case, of course, is one in which only two countries produce and trade in only two commodities, and this I will discuss first. However, Table 6.1 shows the technology for a 3×3 case with three countries, A (America), B (Britain) and country C (Continental Europe), and there are three commodities that each country would initially produce if no international trade takes place: *Corn (Co), Linen (Lin)* and *Cloth (Cl)*. The numbers indicate the quantity of labor required to produce each commodity. Ricardo assumed that labor is the only factor of production, and the quantity of labor required for each commodity is assumed constant, unless technical change is explicitly assumed.

First consider the 2×2 setting that leaves Continental Europe aside and with America and Britain only producing corn and linen. Neither country has an absolute advantage in the production of corn, but America has an *absolute* advantage in linen production since 5 is lower than 7. However, international trade between this pair of

Table 6.1 Labour requirements in the 3×3 example

	America	Britain	Continental Europe
Corn	10	10	10
Linen	5	7	3
Cloth	4	3	2

This set of numbers for the three-country, three-commodity case was used in Jones (1961), which also examined the case of many commodities and countries. An easy discussion of this paper was provided by Ethier, Helpman, and Neary (1993), Chapter 2.

Fig. 6.1 World production possibilities locus (the 2×2 case)

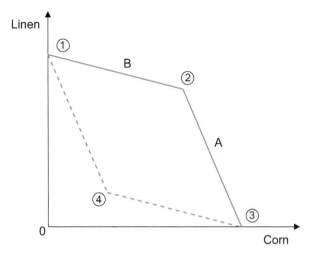

countries is possible because Britain has a *comparative* advantage in producing corn since 10/7 is *lower* than 10/5.[1] As in Ricardo, assume that labor is the only factor of production, and that there are constant returns to scale, so that doubling input of labor doubles the output of the commodity being produced.

The concept of the *world production possibility curve* for this case of two countries and two commodities is well known, and illustrated in Fig. 6.1. Point 1 shows the *world* production of Linen if both countries produce nothing but Linen. That would only be the case if the price of Linen were sufficiently high. If the relative price of Corn should sufficiently increase, which country would be the first to produce some units of Corn? Answer: the country with a *comparative advantage* in the production of Corn, and that is country *B* since 10/7 is less than 10/5. *Comparative advantage reflects a comparison between two cost rankings in one country with a similar comparison of two production costs in the other country.* If the relative price of Corn when trade takes place should rise above 10/7, country *B* has become completely specialized (at point 2), but country *A* would start shifting some of its labor towards producing some Corn only if the relative price of Corn reaches the slope of line {2–3} in the diagram.

Point 4 shows outcomes if country *A* produces nothing but Corn and country *B* is producing only Linen, but this is *not* a combination of production that could be found if *competitive markets* are in equilibrium. Two conditions are required to satisfy equilibrium: (i) In a competitive *equilibrium* no firm produces a commodity that has a lower market price than the cost of production for that firm. Furthermore, (ii) There cannot be an equilibrium if a firm does *not* produce a commodity which

---

[1] 10/7 is the price of corn in Britain expressed not in units of labor but in units of linen if Britain were to produce both commodities. 10/5 would be the price of corn in units of linen in America if it were to produce both commodities.

has a higher price than the cost for that firm to produce the commodity. These two conditions are required for equilibrium in markets if they are purely competitive in Ricardian trade models.

Of particular interest are cases in which *every* country is completely specialized to a single commodity. In the 2×2 case there are three *"classes of complete specialization"*: (i): both countries produce only corn; (ii): both countries produce only linen; (iii): one country is specialized to corn and the other to linen. There is only one possibility in (i) and only one possibility in (ii). However, in (iii) there are two possibilities, with one country producing corn and the other country linen. In this *class* of complete specialization each country is producing the commodity in which that country has a *comparative advantage, A* in Linen and *B* in Corn.

Now let the term a^i_j capture the "man-hours" required to produce a unit of commodity j in country i. The statement that countries A and B have these comparative advantages can be made by the following comparison of each country's cost *ratios* of Corn relative to Linen:

$$\frac{\alpha^B_{co}}{\alpha^B_{Lin}} < \frac{\alpha^A_{co}}{\alpha^A_{Lin}} \tag{6.1}$$

An alternative way of stating this is by cross-multiplying:

$$\alpha^B_{Co} \cdot \alpha^A_{Lin} < \alpha^A_{Co} \cdot \alpha^B_{Lin} \tag{6.2}$$

In words: The assignment of country A in linen and country B in corn is the *minimum product* of labor required in the pair of possible assignments of one country in linen and the other in corn, and this assignment reflects *comparative advantage*. The movement from (6.1) to (6.2) links the concept of comparative advantage to a different form—one that can be used in higher dimensions.

To illustrate, consider the situation in which there are three countries and three different commodities as shown in the table. The kind of comparison of ratios shown in Eq. (6.1) for the 2×2 case seems *not appropriate* for higher dimensions. However, the kind of comparison used in Eq. (6.2) can be used. Unlike the 2×2 case the 3×3 case has more than four *classes of complete specialization*: it has *ten* such classes. In three of them all three countries are producing the same commodity, so that there are no alternatives. Another set of possibilities is that a single country produces Corn and the other two countries produce the same commodity— either Linen or Cloth. Or a single country produces Linen and the other two produce the same other commodity. Or a single country produces Cloth and the other two countries produce in common one of the other two commodities.

Finally, there is a *tenth* possibility: each commodity is only produced by a single unique country. This latter class of complete specializations has a full six number of possibilities. In considering what is the *only* assignment (out of the six) that could be supported in a competitive equilibrium, note that country C has an *absolute* advantage over the other two countries in producing Cloth, and recall that in the two-commodity previous case it was country A that had the comparative advantage in producing Linen and country B in Corn. In the 3×3 setting this assignment (A in linen, B in corn, and C in cloth), is an assignment for all three countries that satisfies *bilateral* comparisons and it has a product of labor requirements of 100. However, this assignment *cannot* satisfy the conditions for *competitive equilibrium!* An alternative assignment, with country A in Corn, B in Cloth and C in Linen has a product of labor requirements of 90. For any class of assignments, *the winner has the minimum value of the product of labor requirements.*[2] This is how to discuss assignments that reflect comparative advantage in dimensions higher than (2×2).

The argument that leads to this result can be easily explained. Suppose the assignment of countries to commodities for the class of complete specialization is indeed the assignment supported by a set of commodity prices. Let p_j be the price of commodity j in equilibrium faced by all three countries, and the wage rates in each country by w^i. Therefore, in equilibrium,

$$w^A \alpha^A_{Co} = p_{Co} \tag{6.3}$$

$$w^B \alpha^B_{Cl} = p_{Cl} \tag{6.4}$$

$$w^C \alpha^C_{Lin} = p_{Lin} \tag{6.5}$$

Furthermore, if that is indeed an *equilibrium* there must *not* be any country that could produce a commodity at a *lower* cost than its market price. For example, consider the alternative to put country A in Linen, country B in Corn and Country C in Cloth (the assignment discussed earlier). If that assignment is ruled out as a contender at given prices, cost of production must be *greater* than price for *at least* one commodity. That is,

$$w^A \alpha^A_{Lin} \geq p_{Lin} \tag{6.6}$$

$$w^B \alpha^B_{Co} \geq p_{Co} \tag{6.7}$$

$$w^C \alpha^C_{Cl} \geq p_{Cl} \tag{6.8}$$

with a strict inequality for at least one industry. Multiply the first set of *equalities* to get:

$$w^A w^B w^C \alpha^A_{Co} \alpha^B_{Cl} \alpha^C_{Lin} = p_{Co} p_{Cl} p_{Lin} \tag{6.9}$$

Multiply the three *inequalities* by comparison to get:

$$w^A w^B w^C \alpha^A_{Lin} \alpha^B_{Co} \alpha^C_{Cl} > p_{Co} p_{Cl} p_{Lin} \tag{6.10}$$

---

[2] As noted in the previous footnote the argument that supports comparative advantage as the significant feature of the Ricardian Model in higher dimensions is explained in Jones (1961).

Fig. 6.2 World production possibilities locus (the 3 × 3 case)

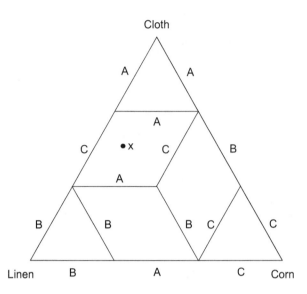

A comparison reveals that the product of labor coefficients that is consistent with equilibrium, $a^A_{Co}\, a^B_{Cl}\, a^C_{Lin}$, is indeed less than all other products of labor coefficients in the *class* in which each country is specialized to a different commodity.

It is important to note that *Comparative Advantage* does *not* by itself reveal which is the overall equilibrium pattern of production, since this depends not only on production technology, but also on world *demand* patterns. What *comparative advantage does* reveal is which trading patterns *cannot* be consistent with equilibrium (and this fraction grows substantially with more countries and commodities).

Return now to the importance of the *world production possibilities locus*. When there are two countries and two commodities Fig. 6.1 not only shows that country *B* has a comparative advantage in producing Corn it shows the extent of *B's* advantage. In the 3 × 3 case the world transformation surface is *three* dimensional. Figure 6.2 is only two-dimensional and thus does *not* show the *extent* of differences between countries, but it does show the *ordering* according to comparative advantage. For simplicity, the effective productive relative *size* of each country is arbitrarily assumed roughly the same. Consider the extreme case in which all three countries are completely specialized in producing Corn. The diagram shows that country *C* is the relatively *worst* producer of Corn, and will be the first country to release labor to produce Linen if it's relative price, p_{Li}/p_{Co}, should increase sufficiently or, if it is the relative price of Cloth that increases, labor moves out of Corn into Cloth.[3] There are 10 *classes of specialization* in Fig. 6.2. Nine of these have only one or two commodities produced and are simple to explain, like in Fig. 6.1. The only class that is

---

[3]Figure 6.2 also shows that countries *A* and *B* are the relatively worst producers of Cloth and Linen respectively. This is what leads to the triangles at each of the corners in Fig. 6.2. This need not be the case with some other technologies for labor's use.

different is the one in which each country is specialized to a *different* commodity. This class has six contenders. The only contender that could be supported in competitive markets has country *A* producing Corn, country *B* Cloth and *C* Linen. As shown in the preceding paragraph, the assignment of *A* into Linen, *B* into Corn and *C* into Cloth does indeed satisfy the *bilateral* conditions for each *pair* of commodities, but does *not* satisfy the requirement that the product of all three assignments be *minimal*, since 90 < 100.

Of course as mentioned earlier the use of *comparative advantage* by Ricardo does not by itself reveal what each country *produces*. That depends upon demand patterns as well as supply, i.e. where in Fig. 6.2 does equilibrium lie? What the Ricardo condition does is to reveal what assignments are *ruled out* in free trade conditions. In the 2 × 2 case there were a total of four possible assignments in which each country was specialized to a single productive activity. Only one assignment, that in which country *A* produced corn and *B* produced linen was ruled out, 25% of the total. In the 3 × 3 case there are 27 possible assignments but 17 are ruled out, i.e. 63%. (In the 4 × 4 case the percentage ruled out would be 86%). The importance of comparative advantage is that the percentage of *possible* production patterns (in the class of complete assignments) that are *ruled out* becomes very high.

Figure 6.2 attempts to show the important features of the three-dimensional world production possibilities, but only has two dimensions in which to show this. The three corner points show *every* country completely specialized in producing the same commodity. Along the edges Fig. 6.2 shows the movements as in Fig. 6.1. Now consider a point such as point **x**, which I assume is the point where a world indifference curve is tangent to the world production possibility surface. Country *A* produces both Linen and Corn, and country *C* produces both Linen and Cloth. What does country *B* produce? Only Cloth, with the relative value of the price of Cloth compared with Linen or with Corn already determined by countries *A* and *C*. Point **x** lies on a "flat" along which relative prices are all the same. For points along the lines only one relative price is constant, while at the point where each country is specialized to a different commodity no single relative price is completely determined, just as in Fig. 6.1 point 2 production would stay the same for a whole range of prices of linen and corn.

6.2 The Heckscher-Ohlin Model

The Ricardian Model was challenged 102 years after its appearance by a Swedish economist, Eli Heckscher, in 1919 and then by one of his students, Bertil Ohlin, in 1933.[4] Their basic purpose was to examine the determinants of the *pattern of trade*, especially when there is more than one factor input. Whereas Ricardo in his model

---

[4]Heckscher's paper was not translated into English until 1949.

assumed that a country's labor force was the only factor of production in any commodity, both Heckscher and Ohlin considered the possibility that in production there is more than just labor: they considered capital and/or land as other production factors[5] (Heckscher, 1919; Ohlin, 1933).

This setting raises several important possible differences between models: (i) The overall *relative quantities* of factor endowments may differ between countries. For example, America has a higher ratio of land to labor than does Sweden. As well, America might be a relatively capital abundant country compared to Sweden. (ii) The relative ratio of factors in which a specific commodity is produced may differ significantly from that in other commodities. (iii) Furthermore, factor ratios used in producing a commodity might be sensitive to changes in the relative prices of land or capital compared with wage rates on labor. All these possibilities were absent in the Ricardian model.

Ricardo assumed that technologies differed from country to country, and that these differences were the *only* basis that determined the pattern of comparative advantages among countries. In order to focus on *other explanations* leading to trade patterns, Heckscher and Ohlin assumed that all countries shared the *same technological knowledge*. And, if relative factor prices should change, so would the techniques of production. For example, if labor costs are reduced, more labor-intensive means of production are apt to be undertaken.[6]

World Production Possibilities used in the Ricardian model (admittedly long after Ricardo's time) can also be used in discussing Heckscher-Ohlin models. However, the *linear* features displayed in Fig. 6.1 or 6.2 are not found in H-O models. Instead, small changes in relative commodity prices might lead to small changes in relative outputs produced by several countries. Nonetheless, the central features found in the Ricardian model survive as well in models in which there are many kinds of inputs used in each of several commodities and countries. Patterns of trade still reflect the difference among countries in *comparative advantage* if we assume that whereas commodities may have global markets, some factors of production are nonetheless exchanged only *within* countries so that *factor* prices need not be similar between countries even if traded *commodity* prices are globally determined. Although the models of Heckscher and Ohlin may differ from the Ricardian model, the importance of comparative advantage comparisons among countries is still found. *Comparative advantage* becomes important when some factors of production have their returns determined in *country* markets. Price changes for commodities that have *global* markets do indeed affect local markets in which factor prices are determined, but *do not* require that factor price changes must be the same between countries.

---

[5]Ricardo, of course, was aware that in reality labor was not the only factor of production. He even used a four-letter word when talking of the price of another productive factor—*rent*. (See, for example, the second chapter of his 200-year old book.)

[6]Some economists later allowed differences in technology in the Heckscher-Ohlin model as well as differences in factor endowments.

Two particular journal articles published in mid-twentieth century had profound effects on the basic Heckscher-Ohlin properties of small-scale models. The first paper was that written by Wolfgang Stolper and Paul Samuelson (1941).[7] Stolper and Samuelson assumed that a country that imports a labor-intensively-produced commodity from another country does so because the foreign country's endowments are relatively more labor-abundant. Their paper concerns the consequences for Home wage rates should the Home country protect production at Home by levying a *tariff on imports* of this commodity (call It commodity X) from the more relatively labor-abundant country. The surprising result: the Home wage rate will rise—indeed it will increase so much that the tariff actually increases the *real* wage rate at Home. The reason? Because the wage rate will increase relatively *more* than the commodity price (assuming a simple 2×2 model). The reasoning behind this result was even more simple than the argument they provided (although that was also clear). The authors assumed that commodity markets were sufficiently competitive so that if a tariff is imposed the *relative* change in the local commodity price must be an *average* of the two relative factor price changes (for labor and capital).[8] If the price increase is only for the more labor-intensive commodity (and Y is the other commodity produced), and if $\hat{p}_X$ is defined as the *relative* change in the price of commodity X, the Home wage rate relative change ($\hat{r}$ is the relative change in the return to capital) is $\hat{w} > \hat{p}_X > \hat{p}_Y > \hat{r}$ so that Home's *real* wage rises, *regardless* of taste patterns of laborers.

The second paper is one that suggested that in the United States the trade pattern comparing exports with import-competing industries seemed to *contradict* the expectations of the Heckscher-Ohlin model. The author was Prof. Wassily Leontief (Harvard University), and the Input-Output figures he used were for the United States (1953). U.S. *exports* seemed to be produced at Home with *more labor-intensive* techniques than found in America's *import-competing sector*. This surprising result (because all agreed that America was the most capital-abundant country) quickly was called the "Leontief Paradox" and many new articles (and Ph.D. theses) from other economists not surprisingly followed. Years later I suggested a simple argument that the kind of result that Leontief obtained is *not* that unusual (Jones, 2008). To keep the argument simple, suppose that only two factors are used in production, capital and labor. Figure 6.3 illustrates the technology for four different commodities, 1 through 4, shown by the four positively

---

[7]The paper had earlier been rejected by the *American Economic Review*. A 50th anniversary celebration led to a *book* entitled, *The Stolper-Samuelson Theorem*. Stolper was my first undergraduate professor (at Swarthmore College), with our textbook the new first edition of Samuelson's text, and Samuelson was my professor for graduate work at M.I.T. This past history urged me to suggest to Alan Deardorff (at the University of Michigan along with Stolper) to have a 50th anniversary celebration there, especially since Alan was a student of mine when I taught a graduate trade course at Cornell.

[8]This presumes that there is *no joint production*. That is, every productive activity requires two inputs to produce a single output. This assumption was so commonly made that often little notice was paid to its importance in affecting factor prices.

Fig. 6.3 Factor endowments and factor prices

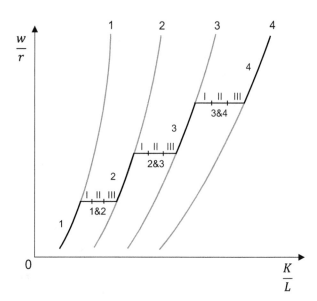

sloped schedules that illustrate that the capital/labor endowment ratio (which increases with growth) would drive up the relative wage/rent ratio *if* the economy produces only a *single* commodity.

Each of the three dark *horizontal* lines illustrate that for some K/L endowment ratios the economy produces a *pair* of commodities. There are three regions in each horizontal line, *regions I, II, and III*, and, because two commodities are being produced with two productive factors, costs in equilibrium are equal to commodity prices and *factor prices are determined*, (but not necessarily the same in different countries).

Consider, now, two countries (among many): *Home's* endowment is relatively labor abundant and suppose it produces commodities 1 and 2 in *region III* of the first horizontal locus. That is, Home produces mostly the second commodity but does also still produce some of the first commodity in its import-competing sector. By contrast, suppose *Foreign* is significantly more capital abundant, and produces commodities 3 and 4 in its *region I*, with *exports* of commodity 3 and local production in *import-competing* sector 4. Region *II* in each country has not been discussed because in those regions each country produces a sufficient amount of two commodities that it exports both of them and has *no* need to produce a commodity it also imports. That is, in *that region* there is no import-competing produced commodity to be compared with the exporting commodities.

Note that Home, a more labor-abundant country, is exporting *its more capital-intensive commodity 2*, and Foreign, a more capital-abundant country, is exporting *its more labor-intensive commodity 3*. This pattern of trade seems to *contradict* expectations of the Heckscher-Ohlin theory. However, comparing factor-intensities for different commodities produced *within a single country* is *not* the same as comparing factor intensities *between* countries with different factor endowments. Ricardo's emphasis on *comparative advantage* requires a comparison of technology *between* countries, and such data were probably at that time not available except for the United States. In his 1953 paper, Leontief compared factor intensities in both its export and import good in the *same* country. If both countries shared the same technologies between countries but the capital/labor ratios actually used depended on relative endowments, the more capital abundant country would use higher capital/labor proportions in *all* its commodities produced than in *any* commodity produced in the other more labor abundant country. (That sounds more like the results desired by Heckscher and Ohlin.)

6.3 Fragmentation and the Role of Services in Production

Recall that in the Ricardian model labor is the only factor of production. Attention was paid to situations in which the only production situations are those in which *final* consumption goods are produced. However, in reality many items that get produced are *parts and components* that need to be assembled before the finished product emerges. Think of two kinds of productive activity. Labor produces a variety of what we can call *"Production Blocks"*, but these "parts" need to be "linked" together, and this we call *"Service Links"*, also requiring labor (see Jones & Kierzkowski, 1990). Do all production blocks that are required to produce a particular final consumption commodity get produced in the same country that exports the final commodity to consumers? Not necessarily. Service Links may bring together parts that are produced in different countries.

It turns out that in the past few years international trade in parts and components have been growing more rapidly than other items, such as final goods. As Ricardo assumed, Labor is often not traded in international markets. However, some of the *items that labor produces may enter global markets*. That is, the objects that labor produces may be traded on world markets without requiring that labor itself do so. Do these remarks suggest that David Ricardo's emphasis on *comparative advantage* as the key explanation of the gains from trade becomes dated, no longer useful? *Just the opposite.* With greater possibilities for parts and components to be traded, who should be producing such parts and components? The answer: countries (and their firms) that have a *comparative advantage* in producing the individual parts and components.

Figure 6.4 may seem to have a strange title, ending with a question mark. Most discussions of competitive markets in international trade rely on an assumption of the way in which improvements in technology take place. If we assume that markets are highly competitive, as is often assumed in discussing international trade, production functions are typically assumed to exhibit *constant returns to scale*. In Fig. 6.4 a positively sloped line from the origin where production costs are shown on the vertical axis and levels of output by the horizontal axis is line 1. Such a line would indeed exhibit constant returns to scale. Line 2 suggests that a *different*

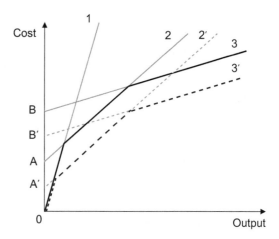

Fig. 6.4 Increasing returns to scale?

technique might be possible, but this entails a set of fixed costs such as shown by line 2 emanating from point *A* on the vertical axis. If such costs are made it is possible that *marginal* costs of production can be lowered (once fixed costs are paid). It would not pay producers to switch to such techniques unless output is large enough, higher output than shown by the intersection of lines 2 and 1.

A further change of techniques is shown by line 3, requiring further types of fixed costs shown by point *B*, after which marginal costs are reduced. The dark portion of three sets of lines 1, 2, and 3 suggest "increasing returns to scale". Sufficiently large firms will have marginal costs of production as shown by line 3. Also shown in Fig. 6.4 are dashed lines 2′ and 3′. Compared with lines 2 and 3, these suggest a significant fall in the costs of *service link activities* that reduce fixed costs *A* and *B* to *A*′ and *B*′ so that lines 2 and 3 drop to 2′ and 3′, the new heavy dashed lines. This is meant to capture the significant lowering of the cost of service link activities (and arbitrarily not to illustrate any reduction in marginal costs). The question mark in the title of Fig. 6.4 is meant to suggest that the remark could be made that the recent lowering in costs are due to increasing returns to scale. I would argue that in a sense that is the case. However, I would prefer that in the lowering of costs that are brought about by the great lowering in service link costs (the lowering of *A* and *B* to *A*′ and *B*′), the heavy dashed parts should be distinguished from any severe technological lowering of marginal costs of activity "on the factory floor".

6.4   Final Remarks

International Trade Theory was a key topic when David Ricardo and friends talked and wrote about economic issues two centuries ago. In the past century much attention has been paid to economic models that extended the Ricardian model in allowing for more than a single input (labor in the Ricardian model) to emphasize that inputs such as capital and land may well be important in production. These more recent trade models typically agreed with the Ricardian model's emphasis that, when considering trade among countries, it frequently makes sense to assume that--with more firms and countries engaged in production--the economic model of perfect competition in global markets often remains quite appropriate, even in more complicated and realistic models than the Ricardian model.

However, although interest in the Ricardian model seemed to fade over time, it became clear that Ricardo's emphasis on the importance of *comparative advantage* remained central to the analysis of global trade. The reason? Some items or productive factors are *not* exchanged in world markets, but are exchanged instead in country markets or even more local markets. This is especially the case often found with labor. Countries are countries for a reason, and many countries prefer to have control over movements of labor (as in the Ricardian model) as well as in many drugs or forms of capital. International trade is clearly important, but the world is far from being "One Country".

Is Ricardo's assumption that labor is the only factor of production still important and useful after 200 years? My vote is yes. Clearly, it is important because his assumption that an important factor of production still remains in a country market supports the basic role of comparative advantage. Furthermore, the fact that it is a very simple model should not be held against it. For example, suppose that the question that is asked is: What is the effect on a country's overall wellbeing if a traded commodity goes up in price because of a change in technology or taste patterns abroad? The Ricardian model suggests that the easy to obtain change in the wage rate suffices to answer the question, since labor is the only factor of production.

To my knowledge the use of the *World Production Possibility Locus* to illustrate possibilities of production with two or three commodities and countries was not developed as long ago as 200 years, but it is very useful in talking about international trade, whether the model is Ricardian, or Heckscher-Ohlin or of another type, such as the *Specific-Factors model* (that allows labor to be used in all firms but in each firm there is another input, e.g. capital, that is *specific* to that firm and no other). There is no doubt that such models can add much to the Ricardian model. As well, a simple model like the Ricardian model can add much to models that may be of higher dimension.

Consider again the (3×3) scenario. The simpler (2×2) model would support the concept of *comparative advantage* introduced by Ricardo, such as in the comparison in Eq. (6.1) between two countries each of them comparing the costs within each country for a pair of commodities. Equation (6.2) states the same comparison and there are six possible assignments for the class in which all three commodities are produced, with a different assignment for each country. We are assuming that world markets are perfectly competitive. The winning assignment was with country A producing corn, country B cloth, and country C linen, because the product of their minimal product, $a^A_{Co} \, a^B_{Cl} \, a^C_{Lin}$ was 90, and the next product was 100, with A in linen, B in corn and C in cloth.

The discussion of comparative advantage that came naturally in (2×2) scenarios was appropriate in higher dimensions by cross-multiplying and selecting the winners that could be found in the assignment that minimized the product of labor costs. This more general selection found in comparative trade markets does not select the pattern of trade in the World Production Possibility Locus, because demand considerations are also important. But the fraction of combinations that do *not* reflect comparative advantage and thus do not get produced gets increasingly larger the number of commodities and countries.

I leave the last word to one of the greatest economic theorists of the past 80 years or so, Prof. Paul Samuelson. On many occasions Prof. Paul Samuelson had talked about the theory of international trade and its connection to the wider field of economic theory. One of these occasions was in 1968 in Montreal, where Samuelson was giving a Presidential Address to the Third World Congress of the International Economic Association. I was fortunate to have been at this occasion, and was struck by Samuelson's remarks:

> Our subject puts its best foot forward when it speaks out on international trade. This was brought home to me years ago when I was in the Society of Fellows at Harvard along with the mathematician Stanislaw Ulam. Ulam, who was to become an originator of the Monte Carlo method and co-discoverer of the hydrogen bomb, was already at a tender age a world famous topologist. And he was a delightful conversationalist, wandering lazily over all domains of knowledge. He used to tease me by saying, *'Name me one proposition in all of the social sciences which is both true and non-trivial'*. This was a test that I always failed. But now, some thirty years later, on the staircase so to speak, an appropriate answer occurs to me: *the Ricardian theory of comparative advantage;* the demonstration that trade is mutually profitable even when one country is absolutely more—or less—productive in terms of every commodity. That it is logically true need not be argued before a mathematician; that it is not trivial is attested by the thousands of important and intelligent men who have never been able to grasp the doctrine for themselves or to believe it after it was explained to them. (Samuelson, 1972, p. 683)

If Ricardo could speak after 200 years he might say, *"Thank you Professor Samuelson, this proves my case."*

References

Ethier, W., Helpman, E., & Neary, J. P. (1993). *Theory, policy and dynamics in international trade*. Cambridge: University Press.

Heckscher, E. (1919). The effect of foreign trade on the distribution of income. *Ekonomisk Tidskrift, 21*, 497–512. Reprinted as Chapter 13 in A.E.A. and Ellis, H.S. (1949). *Readings in the theory of international trade*, 272–300. Philadelphia: Blakiston. With a Translation in: H. Flam & Flanders M. J. (Eds.). (1991). *Heckscher-Ohlin trade theory*, 43–69. Cambridge, MA: MIT Press.

Jones, R. W. (1961). Comparative advantage and the theory of tariffs: A multi-country, multi-commodity model. *The Review of Economic Studies, 28*(3), 161–175.

Jones, R. W. (2008). Heckscher-Ohlin trade flows: A re-appraisal. *Trade and Development Review, 1*(1), 1–6.

Jones, R. W., & Kierzkowski, H. (1990). The role of services in production and international trade: A theoretical framework, Chapter 3. In R. W. Jones & A. O. Krueger (Eds.), *The political economy of international trade*. Cambridge, MA: Blackwell.

Leontief, W. (1953). Domestic production and foreign trade; the American capital position re-examined. *Proceedings of the American Philosophical Society, 97*(4), 332–349.

Ohlin, B. (1933). *Interregional and international trade*. Cambridge, MA: Harvard University Press.

Ricardo, D. (1817). *On the principles of political economy and taxation*. London: John Murray Publishers.

Samuelson, P. A. (1972). The way of an economist. In R. C. Merton (Ed.), *The collected scientific papers of Paul A. Samuelson* (Vol. 3). Cambridge, MA: MIT Press.

Stolper, W. F., & Samuelson, P. A. (1941). Protection and real wages. *The Review of Economic Studies, 9*(1), 58–73.

Chapter 7
Comments on the "The Main Contribution of the Ricardian Trade Theory" by Ronald W. Jones

M. Scott Taylor

Abstract The aim of this chapter is a critical assessment of the Ricardian model and its usefulness in research. It starts with explaining the analytical difficulties by which the two-by-two model is characterized in comparison to an endowment model. Further, it is examined why it is challenging to add further dimensions and extend the basic example to a three-by-three case. Three possible solutions of the challenges related to many-good and many-country cases are discussed. Firstly, understand the possible efficient outcomes of these cases based on Jones (*The Review of Economic Studies* 28(3):161–175, 1961). Secondly, introduce the many-good-continuum model of Dornbusch, Fischer and Samuelson (*The American Economic Review* 67(5):823–839, 1977). Thirdly, find an empirical approach such as Eaton and Kortum (*Econometrica* 70(5):1741–1779, 2002).

Thank you to Rolf for inviting me as it's an honor to discuss a paper by Ron Jones. I discussed one of his papers quite a while ago, when I was an assistant professor. It was also on comparative advantage and Paul Samuelson was in the room. At that time, I had to explain how comparative advantage works in front of Paul, and that was a little frightening. So today things are somewhat similar. Today I have Jonathan Eaton here, but I'm a little older and a little less worried now. So, what I'm going to do with these comments, is what I thought would be the most productive use of my time, and this is to provide a bridge between Ron's presentation and the later presentation of Jonathan. I'm going to start out being slightly contrarian about Ricardo and the usefulness of his model, but I should let you know that Ricardo is paying my mortgage, he is paying my kids' school tuition, and he has bought all my clothes. This is true because almost all of my papers in one way

---

Note: This chapter is based on a transcription of the presentation given at the Conference "Celebrating 200 Years of Ricardian Trade Theory" on May 12, 2017, at the University of Basel, Switzerland. It is a comment to the paper by Ronald W. Jones, i.e., to Chap. 6 of this book.

M.S. Taylor (✉)
Department of Economics, University of Calgary, Calgary, AB, Canada
e-mail: mstaylor@ucalgary.ca

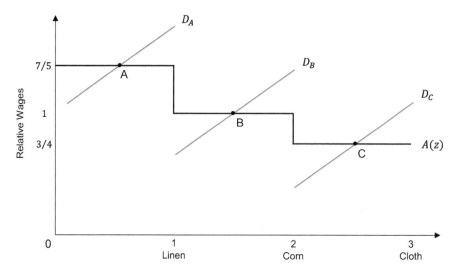

Fig. 7.1 Ron Jones's numerical example in terms of Dornbusch-Fischer-Samuelson. Source: Own figure

or another use or elaborate on the Ricardian model. So while I'm being slightly contrarian to start with, you should understand that it will turn around at the end.

Ron's presentation started with the two-by-two Ricardian model that we use to teach undergraduates. We use this model to explain comparative advantage to the uninitiated, and while it's a beautiful thing to behold, it's really not that useful as a tool. Frankly it's not that useful either analytically or empirically.

It's tremendously insightful but it used to be almost the end of the road for Ricardo. In some sense I feel like, if you had a graduate student bring the model to you with a two by two example, you'd go: "That's quite good, now can you go on and expand it to a whole bunch of countries or tell me what aspects of world trade this can explain that previous theories cannot?" The graduate student would have a hard time doing this I think, so let's review what these deficiencies are.

To start let's review Ron's example or at least part of it (see Fig. 7.1). He has the three-by-three case in his paper but started talking about the two-by-two case. And all I have done in the figure is to put his example into the formulation of the $A(z)$ schedule, that Dornbusch-Fischer-Samuelson (1977) brought to Ricardian trade theory. Ignore for the moment cloth and ignore continental Europe to make this truly a two by two example. I've assumed home is North America and so it's ordered in terms of home country comparative advantage which is first linen and then corn. The exact numbers are Ron's. The equilibrium is then determined by demand conditions which pick out whether we are at A, B or C. So, if the demand for linen is really high, then both countries are going to be producing it at an equilibrium like A, and the US is going to have really high wages. Alternatively, they both could be specialized at B. Or they both could be diversified in corn at C. So that's pretty well the two-by-two case.

Now, what's the problem with this two-by-two case? Well in the specialization case at B, if you do local comparative statics, the model is identical to an endowment model. It really doesn't carry with it any more information than that. So why use a model with production anyway if we are at B? Although the Ricardian model is the simplest general equilibrium model with production, comparative statics around B don't exploit this feature. But what about points A and C? In these cases, one country operates just like an endowment economy, because it is specialized and the other one operates as if it was in autarky. And as you know, autarky isn't trade so the welfare properties of these equilibria are somewhat strange since all the gains go to one country. Finally, at A or C where countries are diversified, local comparative statics either do very little and alter only the amount of one good produced, and or do too much by affecting the set of goods produced in each country in a discontinuous way. So analytically, the simple two by two is a difficult animal to deal with, much harder than say the endowment model is. It's great as an example, but if you want to do comparative statics to learn from it, it is probably not the model you want to use. So, what happens if you add more countries or more goods? Maybe these changes will solve the problem.

So what I have shown is Ron's second case (Fig. 7.2) where now I have added Continental Europe. And I have constructed an America vs. Europe $A(z)$ schedule (red), and an America vs. Britain $A(z)$ schedule (black). Relative wages now are a little bit confusing to think about because the vertical axis has to represent first an America relative to Britain relative wage and then an America relative to Europe relative wage. But the purpose of the slide is to show how difficult it is to add more dimensions, so that's a goal rather than a flaw. Finally there is one more complication. Notice the ordering of comparative advantage has to be different: For the

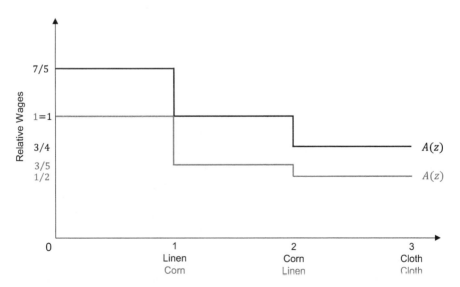

Fig. 7.2 Three countries: adding America versus Europe. Source: Own figure

black schedule, America vs. Britain, the ordering is linen, corn and then cloth. And for the red schedule, America vs. Europe, it's corn first, linen second and then cloth. So, if you were to stick three countries and three goods together and used the same apparatus that I used in the previous slide and then extrapolate, you are going to be in trouble because the vertical axis has two different relative wages, and as we will see bilateral comparisons of comparative advantage can lead you astray.

In fact, figuring out the set of possible outcomes in trade is very difficult if not impossible, using our previous method unless you could put really strong assumptions on how those two $A(z)$-schedules relate to each other. The ordering of goods is now different than before, so it's hard to know how to proceed and you are tempted to use the two schedules in sequence to find a set of efficient outcomes in free trade, but at this point this is more of a hope rather than a plan—hoping that it worked before so maybe it will work again, which is exactly what Ron did earlier in his presentation. It looks good for efficiency if America is in linen, Britain is in corn and Europe is in cloth, because you can think sequentially and use the two schedules to say: "Well, what should America be in relative to Britain? It should be in linen according to the black schedule! And what could Britain be in? It could be in corn or in cloth. But then what does Europe have to be in? It looks as if it has to be in cloth because if America is in linen then this is the right choice for Europe from the red schedule." And by this form of deduction, you end up rationalizing the specialization pattern you started with, but this specialization pattern is not efficient as Ron showed in his 1961 paper.

So how did the profession resolve these problems? There are three things we did. First, we generalized to the extent we could to understand the set of possible efficient outcomes in the many-country and many-good case. Second, we introduced techniques to smooth out the two-good model's comparative static properties, primarily by the introduction of the many-good-continuum model of Dornbusch et al. (1977). And finally we waited for somebody to solve the many-good many-country problem in a tractable, empirically useful and elegant way.

7.1   Solution One

Solution one is something that Ron provided in 1961 (Jones, 1961) and he revisited that result in his paper here today. To understand today's paper I re-read the original 1961 paper—actually I am not sure if I had read it before. The paper is quite dense, and the proof to the main result is beautiful and fantastic but it's still somewhat mysterious to me. The paper begins with the two by two example, and Ron notes that all efficient allocations are situated along the world PPF respectively comparative advantage. We saw that in one of the figures. Then he notes that all such points are also convex combinations of possible specialization allocations which is something I did not realize until I read the paper. Using this he shows you that if the ordering is done respecting comparative advantage, then the product of the unit labor requirements are minimized in any efficient allocation. This seems reasonable in the two by two case, which was clearly his purpose. Next, Ron introduces the third country and the third good and shows you—what Ron said earlier [in his talk]—that respecting bilateral comparative advantage isn't going to be enough, as I tried to show in my example. But then using a mathematical theorem from input-output analysis, he finds there is a way to calculate what efficiency requires in the many-good many-country case. And that is again the minimum product of the unit labor requirements. And furthermore, in that paper—and I think in this paper today—Ron suggests that if we had more countries and more goods, theory would impose more constraints on what represents an efficient division of production worldwide. It looked actually really promising when I read it, as this would really narrow down the number of possibilities for efficiency, but in a world with geography, where you add in source and destination specific based transport costs, then it gets a little harder for theory to impose that strong a set of restrictions. Nevertheless, it's a really beautiful paper, just in the way it is constructed: Starting with the two good example, then going to the three, and carrying the reader through the same logical argument. It's all beautifully straightforward until Ron's ingenious proof of the general result using this Hawkins-Simon condition that comes right out of the left field to save the day. So, Ron's 1961 paper is the solution to our first problem, and this is about as far as we could go with the many-good many-country framework by providing this result on efficiency.

7.2 Solution Two

The second solution was to introduce a method to make comparative statics easier and more useful while retaining a Ricardian structure. And this was done in a paper written by Dornbusch, Fischer, Samuelson in the mid 1970s. They retained the two country assumption, with one factor; and they introduced a continuum of goods z— that's why I introduced the $A(z)$-schedule earlier—except that now $A(z)$ is going to

Fig. 7.3 The Ricardian model until 2002. Source: Dornbusch et al. (1977)

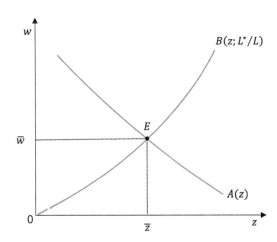

be smooth (see Fig. 7.3) and is assumed to be continuous—and differentiable. These assumptions ensure that no good will be produced by two countries at the same time. Then they also introduce iceberg transportation costs and revenue raising trade barriers. The transportation costs were especially innovative at that time, because it allowed a set of non-traded goods to be determined endogenously, where previously we used to just assume for example "Good z is non-traded and the other two are traded." Importantly, it allowed the set of non-traded goods to change with comparative statics. That was very nice. And tastes were assumed to be Cobb-Douglas.

So, what this model looks like now, is that we have home relative wages on the vertical axis and we have the goods ranked along the $A(z)$'s schedule in terms of declining home country comparative advantage. This is just a smooth continuum version of the graph with flats I showed a few slides ago. And then the $B(z)$ schedule reflects demand for home vs. foreign labor conditional on the set of goods produced. $B(z)$ takes into account the potentially differing budget shares consumer's have across all goods and it also reflects relative country size as captured by labor force sizes.

Until 2002—and there were many elaborations of this—this was the Ricardian model that was taught in graduate schools everywhere. And this was because the model provided a very productive setting to examine many questions. While the model has been used in many different ways, I'll give you just three examples of papers using this framework. The three I chose represent the three most cited papers (Google Scholar citations) that employ and extend the DFS model. Fortunately all three are quite different as well.

The first example is Paul Krugman's (1987) paper 'The narrow moving band, the Dutch disease and the competitive consequences of Mrs. Thatcher', published in the Journal of Development Economics. It's a very interesting paper to read. It's kind of amazing to see, how much Paul got away with in this paper. It's a big think paper with a lot of missing details, none of which I will talk about today. The basic idea can be conveyed by (Fig. 7.4), where along the horizontal axis, it's not z anymore,

Fig. 7.4 Narrow moving band, Dutch disease and competiveness consequences. Source: Krugman (1987)

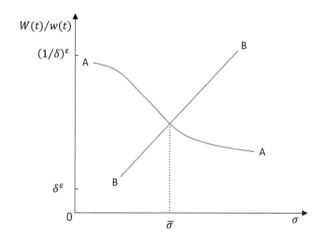

but it's the share of spending falling on home produced goods and along the vertical axis it's again relative wages. What happens in this model is that when you produce more of a good, you accumulate knowledge capital. This knowledge capital is external to the firm, it accumulates and of course the more knowledge capital you have the more productive you and every other firm are in producing that good. This knowledge spills across borders, and the extent of these international spillovers is determined by the parameter δ. So, if δ was one, everything that I know, somebody else living in another country learns too and vice and versa. Spillovers are completely international. If δ is less than one, then Rolf gets part of my knowledge capital from production but doesn't benefit from it completely. And in the steady state this parameter is going to bound wages because it's going to determine ultimate productivity differentials between the two trading countries in any steady state. Paul Krugman used this as a means to talk about three things that people had talked about in trade theory but didn't have a way to model. And the first one was the effects of temporary protection on long run outcomes. He suggested that if a country was to refuse to import one of the goods exported by the partner country, it may in fact become more competitive in this industry over time. In this sense temporary protection could work to generate longer run comparative advantage which is often at the heart of infant industry arguments for protection. So, if you are the home country here, if you refuse to import one of the goods you are currently importing [any good to the right from the intersection], then what would happen is, if you are large enough, you would be gaining more experience in that good because of your relatively large domestic production, than would the foreign country with relative small domestic production. Over time, this will affect the $A(z)$ schedule and may turn it in your favor.

For example, in this model with learning by doing, the $A(z)$ schedule to the left of the intersection moves up because only Home is producing these goods and they are getting relatively more productive at doing so. Conversely, everything to the right of the intersection moves down, so the limiting $A(z)$ schedule looks something like a step function with a vertical section at the intersection point. The narrow moving band of the title is just suggestive of the possibility of a country selectively protecting a group of industries near the intersection so that over time this step function moves rightwards. In essence, it's an argument about the importance of hysteresis since temporary protection can have long run consequences for trade patterns. At the time this was—I think—pretty novel to international trade. The details were left for others to work out.

The second example of Paul's involved the Dutch disease and to model this he used what we already knew about the impact of international transfers. In fact, the element of the transfer problem he used, Ron worked on quite a bit.[1] A resource boom was modeled as delivering a flow of offshore income coming into the country. To get these resource transfer payments to affect the competitive margin, and hence long run comparative advantage, Paul probably read one of Ron's earlier

---

[1]See, for example, Jones (1975).

papers and recognized that, with identical homothetic tastes, transfers are going to do nothing. World demand is unaffected by income distribution in that case, so what did he do? Paul introduces non-traded goods, and this gets him around the problem. With non-traded goods in the mix, the BB schedule shifts up when the home country receives a transfer because a greater share of world income is then spent on home produced goods. The transfer of these resource rents consequently affects the economy's competitive margin and over time it can make this country less competitive in these industries. If the transfers continue for long enough, then when resource rents are gone the economy moves back to a world where it has lost comparative advantage in a set of other industries. Again, a temporary change in the competitive margin has long run effects because of learning by doing. A similar result can follow from overly tight monetary policy that likewise affects the set of goods produced, and this was the paper's last example and the genesis for the "Mrs. Thatcher" in the title.

This application of the Dornbusch, Fischer and Samuelson (DFS) 1977 paper stimulated a large literature by many academics. The Ricardian structure was simple enough so that we could sensibly add the complications of learning by doing, and the efficient pattern of production was also simple to track given our understanding of comparative advantage. The paper led to a large industry of followers who picked up all the pieces and filled in all the missing details having to do with whether temporary protection matters for welfare, about the permanence of resource boom impacts and, I think, even about the long run competitiveness consequences of tight monetary policy. Paul's paper was in some sense completely Ricardian since only one factor earned income and this factor's productivity alone determined trading patterns. The next two applications of DFS moved a little bit away but still retained a strong Ricardian flavor.

The second application of Ricardian trade theory is actually a paper of mine (Copeland and Taylor, 1994). It is very Ricardian in the sense that industries are ordered by their pollution intensity, and ordering these industries in terms of their pollution intensity plays a key role in determining trade patterns. Everyone world-wide has the same technology, but if the North imposes a higher pollution tax than does the South, then the costs of producing pollution intensive goods are relatively higher in the North than they are in the South. And that's what this $S(z)$-schedule reflects here (see Fig. 7.5), and it is the analog to the earlier $A(z)$. The North is the country with the higher pollution tax and the $S(z)$-schedule shows declining Northern comparative advantage as the goods become dirtier and dirtier moving to higher and higher z goods.

It's still Ricardian although with another intermediate step determining comparative advantage, but it would not have been published had I stopped at the exogenous pollution tax case. Another Ricardian component creeps in when we allow for endogenous pollution taxes. The North is the North for a reason, and we assume the two countries differ in absolute advantage. We model this difference by giving the North greater human capital per person, so that the North is much richer than the South. The North, because it's richer, has a higher marginal damage from pollution, so it imposes endogenously higher pollution taxes. And so the fixed

Fig. 7.5 North-South trade.
Source: Copeland and
Taylor (1994)

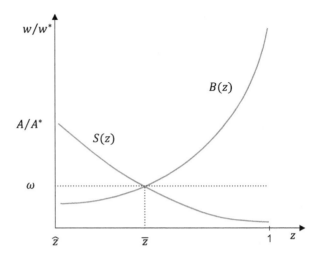

pollution taxes which gave you comparative advantage à la Ricardo become
endogenous pollution taxes that also give you the same pattern, as long as the
North is sufficiently richer than the South. The model replicated the trade pattern
Larry Summers wrote about in his 1993 memo that got him into a lot of trouble. The
rich North gave up production of dirty goods that were in turn produced by the poor
South. It gave the first formal proof or demonstration that the pollution haven
hypothesis could in fact work in a general-equilibrium context. Apart from this
contribution, the paper decomposed the changes in pollution created by trade or
economic growth into the now common mantra of Scale, Composition and Technique effects, and showed how income gains created by international trade had a
fundamentally different effect on environmental outcomes than did say economic
growth. Just like Paul's earlier paper, we also considered transfers but in this case to
examine the impact of foreign aid on environmental outcomes.

This paper also stimulated a large literature that extended the analysis to allow
for additional factors, to consider strategic policy choices across countries, and to
empirical work examining the strength of trade-related changes in the environment.
As such, it was again a very successful application of Ricardo's basic ideas to
important and timely present day questions.

The final example of Ricardo's continuing legacy that I was going to discuss was
an important paper by Feenstra and Hanson published in 1995. Their paper is even
further a field from a typical Ricardian model because there is another factor
endowment and this factor is in inelastic supply, but Feenstra and Hanson employed
the DFS trick to order all of their continuum of intermediates according to their skill
intensity much like Copeland and Taylor did in terms of pollution intensity. The
continuum again divides up the intermediate good production across countries, and
shifts in the additional endowment—capital—which alters the competitive margin.
An increase in foreign direct investment to Mexico or additional capital accumulation in Mexico stimulated by the prospects of NAFTA would then increase the

demand for skill in both countries. It did so because Mexico took over a set of industries on the margin of their competitiveness, and these were the most skill intensive relative to Mexico's existing production. This raises the relative demand for skill in Mexico. The US in turn loses the least skill intensive of its industries, so this raises the relative demand for skill in the US. The model has a factor endowments flavor, but the prospect of trade liberalization—if it induces changes in capital stocks—ensures that both countries post-liberalization could see a rise in the relative return to skill. This was the paper's key result, and it follows from the ranking of sectors, the continuum assumption made popular by DFS, and by the movement of capital with trade. This paper provided a very nice explanation for why the skill premium in both Mexico and the United States could rise with trade, and stimulated a large literature examining the labor market effects of trade liberalization that continues today.

While all of this is great stuff and important work, all of these papers were about two countries or regions. And although they stimulated empirical work, none of them really provided a tight test of the theories that they put forth. They were suggestive and illuminating, but none of them provided guidance for structural estimation. Adding more than two countries to a many good analysis remained difficult without very strong assumptions and extreme patterns of specialization remained in all of them. And without a better way to map theory into empirics, this branch of trade theory was destined to dwindle and be eclipsed first by a renaissance of the empirical Heckscher-Ohnlin-Vanek (HOV) tradition and then later by a surge of interest in models of monopolistic competition stressing firm level behavior. What the Ricardian model desperately needed was a way to take Ricardo's key insights seriously, move them to a world with many countries and goods, and then allow for a rigorous empirical evaluation of their merits.

7.3   Solution Three

The solution to problem three, that I alluded to above, has been provided by Eaton and Kortum (2002) and their subsequent work, but Jonathan is going to talk about this later today so there is no need for me to talk about it here. Suffice to say, their work provides a brilliant solution to this last key problem, and it has reinvigorated interest in the Ricardian model.

7.4   Conclusion

In closing, what are the nagging questions and the missing-in-action components I have ignored in this fly-by review of Ron's paper and Ricardian trade theory? First of all I ignored all applications of the two-good model, for which there are many, many great ones. Actually, I think, my favorite is Bill Ethier's "Decreasing Costs in

International Trade and Frank Graham's Argument for Protection" (Ethier, 1982). There were many other applications. John McLaren's Judge Bowker's argument against free trade (McLaren, 1997) being another. And I ignored all those. So, the Ricardian model played a big role—even the two-good Ricardian model—in allowing trade theorists to go into new areas and bring them into the fold of trade theory.

A second omission, is that I did not ask how far can Ricardo go in explaining the world pattern of production and trade? What fraction of world trade is left to be explained by increasing returns or by models stressing factor endowment differences? Do we really think that increasing returns and factor endowment differences are no longer important for explaining world trade, or should we think of this new reinvigorated Ricardian approach to trade theory as providing us with a far better, but still only partial, guide to reality?

References

Copeland, B. R., & Taylor, M. S. (1994). North-South trade and the environment. *The Quarterly Journal of Economics, 109*(3), 755–787.

Dornbusch, R., Fischer, S., & Samuelson, P. A. (1977). Comparative advantage, trade, and payments in a Ricardian model with a continuum of goods. *The American Economic Review, 67*(5), 823–839.

Eaton, J., & Kortum, S. (2002). Technology, geography, and trade. *Econometrica, 70*(5), 1741–1779.

Ethier, W. J. (1982). Decreasing costs in international trade and Frank Graham's argument for protection. *Econometrica: Journal of the Econometric Society, 50*, 1243–1268.

Feenstra, R. C., & Gordon, H. H. (1995). Foreign investment, outsourcing and relative wages: Evidence from Mexico's Maquiladoras. *Journal of International Economics, 42*, 371–393.

Jones, R. W. (1961). Comparative advantage and the theory of tariffs: A multi-country, multi-commodity model. *The Review of Economic Studies, 28*(3), 161–175.

Jones, R. W. (1975). Presumption and the transfer problem. *Journal of International Economics, 5* (3), 263–277.

Krugman, P. (1987). The narrow moving band, the Dutch disease, and the competitive consequences of Mrs. Thatcher: Notes on trade in the presence of dynamic scale economies. *Journal of Development Economics, 27*(1–2), 41–55.

McLaren, J. (1997). Size, sunk costs, and Judge Bowker's objection to free trade. *The American Economic Review, 87*, 400–420.

Chapter 8
Discussion About "The Main Contribution of the Ricardian Trade Theory"

Harris Dellas

Abstract This chapter includes the discussion of the paper "The Main Contribution of the Ricardian Trade Theory" by Ronald W. Jones (Chap. 6 of this book) and of the comments to this paper by M. Scott Taylor (Chap. 7 of this book). It is based on the transcription of the discussion. The session was chaired by Harris Dellas, Professor in International and Monetary Economics at the University of Bern. He has a PhD from the University of Rochester.

[In his opening below, Harris Dellas first reacts to a statement by Rolf Weder who had welcomed everyone to the conference. Rolf had said that he still remembers very well when he was first exposed to the Ricardian idea in his undergraduate studies at the University of St. Gallen. He was so impressed when using the four numbers to find out that trade would actually lead to a result where a country does not have to give up anything in order to consume more of something—in fact, it would get more of both goods with trade. At the time, he thought that this was a bit like "magic", but great.]

Harris Dellas We will shortly proceed to the discussion. Let me just start by thanking Rolf, for giving me the opportunity to participate in this absolutely wonderful event. Let me also tell him--he used the words magic and mysterious to describe his trade experience at the University of St. Gallen—that it was magic for us, but it was nothing mysterious because my teacher was the best teacher I have ever had in any field and subject. Ron was absolutely wonderful. I owe him a lot: Personally, because he helped me survive the very harsh winters, giving me work in Rochester. He guided me, he advised me. And of course he is one of the key figures in international trade who has made lots and lots of fundamental contributions. But to me as a student, the most important personal contribution was that he made the style of international trade elegant, easy and fun. And I think there are thousands

---

Note: This chapter is based on a transcription of the discussion held at the Conference "Celebrating 200 Years of Ricardian Trade Theory" on May 12, 2017, at the University of Basel in Switzerland. The discussion in this Chap. 8 refers to the contents in Chaps. 6 and 7 of this book.

H. Dellas (✉)
Department of Economics, University of Bern, Bern, Switzerland
e-mail: harris.dellas@vwi.unibe.ch

and thousands of international trade students out there who share this. Thanks to Ron, we can learn international trade very easily.

So let me open the first session. Our first presenter is Ronald Jones, Professor of Economics at the University of Rochester, who holds a PhD from MIT, and who will talk about the "Main Contribution of the Ricardian Trade Theory". Our second presenter is Prof. M. Scott Taylor from the University of Calgary, with a PhD from Queen's University in Canada, who comments on Ron's paper.

[The following is the discussion on both contributions (see Chaps. 6 and 7 in this book). We start with a reaction by Professor Jones to Professor Taylor's comments.]

Ronald Jones By the way, the Dornbusch-Fischer-Samuelson (1977) paper you mentioned. I was the referee of this paper. There was one problem with the paper. It had already been done. Samuelson, had a paper about this about ten years before.[1] I guess he forgot that he had done some of it before.

Scott Taylor Every paper is a kind of moving average paper. If you are writing a series. . .

Jonathan Eaton Was the Samuelson paper published?

Roy Ruffin This was the three goods case. It was in RESTAT: many goods and two countries.

Scott Taylor Really?

Roy Ruffin He just made a continuum. I think it was in RESTAT in 1964.

Harris Dellas What about bringing absolute and comparative advantage together? What Ron has in his footloose factor model. Could that be implemented with this?

Scott Taylor Oh, the connection between the two of them.

Harris Dellas No, the combination of them—the Dornbusch-Fischer-Samuelson model and the model with the footloose factor.

Scott Taylor I don't know. Is this a question for Ron?

Harris Dellas I think Ron has done it, so I don't know what the rest of the profession is making of it. The footloose factor is a combination of absolute and comparative advantage, both of them mattering.

Ronald Jones Comparative advantage matters. Well, if you have footloose factors (e.g., you can have capital moving), that changes the result. It turns out that both matter, absolute as well as comparative advantage. But what I wanted to say in my talk is the following: Suppose you have international trade in parts and components, does this make Ricardo's arguments weaker? The answer: No, it doesn't. What it does is the following: You have more trade responsible on comparative advantage.

---

[1]Samuelson (1964).

If the cost of moving stuff like parts and components went down a lot, well, then who's going to produce it? You produce it if you've got a comparative advantage.

Scott Taylor It also depends on whether you think that when a factor moves does it take the old country's technology or does it have the new country's technology? Are those technologies or skill levels country-specific or individual-specific? If they are individual-specific, then it's a different story.

Rolf Weder I'd like to ask a question to Scott Taylor. You said that in your work you very often applying the Ricardian model, but sometimes also the Heckscher-Ohlin model. So, for example, in the model you weren't talking about now, the model with open-access renewable resources with Jim Brander,[2] you were using the Ricardian model with a production possibility frontier that is in a way endogenous depending on the stock of the resource. My question is this: Why did you sometimes use the Ricardian model and sometimes the Heckscher-Ohlin model? Why did you very often use the Ricardian model? What was the reason?

Scott Taylor I think the answer is just that: Someone said to me once, and I remembered, that the two-good Ricardian model is the simplest GE-model with production, so that entire branch of literature with the Ricardian and the renewable resources started because I had to discuss a paper by Jim Brander. And Jim Brander had this strategic trade policy thing between these two resource countries. One was importing and exporting and I had to say something and I thought how would I do it. And so I just started with the two-good Ricardian model. And then I just added the renewable sector to it and it happened to marry up quite nicely to the Ricardian model and then it did have these implications that when you get some dynamic accumulation going on, now you can have two factors, right, and the same is true of Krugman's in the way that has some factor endowment features to it as well. But, you know, necessity is the mother of invention. So, I had to discuss the paper and I thought this is the simplest way for me to do the thing I had to do.

Peter Bernholz[3] Isn't it true that all these results depend on the assumption that the value of exports is equal to the value of imports, that you have a balanced situation? What would happen if there would be, for instance, a very big surplus of trade and if you could go the extreme, it would be equal to the volume of exports, and that certainly would be a loss of utility for the country. One would have to go too far, but there must be some break there that there is no longer a variable to have this international division of labor. Of course, you could argue that this in time would equalize inter-temporally. But there is a lot of empirical evidence which seems at least to certainly contradict this. So, I wonder what this would mean for the models?

---

[2]Brander and Taylor (1997).
[3]Professor Emeritus of Economics, University of Basel.

Scott Taylor Well, a simple way--I think you a kind of answered your own question, in a way. A simple way to think about it was when I discussed the resource boom in the Krugman model. So, you can think of it as an ongoing continual transfer as the foreign country paying for your excess imports. So, this country is growing in debt over time with this transfer. So, it's just going to shift that B(z) schedule over time. It's going to increase the demand for foreign goods, but that transfer is going to be accumulated over time in debt that will eventually have to be paid off, which is your point, and that schedule is in some way going to have to move back over time. Whether this has real consequences or not, depends on the other model assumptions. So, maybe, in the model that Krugman had, where the allocation of labor affected long-run comparative advantage, maybe in those cases, maybe it would make a difference. I'm sure there are many papers that investigate that. I'm not an expert in that area. But it's nothing inconsistent with the model itself. That's the simplest way to think of it. It's just shifting this B(z) schedule and thinking of a trade deficit as being an ongoing transfer from the rest of the world.

Harris Dellas Any other questions? No, so then we have a coffee break.

References

Brander, J. A., & Taylor, M. S. (1997). International trade and open access renewable resources: The small open economy case. *The Canadian Journal of Economics/Revue Canadienne Economique, 30*(3), 526–552.

Samuelson, P. A. (1964). Theoretical notes on trade problems. *The Review of Economics and Statistics, 46*(2), 145–154.

Chapter 9
Mill and Ricardo: The Genesis of Comparative Advantage

Roy J. Ruffin

*I have no other encouragement to pursue the study of
Political Economy than the pleasure which the study itself
affords me, for never shall I be so fortunate however correct
my opinions may become as to produce a work which shall
procure me fame and distinction (Ricardo, Vol. 6, p. 315).*
David Ricardo to Hutches Trower, October 1815

*My object was to elucidate principles, and to do this I
imagined strong cases that I might shew the operation of
those principles (Ricardo, Vol. 8, p. 184).*
Ricardo to Malthus, May 1820

Abstract Britain suspended the gold standard in its war with France in 1797. This led to an inflation controversy that created Ricardo the economist. He entered the discussion in 1809 arguing that the inflation was caused by too much paper money. His impressive argument attracted the attention of James Mill and Thomas Malthus who both became life-long friends and correspondents. In its early days economics was unsettled with vague terms and loose reasoning. James Mill, impressed with Ricardo's logical mind and brilliance, convinced him to write a book to settle the issues. It was during the writing of this book in 1816 that Ricardo discovered comparative advantage. I tell the story.

David Ricardo (1772–1823) discovered the law of comparative advantage in 1816 and published it in his *Principles of Political Economy and Taxation* in 1817. At this time the understanding of trade was based on Adam Smith's correct exposition of the gains from trade. The incorrect absolute advantage explanation of international trade was still vigorously pushed by Torrens in 1815. This paper will try to

R.J. Ruffin (✉)
Department of Economics, University of Houston, Houston, TX, USA
e mail: roy.j.ruffin@gmail.com

© Springer International Publishing AG 2017
R.W. Jones, R. Weder (eds.), *200 Years of Ricardian Trade Theory*,
https://doi.org/10.1007/978-3-319-60606-4_9

explain how it happened to be Ricardo who discovered comparative advantage and why did it happen in 1817.

Examining an episode in the history of economic thought is very similar to developing an economic theory paper. An economic theory paper is usually fairly self-contained, with definitions, assumptions, and conclusions. The subject matter of the history of thought is on the contributions of some economist and, if available, how the economist discovered his ideas. A fairly self-contained paper in doing history means that one should use primary sources and use extensive quotation to support one's argument. Secondary sources in the history of economic thought are in my experience unreliable, and I will give examples. Thus, I will assume the reader of this essay may not be so familiar with my earlier work (Ruffin, 2002, 2005) that I will present my answers as if they did not exist, but will simply indicate if I am replicating earlier work. Thus, I will rely almost exclusively on the 11 volume *Works and Correspondence of David Ricardo*, which contains his major works together with his letters to and from contemporaries. Fortunately, this is available free of charge on the internet.

9.1   The Setting

Ricardo ended his formal education at age 14 when he entered his father's business. But he married in 1793 at age 21 and due to his father's disapproval of the marriage set out on his own in business. His ability in finance was so acute that by 1795 his family was living in an expensive style. In 1798 letter, at age 26, Ricardo refers to how "bountiful" Fortune has been to him. In letters of 1802 he refers to his wealth and again "one of Fortune's chief favorites" (Ricardo, Vol. 10, p. 47). In 1814, Ricardo and his family moved their principal residence to Gatcomb Park, a palatial estate currently occupied by British royalty.

Ricardo showed early interests in chemistry and geology, but settled on political economy when he chanced upon Adam Smith's *Wealth of Nations* in 1797 and that became his favorite subject. By the time he took up economics, mercantilism, the doctrine that there should be an export surplus, was long dead after David Hume (1711–1776) and Adam Smith (1723–1790) had shown there a tendency towards equilibrium. Smith had also argued that it is imports that are vital. Indeed, the very first line of Smith's Wealth of Nations indicated that it is imports that are important:

> The annual labour of every nation is the fund which originally supplies it with all the necessaries and conveniences of life which it annually consumes, and which consist always either in the immediate produce of that labour, or in what is purchased with that produce from other nations (Smith, 2003, Ch. I).

What is interesting is that Smith did not engage in polemics against the mercantilists, as he does later in the book, but considers it obvious that the "conveniences of life consist always" of their domestic production or "what is purchased with that produce." Presumably, Smith would have been surprised by conventional national income accounts adding exports and subtracting imports.

Smith was so persuasive that an influential economist, the Earl of Lauderdale, pointed out in 1804 that were we to measure the profit from foreign trade in the same way that businesses do we would examine "how much the returns imported are worth more than the commodities exported (Lauderdale, 1804, p. 4)." With the emphasis on imports, it is a short step for Smith to understand the gains from trade consisted of devoting fewer home resources exporting other goods to pay for imports. This is clear from one of his most memorable quotes:

> By means of glasses, hotbeds, and hot walls, very good grapes can be raised in Scotland, and very good wine too can be made of them at about thirty times the expense for which at least equally good can be brought from foreign countries. .... But if there would be a manifest absurdity in turning towards any employment thirty times more of the capital and industry of the country than would be necessary to purchase from foreign countries an equal quantity of the commodities wanted, there must be an absurdity, though not altogether so glaring, yet exactly of the same kind, in turning towards any such employment a thirtieth, or even a three-hundredth part more of either. (Smith, 2003, Book IV).

Notice he said in the very first sentence it takes more resources to produce wine in Scotland than to *buy* it from foreign countries. Smith did not say it takes more resources to produce wine in Scotland than to *produce* wine in foreign countries, although undoubtedly true, which is absolute advantage, but to *buy* wine. Jacob Viner (1937, p. 440) called the idea that fewer resources are used to pay for imports with exports the "eighteenth century rule." This rule was also restated in 1808 by James Mill (1773–1836) and Colonel Robert Torrens (1780–1864).[1] It is a twisted story to get into the various claims that Mill gave comparative advantage to Ricardo (Theawatt, 1976), that Torrens discovered comparative advantage in 1815 (Chipman, 1965), or that Ricardo's account is illogical (Chipman, 1965). I discussed these in a pair of papers that simply looked at Ricardo's letters and book (Ruffin, 2002) and the repeated support of absolute advantage in Torrens' book (Ruffin, 2005). Ironically, evidently the first completely clear statement of the principle of absolute advantage was made by Colonel Robert Torrens, writing in 1815:

> When any given portion of capital can, in England, fabricate a greater quantity of cloth, than in Poland; and can, in Poland, produce a greater supply of corn, than in England; then the absence of regulation is all that is necessary to establishing between the two countries in active and mutually beneficial commerce (Torrens, 1815, p. 297).

Those who argue Torrens anticipated Ricardo simply quoted Torrens out of context (Ruffin, 2005). The above statement of absolute advantage appeared *after* Torrens allegedly discovered comparative advantage when he briefly eluded to the possibility of importing corn "even though they [British corn land] should be superior to the lands of Poland" (Torrens, 1815, p. 264–265). Not even 10 pages later Torrens discussed corn imports again driving land out of production "which require, in order to raise a given produce, a greater quantity of labour and capital than the lands under tillage in other countries (Torrens, 1815, p. 272–73)." Torrens

---

[1]Mill (1808) and Torrens (1808). Thweatt (1976, p. 212) conveniently contains their statements.

was a strong advocate of free trade, but he was a polemist not a disinterested scientist. When confronted with the negative effects of free trade, he simply made things up: He argued several times in his book that corn imports would at first reduce agricultural rents, but later raise them (Torrens, 1815, pp. 252–53, 270–71, 303–304)!

Smith has been accused of advancing absolute advantage by nearly every textbook in trade theory.[2] I do not know the source of this, but it may just be a misreading of his famous quote above about "glasses, hot beds, and hot walls."[3] As George Stigler famously said, "It's all in Adam Smith." Indeed, in the first chapter of Smith's *Wealth of Nations* we find an early intuitive understanding of the possibility of comparative advantage:

> The most opulent nations, indeed, generally excel all their neighbours in agriculture as well as in manufactures; but they are commonly more distinguished by their superiority in the latter than in the former. . . . .But though the poor country, notwithstanding the inferiority of its cultivation, can, in some measure, rival the rich in the cheapness and goodness of its corn, it can pretend to no such competition in its manufactures; at least if those manufactures suit the soil, climate, and situation of the rich country. (Smith, Ch. I, Book I).

Smith's intuition was so acute that he never seemed to fall into the absolute advantage trap. It is one thing to have an intuition about comparative advantage, it is quite another to actually prove it!

9.2   Why Ricardo

When Ricardo made his fortune as a stock broker he devoted time to political economy. It was not unusual in the eighteenth and nineteenth centuries for rich business men to retire young and devote themselves to other activities. Economics was enriched by this practice. The first book on economics was written in the early 1700s by Richard Cantillon, an extremely rich banker. Ricardo was no exception in this regard. But why did he discover comparative advantage?

It is safe to say that Britain's war with France led to David Ricardo. The war forced Britain to go off the gold standard and subsequently the inflation from the issue of paper currency caused what is called the Bullion controversy. Already a well-known business man, on August 29, 1809 Ricardo published a long letter to the *Morning Chronicle*. He opened with these words:

> The present high market price above the mint price of gold, appears to have engrossed a great portion of the attention of the public; but they do not seem to be sufficiently impressed with the importance of the subject, nor of the disastrous consequences which may attend the

---

[2]At least since the classic text book by Ellsworth (1938).

[3]In an early debate between Edwin Seligman and Jacob Hollander (1911, p. 457), Hollander misinterprets "thirty times the expense for which at least equally good can be *brought* from foreign countries" as 30 times the *cost* in Portugal.

further depreciation of paper. I am anxious, whilst there is yet time, that we should retrace our steps and restore the currency to that healthful state which so long existed in this country, and the departure from which is pregnant with present evil and future (Ricardo, Vol. 3, p. 15).

He then went on to explain how the gold standard worked and displayed a complete mastery of the practical details of international finance. Two other letters followed and in 1810 he published a pamphlet on "The High Price of Bullion," which showed a mastery of the writings of not only Adam Smith, but also Henry Thornton (1760–1815), a banker and highly regarded monetary economist. That pamphlet shows Ricardo thought a great deal about monetary matters and could see through the veil of money.

It was his obvious understanding of international finance and money that brought him to the attention of James Mill and Thomas Malthus, thus beginning in 1811 a famous series of letters. It is in these letters that we know a lot about how Ricardo the economist came to be and how he discovered comparative advantage.

We learn from Ricardo's pamphlets that he understood that all trade boiled down to trading exports for imports once monetary adjustments take their full effects. In a letter to Malthus 22 October 1811 he also indicated the role of relative commodity prices:

> . . .it is the relative prices of commodities which regulates their exportation. Is it not certain that money will go to that country where the major part of goods are cheap, as goods will go to any other country where the major part of goods are dear. I say the major part because if the cheapness of one half the exportable commodities be balanced by the dearness of the other half, in both countries, it is obvious that the commerce of such countries will be confined to the exchange of goods only (Ricardo, Vol. 6, p. 64).

Clearly, Ricardo was a prime candidate for discovering comparative advantage, though he may not have been there in 1811.

Mill was Ricardo's taskmaster. His letters often deal with personal matters rather than economics. Mill and Ricardo were very close. In a letter to Malthus 25 May 1818, he wrote: "My walks with Mill continue almost daily (Ricardo, Vol. 7, p. 263)." Their friendship was cemented much earlier than 1818. On August 13, 1815 Mill wrote to Ricardo and took the liberty to *say "as you have now made quite as much money for all your family . . . , you will now have the leisure for other pursuits* (Ricardo, Vol. 6, p. 251)." In particular,

> . . . you can improve so important a science far more than any other man who is devoting his attention to it, or likely to do so, for Lord knows how many years—my friendship for you, for mankind, and for science, all prompt me to give you no rest, till you are plunged over a head and ears in political economy. (Ricardo, Vol. 6, p. 252)

Thus begins Mill's urging of Ricardo to write a book on political economy. It is evident that Ricardo's personal brilliance made an enormous impression on Mill. He kept after Ricardo. On November 9, 1815 Mill instructed him as follows:

> You want some practice in the art of laying down your thoughts, in the way most easy of apprehension to those who have little knowledge, and little attention; and this is to be got infallibly by a little practice. As I am accustomed to wield the authority of a schoolmaster, I therefore, in the genuine exercise of this honourable capacity, lay upon you my commands, to begin to the first of the three heads of your proposed work, rent, profit, wages—viz. *rent,*

without an hours delay. If you entrust the inspection of it to me, depend upon it I shall compel you to make it all right, before you have done with it (Ricardo, Vol. 6, p. 321).

The first sentence of the above quote is interesting because Ricardo is regarded as the first economist to lay out economics in a way that can be completely understood. Knut Wicksell, the great Swedish economist, said Ricardo "appeals to the understanding of his readers instead of their emotions (Wicksell, 1893, p. 17)."

It was not only the great Wicksell who pointed this out. One of the greatest theorists of the twentieth century John R. Hicks said Ricardo "had given a shape to economic theory, so that it had become something teachable, a possible academic discipline (Hicks, 1953, p. 117)."

Ricardo wanted to be completely logical. Mill repeated his injunction on December 22, 1815 when commenting on an argument of Ricardo said: "*But you have no where stated the proof* (Ricardo, Vol. 6, p. 339)." The same letter contained more encouragement: "*... you are already the best thinker on political economy. I am resolved that you shall also be the best writer* (Ricardo, Vol. 6, p. 340)." Thus James Mill's high regard for Ricardo and advice on explaining theories helped set the stage for what was to come.

Finally, on 14 August 1816 after Ricardo indicated some trepidation about finishing his book, Mill wrote a long letter encouraging him to continue with this remarkable prediction:

... your talents are admirable; your capacity is immense—only do write and astonish the world! (Ricardo, Vol. 7, p. 59)

This letter was written a few months before Ricardo's most creative work.

9.3   Ricardo's Discovery of Comparative Advantage

We know about when Ricardo's discovered comparative advantage by his letters to Malthus and Mill. Malthus introduced himself to Ricardo in a letter on June 16, 1811, and thus begun an important series of letters between these two giants of economics.

Every academic economist presumably knows that the Ricardian model of trade is based on a single input, labor. Thus it was very convenient for Ricardo to have a labor theory of value. But he did not adopt this labor theory until March 1816, as we know from letters to and from Malthus (Ruffin, 2002). In a letter to Malthus, 7 February 1816 he said:

"*If I could overcome the obstacles in the way of giving a clear insight into the origin and law of relative or exchangeable value I should have gained half the battle* (Ricardo, Vol. 6, p. 20)." Therefore, it is highly unlikely that Ricardo developed comparative advantage before that time. Shortly after a March 1816 visit to Ricardo, Malthus wrote on 28 April 1816: "*On the subject of determining all values by labour...I think you must have swerved a little from the right course*

(Ricardo, Vol. 6, p. 30)." Thus we know almost for certain that he discovered comparative advantage between March 1816 and October 1816 when he sent his foreign trade chapter to Mill, who commented on comparative advantage. Ruffin (2002) argues that this most likely occurred in October, 1816.

Remarkably, it was Ricardo himself who introduced the phrase, comparative advantage in his book: *"A new tax too may destroy the comparative advantage which a country before possessed in the manufacture of a particular commodity* (Ricardo, Vol. 1, p. 263)."

We know why Ricardo wrote his 1817 book, but why did Ricardo discover comparative advantage and not someone else? A possible answer lies in Ricardo's training in business and his need to be logical. In business one faces complicated situations with lots of contradictory cross-currents. It is necessary for one to concentrate on the most important fact or facts or the dominating principle. Ricardo was quite aware that factors other than labor determined the price of a good, but clearly labor is the most important cost of production. Once he adopted the labor theory of value, he was on his way to comparative advantage.

Some light is thrown on this by a letter he wrote to Malthus in May 1820 in which he stated his methodological orientation in his book: "My object was to elucidate principles, and to do this I imagined strong cases that I might shew the operation of those principles (Ricardo, Vol. 8, p. 184)." Thus, Ricardo was there with this orientation long before Paul Samuelson, Abba Lerner, and Ronald Jones utilized this approach in trade theory.

The letters to Malthus and Mill tell a remarkable story. In brief, what happened is he started writing his book in 1816, presumably in sequence, and when he got to the chapter on foreign trade he ran into a problem. On 5 October 1816 he wrote to Malthus: "I have been very much impeded by the question of price and value, my former ideas on these points not being correct. My present view may be equally faulty, for it leads to conclusions at variance to all my preconceived opinions (Ricardo, Vol. 7, pp. 71–72)." Two weeks later he wrote a letter to Mill and enclosed the first seven chapters of his book, the seventh being on foreign trade. On 14 October 1816 he said to Mill:

> I have been beyond measure puzzled to find out the law of price. I found on a reference to figures that my former opinion could not be correct and I was full a fortnight pondering on my difficulty before I knew how to solve it. . . . I shall now consider the subject of taxation (Ricardo, Vol. 7, p. 84).

The chapter on taxation follows the chapter on foreign trade.

I conjecture that he had to be talking about the law of comparative advantage because he begins his discussion of comparative advantage in his book with the statement: "The same rule which regulates the relative value of commodities in one country, does not regulate the relative value of commodities exchange between two or more countries (Ricardo, Vol. 1, p. 133)." Why? His answer is that factors of production do not move as easily between "England to Holland, or Spain, or Russia" as between "London to Yorkshire" (Ricardo, Vol. 1, p. 134).

What seems to have happened is when Ricardo turned to foreign trade he realized that the labor content of exports did not match the labor contact of imports. It took him "a fortnight" to conclude that "the same rule" does not apply to foreign trade due to factor immobility. Reconciling his labor theory of value with the facts forced him to introduce a new assumption. Thus he is explicit:

> The labour of 100 Englishmen cannot be given for that of 80 Englishmen, but the produce of the labour of 100 Englishmen may be given for the produce of the labour of 80 Portuguese, 60 Russians, or 120 East Indians (Ricardo, Vol. 1, p. 135).

9.4 Ricardo's Proof

Ricardo proved the law of comparative advantage by *starting* with the terms of trade and the implicit labor contained in the trading bundle. This was a key simplification because he did not have to build the model up from resources and preferences, as did John Stuart Mill (1852) in his rational reconstruction of the Ricardian model. Here is his proof:

> The quantity of wine which she [Portugal] will give in exchange for the cloth of England, is not determined by the respective quantities of labour devoted to the production of each, as it would be if both were manufactured in England, or both in Portugal. England to produce *the cloth* may require the labour of 100 men for one year; and if she attempted to make *the wine*, it might require the labour of 120 men for the same time. England would therefore find it in her interest to import wine, and to purchase it by the export of cloth. To produce *the wine* in Portugal, might require only the labour of 80 men for one year, and to produce *the cloth* might require the labour of 90 men for the same time. It would therefore be advantageous for her to export wine in exchange for cloth. (Ricardo, Vol. 1, pp. 134–135, italics added)

Ricardo did not consider, as John Stuart Mill and modern textbooks, the amount of labor contained in a unit of production but the amount of labor contained in exports versus the labor that would be used if the imports were produced domestically. The next paragraph then contained the line about England being able to trade 100 Englishmen for smaller or larger amounts of labor in other countries. What is interesting about his proof is that it applies to any number of goods or countries.

Ricardo grasped comparative advantage so solidly that much later in the book he stated: "Foreign trade will always continue, whatever may be the comparative difficulty of production in different countries (Ricardo, I, p. 343)." Also in the book he was able to correctly criticize what has been called Adam Smith's "vent for surplus" approach:

> Adam Smith concluded we were under some necessity of producing a surplus of corn, woollen goods, and hardware, and that the capital which produced them could not be otherwise employed. It is, however, always a matter of choice in what way a capital shall be employed, and therefore there can never, for any length of time, be a surplus of any commodity; for if there were, it would fall below its natural price, and capital would be removed to some more profitable employment. (Ricardo, Vol. 1, p. 291n)

Thus, Ricardo did not even allow his enormous respect for Adam Smith from spotting errors in reasoning in the master.

9.5   Post-Ricardo

Three years after Ricardo published his book in 1817, Malthus' *Principle of Political Economy* (1820) still embraced absolute advantage in which he asserted that America's export growth in raw produce was explained by lower labor costs than Europe. To this Ricardo replied in his "Notes on Malthus":

> It can be of no consequence to America, whether the commodities she obtains in return for her own, cost Europeans much, or little labour, all she is interested in, is that they shall cost her less labour by purchasing than by manufacturing them herself. (Ricardo, Vol. 2, p. 383)

It is always surprising to me that after teaching students comparative advantage they still have a hard time remembering it on exams, but Ricardo himself never had any problem keeping it firmly in mind despite the intervening years of working on politics (a member of Parliament) and writing extensively on monetary issues.

It is my conjecture that Malthus and Ricardo did not really learn a lot of each other as both were highly independent minds. This at least partially explains why Malthus did not embrace comparative advantage. The writers who picked up the ball after Ricardo were Nassau Senior (1790–1864) and Mountifort Longfield (1802–1884). Senior's "Cost of Obtaining Money" (1830) is probably the best introduction to the practical aspects of comparative advantage, relating money wages to productivity, and Longfield (1835) extended the Ricardian model to many goods and two countries in a fashion that is familiar to all trade theorists. Longfield is also well-known for anticipating the Heckscher-Ohlin model of trade (Ohlin, 1933, Ch. 1).

9.6   Conclusion

The Ricardian trade model is still popular after 200 years. A fitting tribute after two centuries. Ruffin (1988) applied the model to the factor endowment theory of trade, Costinot and Vogel (2015) and Eaton and Kortum (2012) to the world of many goods and countries. Ruffin (2014) applied the model to purchasing power parity with non-traded goods, a subject to which even Ricardo had surprising insight given his brief involvement with trade theory. Samuelson (1994, p. 206) has said that it was "of course" Ricardo who made the first contribution to comparing international prices.

Ricardo was a member of Parliament from 1819 to his death 11 September 1823. He represented a county in Ireland that he probably never visited (Cannan, 1894). During this period he strongly supported free trade at every opportunity. One of the most interesting occurred on the coronation of the king in which Ricardo suggested that the items of consumption should be imported when cheaper because, as reported, "they must be purchased by the produce of our own industry (Ricardo, Vol. 5, p. 69)." This is an allusion to the Adam Smith version of the gains from trade.

Also interestingly to trade theorists, on 7 March 1821 an issue arose which stimulated Ricardo's interest in factor specificity. Since he seemed indifferent to the effect of imported corn prices on agricultural capital, a colleague remarked, "Where has the honorable member (Mr. Ricardo) been? Has a just descended from another planet? Does he know that a great deal of capital is engaged in agriculture, which would then be thrown out of employment? " (Ricardo, Vol. 5, pp. 85–86). Ricardo responded in Parliament but saw fit to add a note to the third edition of his Principles dealing with factor specificity.

Ricardo contributed many fundamental ideas in economics. He anticipated the concern of trade theorists for the distribution of income, he formulated the laws governing the distribution of monetary assets, how a central bank should operate, the symmetry between uniform export duties and import duties, and the issues involved in taxation or deficit financing (Ruffin, 2002). How is was capable of focusing his attention on fundamental issues is remarkable given the demands on his time. We see only his writings, but in his letters we get a glimpse into what must have remarkable powers of concentration. In a letter he wrote to Mill on 24 October 1815 he confessed:

> Here at Gatcomb we go on much as usual,—we are always full of visitors, some of which make great demands on my time. I often say that I must go to London for retirement, for here not only have I to entertain the visitors who are staying with us, but all our Glouces-tershire neighbours, living within 10 miles, in all directions, are very much inclined to be sociable, so that with them we have to find time, not only for the visit, but for the journey also. At the present moment we are full to overflowing. Last night we had a dance and sat down to supper a party of no less than 49 which did not disperse before 4 o'clock this morning (Ricardo, Vol. 6, p. 312).

Perhaps in the simpler world without the modern conveniences of radio, television, cell phones, the internet, cars and planes, people had more time to think. But it makes one wonder if we will ever see his kind again.

References

Cannan, E. (1894). Ricardo in parliament. *Economic Journal, 4*(14), 249–261.

Chipman, J. S. (1965). A survey of the theory of international trade: Part 1, The classical theory. *Econometrica, 33*(3), 477–519.

Costinot, A., & Vogel, J. (2015). Beyond ricardo: Assignment models in international trade. *Economics, 7*(1), 31–62.

Eaton, J., & Kortum, S. (2012). Putting Ricardo to work. *The Journal of Economic Perspectives, 26*(2), 65–89.

Ellsworth, P. T. (1938). *International economics*. New York: Macmillan.

Hicks, J. R. (1953). An inaugural lecture. *Oxford Economic Papers, 5*(2), 117–135.

Lauderdale, J. M. (1804). *An inquiry into the nature and origin of public wealth* (2nd ed.). Edinburgh: Archibald Constable and Co..

Longfield, M. (1835). *Three lectures on commerce and one on absenteeism.* Dublin: Richard Milliken & Son.

Mill, J. S. (1852). *Principles of political economy* (3rd ed.). London: Longman and Green.

Ohlin, B. (1933). *Interregional and international trade.* Cambridge: Harvard University Press.

Ricardo, D. (1951). *The works and correspondence of David Ricardo.* Cambridge: Cambridge University Press.

Ruffin, R. J. (1988). The missing link: The Ricardian approach to the factor endowments theory of trade. *The American Economic Review, 78*(4), 759–772.

Ruffin, R. (2002). David Ricardo's discovery of comparative advantage. *History of Political Economy, 34*(4), 727–748.

Ruffin, R. J. (2005). Debunking a myth: Torrens on comparative advantage. *History of Political Economy, 37*(4), 711–722.

Ruffin, R. J. (2014). Nontraded goods and real exchange rates in a multi-good Ricardian model. *Review of International Economics, 22*(1), 105–115.

Samuelson, P. A. (1994). Facets of Balassa-Samuelson thirty years later. *Review of International Economics, 2*(3), 201–226.

Seligman, E., & Hollander, J. (1911). Ricardo and Torrens. *Economic Journal, 21,* 448–455.

Senior, N. W. (1830). *Three lectures on the cost of obtaining money.* London: William Clowes.

Smith, A. (2003). *The wealth of nations.* New York: Bantam Classics.

Thweatt, W. O. (1976). James Mill and the early development of comparative advantage. *History of Political Economy, 8*(2), 207–234.

Torrens, R. (1815). *An essay on the external corn trade.* London: J. Hatchard.

Viner, J. (1937). *Studies in the theory of international trade.* New York: Harper and Brothers.

Wicksell, K. (1893). *UBER WERT, KAPITAL UND RENTE.* Jena: J. Fischer.

Chapter 10
Comments on "Mill and Ricardo: The Genesis of Comparative Advantage" by Roy J. Ruffin

Antonio Loprieno

Abstract While economists tend to interpret the appearance of a new theoretical frame as "discovery" or as "invention," historians prefer to consider them as the result of pressures from within their cultural context in which they originate. In this sense, there are very specific reasons why Ricardo's Comparative Advantage emerged around 1816–1817. These reasons have a biographical (why Ricardo and not someone else), a historical (why in 1816–1817, and not before), or a philosophical background (why a Comparative, and not the already pre-existing Absolute Advantage). These reasons are shortly presented in this response to Roy J. Ruffin's paper, printed as Chap. 9 of this book.

Dear colleagues, ladies and gentlemen, thank you for inviting me. As you see, I have given to my response the title 'A Learner's Response' and I want to explain to you why. Actually, the reason was contained in the presentation by the Chair (Prof. Hefeker) of this session; and that is that I am by no means a specialist on Ricardo. In fact, I am probably the least competent to make a response to Roy [Ruffin] in this room today. I am afraid that I owe my presence to Rolf's [Rolf Weder] evilness or evil spirit, because I think that he, as the host, said—well, you know he didn't really say it this way—but that's what he implied: 'I really want to test you, I would like to see whether you are worthy of sitting with us. Well, I gave you a small job to perform.' And now, without jokes: What can I do? The chair said it: I am a historian of culture by formation, so what I can perhaps contribute is to provide a reading of Roy's paper with the biases that I carry with me because of my own intellectual background.

And to put it in a nutshell, I think the basic difference is that in the type of scholar socialization I have, we tend to look at intellectual developments as processes, in which usually many scholars or people are implied, and not as punctual discoveries as it is presented in this case, for certainly very good reasons. So, I will start by

Note: This chapter is based on a transcription of the presentation given at the Conference "Celebrating 200 Years of Ricardian Trade Theory" on May 12, 2017, at the University of Basel, Switzerland. It is a comment to the paper by Roy J. Ruffin, i.e., to Chap. 9 of this book.

A. Loprieno (✉)
Faculty of Business and Economics, University of Basel, Basel, Switzerland
e-mail: a.loprieno@unibas.ch

© Springer International Publishing AG 2017   145
R.W. Jones, R. Weder (eds.), *200 Years of Ricardian Trade Theory*,
https://doi.org/10.1007/978-3-319-60606-4_10

presenting it as a result of my own biases, one of these being that I am somewhat skeptical when complex phenomena are dated to a very late date, because that tends to be true in terms of immediate cause, but not necessarily in terms of ultimate cause. So, for example, the absolute advantage, if interpreted in a more general way, was actually a form of knowledge already known in the ancient world—not the relative, but the absolute advantage. Xenophon, who was the person who actually gave us the word "economics" in terms of administration of a household, in his fictional biography of the Persian Emperor Cyrus, has this very interesting statement that I would like to read. It discusses the differences in production and in economics in this micro-economic sense between large cities and small villages, and it says:

> And it is, of course impossible, for a man of many trades to be proficient in all of them. In large cities, on the other hand, in as much as many people have demand to make upon each branch of industry, one trade alone, and very often even less than a whole trade is enough to support one man. For instance, one man makes shoes for men, and another for women; and there are places even where one man earns a living by only stitching shoes, another by cutting them out, another by sewing the uppers together, while there is another who performs none of these operations but only assembles the parts. It follows, therefore, as a matter of course, that he who devotes himself to a very highly specialized line of work is bound to do it in the best possible manner.[1]

It is, of course, at the micro-level, but it contains, if you want, the seed of what would become the theory or the model of comparative advantage. Now, we come to Roy's paper. I admire, of course, the very precise formulation of his goal, which I restate here,[2] and I would like to look at it and ask three questions that are implied within his statement and that are very well developed in his argumentation. Here are the three questions—and I'll give you in a nutshell my answers which I shall presently dwell on:

(1) **"Was the law of comparative advantage discovered in 1816?"** I emphasize here the terms 'law' and 'discover' for the reasons that I provided in my short introduction, i.e. because I'm not so sure, even following the discussions in this room, that we can describe this intuition or this model as a *law*, nor am I sure that we can really speak of a *discovery* in the strict sense. So, my point is that perhaps in a sense 'yes', and in a sense 'no'. Many factors contributed to this scientific development rather than discovery. The second question that is entailed in Roy's presentation is:

(2) **"How did Ricardo happen to be the one who discovered this law?"** My answer in this case is because he was also the one—this is included in Roy's

---

[1] Xenophon, *Cyropaedia* VIII, 2.5.

[2] "David Ricardo (1772–1823) discovered the law of comparative advantage in 1816 and published it in his Principles of Political Economy and Taxation in 1817. At the time the understanding of trade was based on Adam Smith's correct exposition of the gains from trade. The incorrect absolute advantage explanation of international trade was still vigorously pushed by Torrens in 1815. This paper will try to explain how it happened to be Ricardo who discovered comparative advantage and why it happened in 1817."

presentation—who changed economics from a background of philosophy in the general sense, from a more descriptive mode, to a scientific perspective in a more prescriptive, explanatory mode. Now, the third question is:

(3) **"Why did it happen in 1816?"** There is an interesting assumption in what Roy writes, that it may have had something to do with the war between France and England. And I would like to claim at the end that it had very much to do with the Congress of Vienna, which is the reason why it happened precisely in that year.

So, let's look at the three topics.

10.1   Was the Law of Comparative Advantage Discovered in 1816?

In his statement, Roy emphasizes the fact that, basically, you have to write a paper in economic history according to the same criteria with which you write a paper in economics, starting with a model that is closed in itself. Well, here I have to defend a little bit my profession: I'm not so sure the history of economic thought is similar to economic history, because there isn't really the same distribution of predicate and complement at stake: the history of economic thought is basically primarily a history and then of economic thought. So, I think that we need to put the emphasis here in the right way.

The reason is that the history of economic thought is about contributions and their discovery by economists. Here, I would like to specify something of a historical development that is frequently disregarded, but which is very important, because what we understand as discovery is not the same depending on the cultural context. It depends on the 'warmth' or the 'coldness' of a society. 'Hot' and 'cold' are terms introduced by the French anthropologist Lévi-Strauss. A hot society is a society that cherishes innovation very much, where innovation is written on top, and cold societies are societies that cherish tradition, and then you can organize them on a model. Now, the point is that our western society moves from coldness to hotness, so at the beginning of the nineteenth century we can consider that our society was less hot than it is now; that is, cherished, or privileged, or emphasized individual innovation less than we do today.

So, Roy's very interesting joke on never having seen an academician giving away ideas so freely is completely correct in the hottest of our possible societies that have ever existed in the world, and that's ours, but was certainly less true 200 years ago, and to go even further, was not at all true 2000 years ago, where quite the contrary happened: It would have been pretty stupid for you to say that you are the author of a book, because the author of a book was always a person of the past who could guarantee the quality of the book. The psalms by David were certainly not written by king David or the Wisdom of Solomon, certainly not by Solomon himself. But the author of these books thought that it was in his best interest, comparative advantage, to say that not he, unknown, was the author, but rather a known person of the past was the author. And you can see a development whereby this emphasis tends to play a greater role right now.

Another—for a historian—very difficult separation to accept, prima facie, is the opposition between primary and secondary sources. Roy said something that is frequently claimed, and that is that primary sources are, to a certain extent, more reliable to sustain a theory than secondary sources. Well, I'm afraid that's not so, because, in fact, the real opposition of historical sources is not between primary and secondary sources, but is between what I would call *traces* and *messages*. Traces are remnants of history that are conveyed without willfully or ideologically wanting to refer to them. So, information on the side, that we derive. And messages are things that I want an addressee to know. So, a letter, for example, regardless who writes it, a letter is a pure message, because a letter is written in order to persuade someone, regardless of who the author is.

So, the origin of a source is one factor, but very important in order to study the reliability of a historical source is whether it was meant to say something that it says, or whether it was meant to say something else, in which case, it is actually *more* interesting for us historically, and not *less* interesting, because it is less tainted by ideology in the general sense. Understand me correctly, what I want to say is that both need to be figured into the analysis, but without an automatic privilege or advantage for primary sources or secondary sources; rather, what counts is the willfulness, the ideological background that these sources provide.

10.2 How Did Ricardo Happen to Be the One Who Discovered It?

This is the second question. It is actually a question where Roy brilliantly argues and shows us the paths that led him. I would like to add three points here: (1) Ricardo acted in an intellectual climate in which professional competence was not any longer embedded in a philosophical position, but rather was developed dialectically or collegially. That is, we are in a period of transition between a way of doing economics à la Adam Smith, which was a way of basically embedding economics into an overall view of the world, and creating economics as a self-contained discipline: an economic discourse in itself. (2) The second reason is because Ricardo was the first professional economist interested in predictable— Roy says that very clearly—formal principles or laws which makes it easier to attribute to him a well-defined theoretical framework: He refers to his work as "my doctrine", as having wanted to present a self-contained model. So, we could say that Ricardo was the first one to adopt a prescriptive, or you could say normative—we would also say "scientific"—and not just scholarly style in his writing.

By the way, I am surprised how rarely, and how little attention is paid to one feature that, in my opinion, plays a major role in this development, and that is

Ricardo's own background. The reason why Ricardo was disinherited by his father is because he was a Jew who married a Christian. Now, as we see it, he had married a Christian—who knows—probably for love or probably also because she was certainly not poor, but at any rate, Ricardo had been socialized in a tradition of analysis, of analyzing texts and organizing them even if they have an ideological feature into a very well-structured form of discussion, which certainly favored his own professional approach. So, to a certain extent, he had a predestination, as it were, an intellectual, cultural and formative predestination to be the first scientist in the history of economic thought.

(3) As we are all professors, we should also speak of our own profession in a positive way: Ricardo had an academic supervisor, and that was James Mill. And, to have an academic supervisor—to speak in modern terms—certainly favored the dialectic, and Roy presented very clearly how much he owed to James Mill. But I would also say that he owed this dialectical position, having to answer questions, to have a coach, which is so important in the formation of a mind. Let us come to the third question.

10.3   Why Did It Happen in 1816?

Roy points to a very important line of argument, which is the war between France and Britain. I would add, to this point, a more contextual reason, and that is the Congress of Vienna that had just been concluded. The Congress of Vienna is, to a certain extent, the event that created Europe in terms of the division of national states the way we know it now in a series of sequences. Why? Because, at the Congress of Vienna a certain number of political principles were debated and agreed upon that indirectly had an impact also on the development of economic laws. For example, there is one, a strategy of continental solidarity to avoid revolutions, so there was inherent in the Congress of Vienna the invitation to states to come to some kind of formal agreement which was not part of the traditional Ancien Régime before Napoleon, when these things were not known. The second thing is a restorative approach to national boundaries—these national boundaries that Napoleon and generally the French revolution had questioned. What happens in the Congress of Vienna is that, all of a sudden, the era of nationalism begins; understand me correctly, not because there was no nationalism before, but in the Ancien Régime the tendency was to speak of nations—Adam Smith speaks of nations—or of societies. Of course, there were already national states, but they hadn't been thematized. The Congress of Vienna makes the national states the center of political and economic life. And it's not by chance in my opinion that, precisely, soon thereafter the first economic models in which countries appear as dialectical poles, begin to play a role.

And thirdly, the balance of power to prevent future wars in the Acts of the Congress of Vienna is the idea of the balance that power plays a central role, and the model of comparative advantage is to a certain sense a balancing model. It is an idea of guaranteeing a form of equilibrium. And the third and last point is that the traces and messages mentioned by Roy point to the fact that both candidates for this discovery, let's say the true candidate, Ricardo, and perhaps the false one, Torrens, had a very strong nationalistic involvement, both of them thought intensely about economics also in terms of the advantage for their own country, and thus were certainly prone to this type of formalization.

With this, I thank Rolf very much for having given me the possibility to do my Bachelor's presentation in this area and to Roy for having caused me to understand what I was supposed to talk about. Thank you very much.

Chapter 11
Discussion on "Mill and Ricardo: The Genesis of Comparative Advantage"

Carsten Hefeker

Abstract This chapter includes the discussion of the paper "Mill and Ricardo: The Genesis of Comparative Advantage" by Roy J. Ruffin (Chap. 9 of this book) and of the comments to this paper by Antonio Loprieno (Chap. 10 of this book). It is based on the transcription of the discussion. The session was chaired by Carsten Hefeker, Professor of Economic Policy at the University of Siegen. He has a PhD from the University of Konstanz.

[This chapter starts with an introduction by Professor Hefeker to the second session of the conference "Mill and Ricardo: The Genesis of Comparative Advantage" and then proceeds to the discussion.]

Carsten Hefeker Ladies and Gentlemen, I would like to welcome you to the second session of this conference. It is an honor to be the chair of it. In this session, we want to discuss what environment existed when the idea of *comparative advantage* was discovered and whether David Ricardo was indeed the one who discovered it.

I first introduce the speakers. The paper is given by Roy J. Ruffin, Professor of Economics at the University of Houston with a PhD from Northwestern University. He is a trade theorist but has also written on the history of thoughts in international trade, particularly on David Ricardo. There is his famous paper published in the *History of Political Economy* in 2002 in which he showed when and how Ricardo came up with the idea of comparative advantage. And the second speaker, the comments, will be provided by Antonio Loprieno, who is actually Egyptologist and Linguist. He wrote his PhD at Turin University and then held professorships in Göttingen, and at UCLA, before coming to Basel. And he used to be the president of this University for about 10 years. Now he is a professor of the history of institutions at the Faculty of Business and Economics at the University of Basel.

Note: This chapter is based on a transcription of the discussion held at the Conference "Celebrating 200 Years of Ricardian Trade Theory" on May 12, 2017, at the University of Basel in Switzerland. The discussion in this Chap. 11 refers to the contents in Chaps. 9 and 10 of this book.

C. Hefeker (✉)
Department of Economics, University of Siegen, Siegen, Germany
e-mail: carsten.hefeker@uni-siegen.de

© Springer International Publishing AG 2017
R.W. Jones, R. Weder (eds.), *200 Years of Ricardian Trade Theory*,
https://doi.org/10.1007/978-3-319-60606-4_11

[The following is the discussion on both contributions (see Chaps. 9 and 10 in this book). We start with a reaction by Professor Roy J. Ruffin to Professor Loprieno's comments.]

Roy Ruffin Thank you very much for your comment, Antonio. I would like to just say one thing about secondary sources and primary sources, and this type of thing. I said in my paper that doing an economic theory paper is like doing the history of economic thought, and I'd never done the history of economic thought at all. But the similarity is this—and I think that people who do economic theory would all agree with me: An economist theorist usually doesn't believe anything he reads. I don't believe anything I read; I don't believe anything I read in theory, Okay? I have to prove it myself, before I'm happy. If anybody says "Joe Blow said this", I'm not going to believe it: It doesn't make any difference what that person says. So, I don't care who it is who says it. Now, Paul Samuelson—God I worship at his feet in terms of economic theory—but when he says Torrens discovered the law of comparative advantage, I don't believe it. I don't believe anything anybody says. So, when people start saying these things, I say, "Well that is kind of interesting and so I went back and tried to replicate what they said, just like I try to prove a theorem. I want to prove it myself. I don't care about someone else's proof, I want to know that I can prove it.

So I am doing the same type of thinking process, that's how I would do history of economic thought. So, I would go back and read the letters of Ricardo. That's why I was so thankful for that one paper by William Thweatt,[1] where he said James Mill gave the law of comparative advantage to Ricardo. After Ricardo wrote his Chap. 7, he sent them and bundled them off and sent it to James Mill. And then James Mill wrote him a letter. He said "that you discovered the law of comparative advantage"—he didn't use the phrase "the law of comparative advantage", this was not current then—so he said, paraphrasing him, "It was remarkable that you discovered the law of comparative advantage." And so I mentioned this to a historian of thought, I won't mention his name. I said, you know, James Mill congratulated Ricardo on proving the law of comparative advantage, then how is it that he gave it to him? He said, "Well, James Mill was just a nice guy", that was his answer. We don't know the truth—we'll never know the truth. You, Antonio, were talking about different attitudes about that. I thought it was kind of curious to do history of thought. I just did this soldiering into it. I wish I hadn't sometimes, but it has been at times quite controversial. Anyway, thank you very much for your comments.

Rolf Weder So, Antonio, it was not a test at all, and if it was, you passed it [He refers to Antonio Loprieno's introduction in his comments; see Chap. 10]. But the point why I asked you, is really because I wanted to hear from you–and this is what you did—what kind of methodology would somebody like you, in your discipline, use to get as close as possible to the truth to find out who is responsible for something—for a thought, even for a written document, and this is part of your

---

[1]Thweatt (1976).

research, right? Now, you have said that one should be rather broad in trying to identify, but what is your conclusion? I mean, what would be convincing evidence that one should look for? What is your view on the concrete case?

Antonio Loprieno Right, Rolf. But you see, I guess that what I can say as an answer to your question is that probably, your question, posed in this way, cannot have an answer from people like me. Because to come to a conclusion with a particular name would be, in view of what I said, a little bit problematic, because it would show that all this process of contextualisation is to a certain extent useless—because you could use the simplification approach. I think that you can opt for a simplification approach and that is precisely the more theoretical procedure [points to Roy Ruffin]. Or you can opt for a contextualisation approach which is more the heuristic procedure that a historian of culture adopts. In this case, it's somewhat difficult to answer the question that is posed with the premises of a jubilee of 2017—because, for example, in 1817 no one would have ever had the idea of having a conference for the 200 years of a particular theory. You see the point?

You can also look at the number of celebrations of birthdays that institutions have organized in the last years. The University of Basel celebrated its first birthday 200 years after its foundation. And then the other one, 100 years later, and then the next one, again another 100 years later, and then all of a sudden 50 years later. I promise you, now there will be a celebration every 5 or 10 years because that has to do with this hot element of society, because now we privilege very much the moment of discovery, of foundation. That is something that is now rooted in our understanding. So, we consider, we tend to believe that theories or models have a moment of creation, and we are very legitimate in doing so, and I don't want to question that. And if we consider this question legitimate, then my answer cannot be any different from Roy's answer.

My point is, however, that I'm not so sure that, if we really want to understand the world that we are trying to recreate when this development took place, that that is precisely the right question, because probably at that time, neither was James Mill a particularly generous person, the way we would interpret it right now, nor was Torrens a free-rider, someone who was trying to take advantage of a discovery by someone else, nor probably, I would dare to say, was Ricardo himself particularly convinced that he had performed a discovery that would qualify him for a Nobel Prize, if there had been such a prize at that time, which, not by chance, there wasn't. So, I'm trying to question a little bit the legitimacy—no, the legitimacy is certainly there—no the adequacy, of a particular question projected back to 200 years ago.

Peter Bernholz[2] Let me first ask you a question to you Mr. Ruffin and then say something to Mr. Loprieno. As we know, Ricardo—and you hinted at it—also invented the purchasing power parity for the exchange rate. Did you find anywhere a hint that he brought together his comparative advantage law and the purchasing power parity of the determination of the exchange rate?

---

[2]Professor Emeritus of Economics, University of Basel.

Roy Ruffin I think he had a monetary approach to the balance of payments, that the exchange rate was determined by the relative supplies of money in the two countries. I think that that was basically it. But, I don't think he tied it together the way Samuelson did in his 1964 RESTAT paper[3] talking about wages and prices, and things of this nature. He probably could have done that, but I think he didn't make the distinction between the dollar price of something and the resources that were used to establish something. But as far as laying out the dollars and cents of the Ricardian model, combined with the money supply, and all this stuff and the exchange rate—we did that later. There was another writer after Ricardo—see what popularized Ricardo was another British economist named Nassau Senior and Montfort Longfield. If you've read Ohlin, you'll know that Ohlin said that "Longfield anticipated me on the factor endowment theory of international trade". But in any case, these guys extended Ricardo to exchange rates and many goods, and things of this nature, and talked about wages and prices, and so forth. Nassau Senior had a wonderful exposition on the Ricardian model from your point of view, from the point of view of wages and productivity and those types of things. But that was very shortly after Ricardo. I don't think that Ricardo himself thought too much about that in terms of the dollar prices. I don't think so. He might have...

Peter Bernholz I have a certain support for Mr. Loprieno's idea that historical circumstances may have an important influence on at which time an invention was made—not a necessary role, certainly not a sufficient—, but it happens. For instance, as I mentioned already the purchasing power parity theory for the exchange rate of Ricardo. He did not know that at this time already a theory of overshooting of exchange rates existed, and this was in Russia. Because in Russia the convertibility of the bank notes or paper notes into gold had already been ended because of inflation in the 1790s, and so the Baltic German Freiher von Storch found out—and empirically supported it by looking at the exchange rate in St. Petersburg—the theory of overshooting of the exchange rate, already then. And this was not known in London, of course, probably because of bad communication at that time. But the interesting thing is that it was also forgotten afterwards. It has been forgotten for decades until we, with flexible exchange rates, found out about it.

Roy Ruffin Ricardo knew about overshooting, of course. Throughout the letters there is reference to the price of bonds, how the war was going, and the war was going badly, and British bonds became cheap—or somebody's bonds became cheap—and he bought them very cheap, okay? He figured the price would go up if Britain was more successful on the war front. And he bought some of those I think for James Mill, and he bought some bonds at the cheap price for Malthus, and so the letters often talk about this overshooting phenomenon, not in the Dornbusch sense of that article in the *JPE*,[4] but the price of those bonds. Later on the price of those

---

[3]Samuelson (1964).
[4]Dornbusch (1976).

bonds went up and James Mill and Malthus and Ricardo were thrilled by the price of those bonds going up. So I am sure he was quite aware of that overshooting phenomenon.

Scott Taylor Roy, can you fill in some detail. What was the relationship between John Stuart Mill and Ricardo?

Roy Ruffin John Stuart Mill was a child when Ricardo was growing up. Ricardo knew him as a child. They talked about 'John', 'little John' in the letters, and Ricardo took a special interest in him. He thought he was a very bright young man. And of course, John Stuart Mill had great respect for Ricardo. And when John Stuart Mill wrote his essay on international trade[5]—I don't know what the name of it was—in the 1840s—that's where he constructed what we now call the Ricardian model. In his autobiography, he explains how that came about. They used to have meetings, after Ricardo died, of course. John Stuart Mill and a friend of his by the name of George Graham would meet before classes or before whatever they were doing. They'd meet in the morning for coffee, or whatever—get their espressos, or cappuccinos—and they'd talk for 30–40 minutes about trade or whatever they were talking about And John Stuart Mill in his autobiography said: "My theories of international value were based on discussions with George Graham that we had in the morning, but we disagreed about it". He didn't say what it was, "so I considered what I did my own", without putting George Graham's name on it. And so we don't know what their disagreements were—whether George Graham hit him after the book was published—I have no idea—but he said, "I consider the theory of international value my own." But he did it differently than Ricardo. He developed the paradigm of the general equilibrium. According to McKenzie, it was John Stuart Mill who gave us our general equilibrium paradigm. Maybe George Graham–I have no idea what their argument was.

Scott Taylor But he solved the price determination?

Roy Ruffin Yeah he solved it, he put the laws of supply and demand, he had prices determined by supply and demand. That's all I know about it. That's all I know.

Carsten Hefeker So, are there any more questions? It doesn't seem to be the case. So, thank you again!

References

Dornbusch, R. (1976). Expectations and exchange rate dynamics. *Journal of Political Economy, 84*(6), 1161–1176.
Mill, J. S. (1844). On the laws of interchange between nations. In *Essays on some unsettled questions of political economy*. London: John W. Parker.

---

[5]Mill (1844).

Ruffin, R. (2002). David Ricardo's discovery of comparative advantage. *History of Political Economy, 34*(4), 727–748.

Samuelson, P. A. (1964). Theoretical notes on trade problems. *The Review of Economics and Statistics, 46*, 145–154.

Thweatt, W. O. (1976). James Mill and the early development of comparative advantage. *History of Political Economy, 8*(2), 207–234.

Chapter 12
Putting Ricardian Trade Theory to Work in 2017: Current Empirical Analyses

Jonathan Eaton

Abstract This chapter discusses extensions of the simple 2×2 Ricardo model. In particular, it considers extensions to several goods and countries, the possibility of international technology diffusion, and the possibility of imperfect labor mobility between sectors. The chapter shows how these extensions make the Ricardian framework a useful tool for understanding data, and, thus, help to put Ricardian Trade Theory (back) to work.

I was so delighted when Rolf invited me last fall. I said this sounds like so much fun, and it has been so far for me. I especially enjoyed listening to this morning's discussion. I am very bad at reading old texts: I get impatient; I like equations. It was illuminating to hear the discussion from both Roy and Antonio about Ricardo's representing a transition from economics as philosophy to economics as science. To the extent that I have read the Classics, there is something transitional about Ricardo for me. When I try to read Smith or even Malthus, I find lot of words but when I get to Chap. 7 of Ricardo's book, I see a model.

It's very cryptic: two countries, two goods, one factor, the minimum necessary to make the point. We have the 2×2 labor relative requirements and the relative price, taken as given. But at the end it's just three numbers you need: the relative labor requirements and the price. That's it.

But let's take a minute to consider what Ricardo is implicitly assuming here. There are three very strong assumptions that we are still making: (1) Workers can change activities inside a country. (2) They can't move between countries. (3) Technology is sufficiently immobile between countries to generate differences in relative worker requirements.

Part of my charge from Rolf was to discuss tests of Ricardian theory. I tend to stay away from the wording *testing of theories*. All theories are false. It's easy to find a counterexample to reject them. Any good model is sufficiently parsimonious

Note: This chapter is based on a transcription of the presentation given at the Conference "Celebrating 200 Years of Ricardian Trade Theory" on May 12, 2017, at the University of Basel, Switzerland.

J. Eaton (✉)
Department of Economics, Pennsylvania State University, University Park, PA, USA
e-mail: jxe22@psu.edu

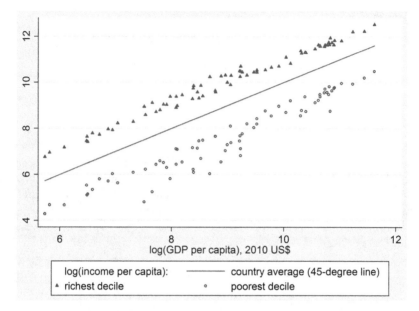

Fig. 12.1 log-GDP per capita in 2010 vs. richest income decile (*red triangles*) and poorest income decile (*blue squares*) in that country. Source: Eaton and Fieler (2017)

that there will be facts that contradict an assumption. With permission, then, I'm reframing the question as, "Is the Ricardian framework a useful tool for understanding data?" and the answer is a resounding yes.

12.1 Confronting Ricardo's Assumption with Data

I first of all want to talk about these obviously false assumptions that are behind the model. How good are they? They are obviously false, and they are also very standard: The lack of factor mobility across countries, factor mobility within-countries, goods being exchangeable across countries, technologies being different are assumptions still at the heart of what we are doing. I've been working with a former student, Cecilia Fieler[1] at Penn. For our project Cecilia has assembled the diagram in Fig. 12.1. It shows log GDP per capita of several countries taken from the World Bank's World Development Indicators (WDI). For each country above and below are the top 90th and the bottom 10th decile of income in that country.

The basic Ricardian model can explain cross-country income differences on the basis of absolute advantage, but would predict no within-country income

---

[1]Cecilia Fieler, Assistant Professor of Economics, University of Pennsylvania, Member of the International Growth Centre (IGC) Trade Program.

differences. Now obviously we have within-country income differences, but they are really swamped by cross-country income differences: The top 90% in a country don't live better than the average person in an only modestly richer country while the poorest 10% don't live worse than the average person in an only modestly poorer country. Internal mobility mitigates internal income inequality, but international immobility maintains inequality across countries. So if we are forced to go to a corner of treating workers as either perfectly mobile or as perfectly immobile between countries and between activities within a country, Ricardo's assumptions, if we had to start somewhere, aren't looking bad, even with 2010 data.

So, what about differences in relative productivities? Figure 12.2 is taken from a paper that I'm going to talk about down the road by Costinot, Donaldson, and Komunjer (2012, CDK hereafter) on relative productivity differences across countries. These data are from OECD countries only. So, we're already looking at a set of countries among which it's reasonable to think that there has been a fair bit of flow in technologies. But in their data, relative labor productivities differ across sectors by a factor of up to four (e.g., for transportation versus food between Japan and Hungary). In other sectors, for example textiles, there is less evidence of heterogeneity, which is a point that I also want to get back to.

While Ricardo's stark assumptions about labor and technological immobility have served us well over the last two centuries, and seem consistent with first-order facts, there are contexts in which we want to relax them, and there is now a large quantitative literature that extends Ricardo's basic framework to do so.

Let's return to the assumption that workers can easily move between activities within a country but can't change countries. We've recently had elections in Britain and the United States that seem to have been influenced by perceptions that contradict Ricardo's assumptions about labor mobility. One is that trade has had a negative effect on workers who can't readily change industries. Another is that immigration has had a negative effect on domestic workers. Oxford's Migration Observatory website reports that, in 2015, 16.7% of the workforce in the UK was foreign-born.

What about technology? Visiting the United States Patent and Trademark Office (USPTO), I was quite stunned that they report that over half the US patents granted in 2015 were to foreign inventors. Kortum and I wrote quite a long time ago about patenting and technology diffusion.[2] Foreigners pay money to file these patent applications. The fee structure reported on the USPTO website is complicated, so I don't have a single number that I could grab, but applying for a patent appears expensive. If foreigners are paying real money to patent their inventions in the US, they must anticipate that their inventions are going to be useful in the US. That is, theirs is a technology that will diffuse to the US.

---

[2]Eaton and Kortum (1999).

	Food	Textiles	Wood	Paper	Fuel	Chemicals	Plastic	Minerals	Metals	Machinery	Electrical	Transport	Misc. Manuf
Australia	1	0.77	0.89	0.85	1.21	0.84	0.81	1	0.84	0.86	0.82	0.74	0.84
Belgium	1	0.84	0.84	1.03	1.7	1.26	1.71	1.49	1.07	0.93	0.86	0.71	1.11
Czech Republic	1	0.8	1.16	0.72	0.66	1.44	1.65	1.88	1.05	0.97	0.93	0.78	0.85
Denmark	1	0.75	0.84	0.63	0.64	1.02	1.01	0.98	0.85	0.85	0.63	0.51	1.35
Spain	1	0.92	1.47	0.91	0.7	1.34	1.38	1.58	1.08	0.99	1.08	1.01	1.15
Finland	1	0.82	1.2	118	0.86	1.69	1.37	1.3	1.18	1.13	0.9	0.65	1.47
France	1	0.76	1.22	0.93	1.11	1.24	1.64	1.28	1.08	1.13	0.93	0.84	0.92
Germany	1	0.67	0.91	0.89	0.94	1.03	1.23	1.2	0.91	0.92	0.8	0.72	0.9
Greece	1	1.07	1.65	1.57	1.13	1.87	1.21	2.19	1.51	1.54	1.26	0.83	1.36
Hungary	1	0.8	1.05	1.08	0.52	0.98	1.32	1.33	0.91	1.52	0.83	0.49	1.14
Ireland	1	0.93	1.03	0.81	1.15	1.49	1.55	1.19	1.11	0.92	0.74	0.62	1.11
Italy	1	0.79	1.02	0.68	0.65	1.26	1.48	1.63	1.17	1.02	0.98	1.14	0.94
Japan	1	1.88	1.37	1.69	1.06	1.84	1.69	1.71	1.85	2.05	1.96	1.96	1.33
Korea	1	1.23	1.56	1.4	1.32	2.74	1.97	2.22	1.5	1.64	1.6	1.72	1.94
Netherlands	1	0.85	0.54	0.76	0.65	1.25	1.26	1.11	1	0.71	0.75	0.61	0.74
Poland	1	1.15	1.12	0.92	1.07	1.24	2.21	1.59	0.91	0.8	0.6	0.68	0.64
Portugal	1	1.18	1.32	1.08	0.62	1.26	2.32	1.66	1.42	1.01	1.01	0.59	0.91
Slovakia	1	0.63	0.82	0.91	0.49	1.04	1.07	1.45	0.71	0.63	0.72	0.65	0.89
Sweden	1	0.68	1.18	0.92	0.78	1.22	1.18	0.92	1.14	0.98	0.89	0.67	1.09
U.K.	1	0.92	0.69	1.23	1.27	1.2	1.74	1.24	1.02	1.29	0.97	0.79	1.8
U.S.	1	1	1	1	1	1	1	1	1	1	1	1	1

Notes: Country and industry productivity, as measured by the inverse of producer prices (as collected by the GGDC Productivity Level Database). Entries are normalized to reflect relative productivity levels. That is, within each industry the U.S. has productivity equal to 1, and within each country, the "Food" industry (ISIC Rev 3.1 code: 15–16) has productivity equal to 1. Belgium is merged with Luxemburg.

Fig. 12.2 Relative productivity levels, by country and industry. Source: Costinot et al. (2012, p. 594)

12.2   Extending Ricardo to Many Goods and Countries

In taking Ricardo to data it helps to extend it beyond his 2×2 example to accommodate multiple countries and goods. I'm also going to talk about how, to the extent that we think we live in a world where Ricardo's strong assumptions don't quite apply, we can extend the Ricardian framework very easily to accommodate internal labor immobility, external labor mobility, and technology diffusion.

When I studied Ricardo as a Ph.D. student, the quantitative work based on it was pretty much one paper, the paper by MacDougall (1951). I went back to look at it, there's a lot more there than I had remembered.

What was MacDougall's exercise? He looked at two countries, the US and the United Kingdom, so, he passed Ron's [Ronald Jones] test: He got data from two countries, not one. So, unlike Leontief,[3] who used just US data, MacDougall was using US and UK data. He had measures of worker productivity, the inverse of Ricardo's worker requirements. Let's denote A_i^j as output per worker in industry j in country i. He then turned to trade data and looked at the US trade share in the rest of the world, which I denote $\pi_{ROW,USA}^j$, compared with the UK share in the rest of the world in sector j, $\pi_{ROW,UK}^j$. He considered the Ricardian model as predicting that, across industries, relative trade shares would vary with relative labor productivities or that:

$$\frac{\pi_{ROW,USA}^j / \pi_{ROW,USA}^{j'}}{\pi_{ROW,UK}^j / \pi_{ROW,UK}^{j'}} \sim \frac{A_{USA}^j / A_{USA}^{j'}}{A_{UK}^j / A_{UK}^{j'}}. \tag{12.1}$$

While I had remembered reading MacDougall in grad school, I had forgotten his wonderful diagram taken from the *Economic Journal* in 1951 (see Fig. 12.3).

Notice that it's hand-drawn. So, what do we have here? I would have switched the axes, but MacDougall must have had his reason for doing it his way. Here the y-axis is the relative productivities of the US to the UK, the ratio of those A's, for the indicated industry. On the x-axis are ratios of the US to the UK trade shares in the rest of the world, the ratio of the π's, for that industry. Starting in the southwest we have woolens, worsted, margarine, and clothing where US productivities and market shares are low, up to tin cans, pig iron and wireless in the northeast, where US productivities and market shares are high, demonstrating the correlation above. Ricardo is not just about trade, it's about trade and technology. Here MacDougall uses the Ricardian framework to connect data on trade with data on technology.

An old criticism of MacDougall's exercise is that it wasn't really about the Ricardian model. If we think of industries in MacDougall's analysis as the goods in Ricardo's example, how could the UK and the US coexist with each other in the same industry in the same market, not to mention coexisting with third countries? Ricardian predictions are binary about market entry. Interpreting the Ricardian model narrowly, MacDougall's diagram should be a step function.

Can we stick to Ricardian principles and still generate the smooth relationship between measured productivity and market share that MacDougall found? Recent work reframes the Ricardian model in a way that is totally consistent with what MacDougall is observing.

---

[3]Leontief (1954).

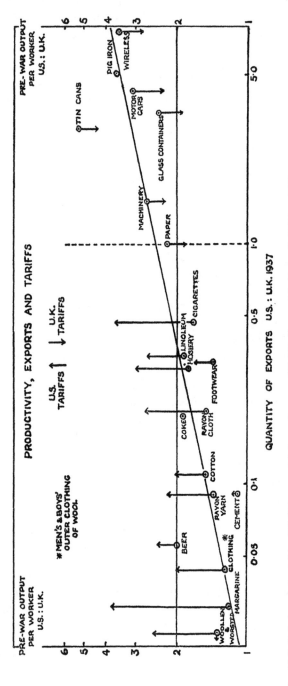

Fig. 12.3 Relative productivities US-UK vs. world share of exports US-UK. Source: MacDougall (1951, p. 703)

A paper in the *Journal of International Economics* by Finicelli, Pagano, and Sbragia (2013, FPS hereafter) shows how we can think about industry productivity levels in a more subtle way than a single number representing output per worker. Building on my 2002 framework with Kortum (Eaton and Kortum, 2002), they represent an industry j not as a single good, but as a whole slew of varieties within this industry. Country i has an efficiency (output per worker) $z_i^j(\omega)$ in making variety ω in sector j. It has a wage w_i that it has to pay its workers. Delivering a unit of the variety to country n requires shipping $d_{ni} \geq 1$ units from country i (the iceberg transport cost). Hence the cost of variety ω in market n if purchased from source i is:

$$p_{ni}(\omega) = \frac{d_{ni} w_i}{z_i^j(\omega)}. \qquad (12.2)$$

Each destination n is going to buy that variety from the lowest cost source:

$$i_n^*(\omega) = \text{argmin} \left\{ \frac{d_{n1} w_1}{z_1^j(\omega)}, \frac{d_{n2} w_2}{z_2^j(\omega)}, \ldots, \frac{d_{nN} w_N}{z_N^j(\omega)} \right\}. \qquad (12.3)$$

Using my trick with Kortum, FPS treat the efficiency z for these individual varieties as realizations from the *Fréchet* extreme value distribution:

$$F_i^j(z) = \Pr\left[Z_i^j(\omega) \leq z \right] = \exp\left(-T_i^j z^{-\theta} \right). \qquad (12.4)$$

We mostly treat these varieties as finer than anything we measure since, when we look at the product categories, we see destinations buying the same products from multiple sources. The parameter θ reflects how diverse productivity is across these varieties within industry j. It represents the force of Ricardian comparative advantage *within* the industry. The parameter T_i^j reflects country i's overall absolute advantage in industry j, and is intimately connected with the A_i^j's that MacDougall was looking at. Doing a little bit of calculus requiring a change of variable gives us country i's average productivity in industry j:

$$\bar{z}_i^j = \int_0^\infty z \, dF_i^j(z) = \Gamma\left(\frac{\theta - 1}{\theta} \right) T_i^{j 1/\theta}. \qquad (12.5)$$

But because of trade, country i won't produce all of the varieties in industry j, just the subset that are not imported. But this subset is not random as country i is more likely to import the varieties for which $z_i^j(\omega)$ is highest.[4]

---

[4]The probability that country i can provide variety ω to destination n at cost less than c is:

$$\Pr\left[\frac{d_{ni} w_i}{Z_i^j} \leq c \right] = 1 - \exp\left[-T_i^j (d_{ni} w_i)^{-\theta} c^\theta \right].$$

If destination n buys each variety from the lowest cost source, country i's trade share in country n in sector j is:

$$\pi_{ni}^j = \frac{T_i^j (d_{ni} w_i)^{-\theta}}{\phi_n^j}, \tag{12.6}$$

where $\phi_n^j = \sum_{i'} T_{i'}^j (d_{ni'} w_{i'})$. The trade share relates to country i's overall efficiency in sector j through the parameter T_i^j, the wage in country i, w_i, and the iceberg cost of getting goods from i to n, d_{ni}, relative to these terms summed over all sellers to country n, ϕ_n.

Let's connect expression (12.6) to the trade shares on MacDougall's x-axis. Think of i as the US, i' is the UK, and n is the rest of the world and j as, maybe, tin cans, and j' as clothing. While we don't see the T's directly in the data, we can take relative trade shares of two countries i and i' in sector j compared with sector j' in destination n and calculate:

$$\frac{\pi_{ni}^j / \pi_{ni}^{j'}}{\pi_{ni'}^j / \pi_{ni'}^{j'}} = \frac{T_i^j / T_i^{j'}}{T_{i'}^j / T_{i'}^{j'}}. \tag{12.7}$$

Equation (12.7) was what MacDougall was looking at on his x-axis. What about the y-axis?

Here, FPS make a point that those T's are about all the varieties. We calculated above average efficiency across all varieties in the country. But, as mentioned, some of those varieties won't be produced because of import competition. When we look only at a country's productivity in the varieties it's producing within an industry, we overstate its innate ability to produce all the varieties in the industry. Going through some math,[5] measured productivity in country i in industry j is:

$$A_i^j = \Gamma\left(\frac{\theta-1}{\theta}\right)\left(\frac{T_i^j}{\pi_{ii}^j}\right)^{\frac{1}{\theta}} > z_i^j = \Gamma\left(\frac{\theta-1}{\theta}\right)\left(T_i^j\right)^{\frac{1}{\theta}}. \tag{12.8}$$

---

[5]Given $z_i^j(\omega)$ the probability that country i is the cheapest source at home is:

$$\Pr\left[\frac{d_{n1} w_1}{Z_1^j} \geq \frac{w_i}{z_i^j(\omega)}\right] \times \Pr\left[\frac{d_{n2} w_2}{Z_2^j} \geq \frac{w_i}{z_i^j(\omega)}\right] \times \ldots \times \Pr\left[\frac{d_{nN} w_N}{Z_N^j} \geq \frac{w_i}{z_i^j(\omega)}\right]$$

$$= \exp\left(-w_i^{\theta} \sum_{i' \neq i} \left[T_{i'}^j (d_{ni'} w_{i'})^{-\theta}\right] z_i^j(\omega)^{-\theta}\right),$$

where we normalize $d_{ii} = 1$. To get the average productivity in the varieties country i actually produces we need to weight each z in expression (12.5) by this probability.

Equation (12.8) shows how we can discern a country's innate ability T_i^j from observed productivity A_i^j using its home share π_{ii}^j in that industry. Taking this equation to data, FPS ask: "To what extent, through the lens of this model, is trade increasing average productivity in different sectors?" They take a value of 6.67 for the parameter θ from Alvarez and Lucas (2007), finding that trade increased measured productivity by 6.1% on average in 1985 up to 11% in 2005. These figures represent the extent to which the productivities we're observing across sectors are higher because these countries are specializing within the sectors in the varieties which they're better at making. A kind of irony here is that as trade barriers fall differences in measured productivity decline as countries specialize in the varieties that they do best. If we actually could eliminate all trade barriers, and have completely flat trade, countries could specialize within industries to an extent that would wipe out differences in measured productivity. MacDougall's diagram would turn into a flat line:

$$\frac{A_i^j/A_i^{j\prime}}{A_{i\prime}^j/A_{i\prime}^{j\prime}} = 1, \tag{12.9}$$

not because countries didn't have differences in their innate ability in different industries, as Ricardo assumed, but simply because trade, by letting countries squeeze into the tails of the distribution where they are best, would just eliminate differences in measured productivity.

Now, combining the expressions above gives:

$$\frac{\pi_{ni}^j/\pi_{ni}^{j\prime}}{\pi_{ni\prime}^j/\pi_{ni\prime}^{j\prime}} = \left(\frac{A_i^j/A_i^{j\prime}}{A_{i\prime}^j/A_{i\prime}^{j\prime}}\right)^{\theta} \frac{\pi_{ii}^j/\pi_{ii}^{j\prime}}{\pi_{i\prime i}^j/\pi_{i\prime i}^{j\prime}}. \tag{12.10}$$

The π_{ni}^j are the trade shares, which we observe. The left-hand side of Eq. (12.10) is MacDougall's x-axis variable. The expression in brackets on the right-hand side of Eq. (12.10) is MacDougall's y-axis variable. But we also have the internal trade shares (the π_{ii}'s). The paper by CDK that I mentioned before, from which I took the data on relative sectoral productivities, looks at this relationship very much as MacDougall did, with the π's here from data, the A's here from data, but making this correction for the extent of internal specialization within a sector (the last fraction in 12.10). Taking it to data they estimate a θ of 6.5. That's quite remarkable as the FPS paper used 6.7 from Alvarez and Lucas (2007) from a number of years before.

CDK's exercise isn't a test of Ricardo in any formal way, but it shows how we can use Ricardian logic to organize our thinking about connections between various types of data, in this case data on relative productivities and data on trade shares. The framework can be taken from Ricardo's three numbers to the hundreds of thousands in the data.

Before CDK, Kortum and I looked at the role of internal trade shares (the π_{ii}'s) in calculating the gains from trade, but ignoring the industry dimension. We needed to make assumptions about preferences, which I haven't needed up until now. Now we have to think about the aggregation of varieties into some final thing. We used standard constant elasticity of substitution (CES):

$$Y = \left[\int_{\omega \in \Omega} q(\omega)^{\frac{\sigma-1}{\sigma}} \, d\omega \right]^{\frac{\sigma}{\sigma-1}}. \tag{12.11}$$

These preferences imply a price index

$$P_n = \gamma^{-1} \phi_n^{-1/\theta}, \tag{12.12}$$

where $\gamma = \left[\Gamma \left(\frac{\theta - (\sigma - 1)}{\theta} \right) \right]^{\frac{1}{\sigma-1}}$.

It depends on this ϕ_n term from above. To take Ricardo closer to the data, we allowed varieties to be intermediates as well as final goods, both aggregating across varieties according to Eq. (12.11). Letting the labor share be β, the expression for the trade share in (12.6) becomes:

$$\pi_{ii} = \frac{T_i \left(w_i^\beta P_i^{1-\beta} \right)^{-\theta}}{\phi_i} = \frac{T_i \left(w_i^\beta P_i^{1-\beta} \right)^{-\theta}}{\gamma P_i^{-\theta}} = \frac{T_i}{\gamma} \left(\frac{w_i}{P_i} \right)^{-\theta \beta} \tag{12.13}$$

giving us an expression for the real wage

$$\frac{w_i}{P_i} = \left(\frac{T_i}{\gamma \pi_{ii}} \right)^{1/\theta\beta}. \tag{12.14}$$

Notice, it depends on the T and the internal trade share. The elasticity is $1/\theta\beta$ rather than $1/\theta$ as in CDK. Since the labor share β is a number less than one (in manufacturing it's about a third as a share of total production costs) intermediates imply a much larger gains from trade.

12.3   Extending Ricardo to Imperfect Labor Mobility Between Sectors

Two recent papers probe a major departure from Ricardo's assumption of perfect internal labor mobility. Trever Tombe[6] and David Lakagos and Michael Waugh[7] probe three stylized facts:

1. Poor countries appear to be much less efficient producing food than manufactures.

---

[6]Tombe (2015).
[7]Lakagos and Waugh (2013).

2. Poor countries tend to have a larger market share in agricultural goods than in manufactures.
3. Poor countries tend to have much lower wages in agriculture than in manufactures.

Facts 1 and 2 imply that, if we drew MacDougall's diagram to rich and poor countries in manufactures and agriculture, it would have the wrong slope. Both Tombe and Lakagos and Waugh attribute the failure to a lack of internal mobility between agriculture and manufacturing. Let's pursue Tombe's characterization of imperfect mobility in more detail, simplifying a bit. Say that each country i has a wage in agriculture w_i but workers need to receive a premium $\tau_i > 1$ in manufacturing so that the manufacturing wage is:

$$w_i^m = \tau_i w_i. \tag{12.15}$$

Tombe's paper accounts how the development literature explores many types of rigidities that rural workers face in a lot of poor countries in moving to the city, motivating τ_i. There are language differences, ethnic differences, trade unions that they might have to join to get work. Hence τ_i is like another iceberg cost, but applying to labor moving internally rather than to goods moving across borders.

Say that poor country i has a Fréchet distribution of efficiencies for manufacturing varieties with a parameter T_i^m and a Fréchet distribution of efficiencies for agricultural varieties with a parameter T_i^a. Then its trade share in country n in agriculture would be:

$$\pi_{ni}^a = \frac{T_i^a (w_i d_{ni})^{-\theta}}{\sum_{i'} T_{i'}^a (w_{i'} d_{ni'})^{-\theta}}, \tag{12.16}$$

and in manufactures:

$$\pi_{ni}^m = \frac{T_i^m (\tau_i w_i d_{ni})^{-\theta}}{\sum_{i'} T_{i'}^m (\tau_{i'} w_{i'} d_{ni'})^{-\theta}}. \tag{12.17}$$

From Eq. (12.8) above, country i's relative measured productivity in manufactures relative to agriculture would be:

$$\frac{A_i^m}{A_i^a} = \frac{\left(\frac{T_i^m}{\pi_{ii}^m}\right)^{\frac{1}{\theta}}}{\left(\frac{T_i^a}{\pi_{ii}^a}\right)^{\frac{1}{\theta}}} = \tau_i \frac{P_i^a}{P_i^m}, \tag{12.18}$$

where P_i^a is country i's agricultural price index and P_i^m is its manufacturing price index. Under autarky

$$\frac{P_i^a}{P_i^m} = \left(\frac{T_i^m}{T_i^a}\right)^{1/\theta} \tau_i^{-1}. \tag{12.19}$$

Hence, in the neighborhood of autarky, measured productivity is proportional to the ratio of the Fréchet parameters. From that point greater openness in manufactures relative to agriculture tends to raise observed productivity in manufactures relative to agriculture. The term τ_i doesn't matter.

But note from expressions (12.16) and (12.17) that τ_i drags down country i's manufacturing share relative to its share in agriculture. Hence the τ_i's can qualitatively explain the three stylized facts enumerated at the beginning of this section.

Beyond making this qualitative point Tombe goes on to connect his analysis to data on differences between urban and rural wages and finds that they correspond quite well to these τ's. Hence Tombe's exercises combines data on these three quite different things, international trade, relative productivity, relative wages, in a single framework. Moreover, the framework allows for counterfactual analysis, such as examining the gains from lower trade barriers and greater internal labor market integration.

Here Tombe is following in Ricardo's tradition of using a model to conduct a counterfactual exercise. In Ricardo's case it was to demonstrate the gains from trade (for a small, world price-taking countries) by comparing international prices with what prices would be under autarky.

Lakagos and Waugh (2013) have a slightly different take on internal labor immobility. They use the Roy (1951) model. But the Roy model is really Ricardo's model applied to individual workers instead of industries. Workers have different abilities in different industries so sort according to comparative advantage. Lakagos and Waugh use the Fréchet extreme value assumption for workers' efficiencies in different sectors.[8,9] Lorenzo Caliendo and co-authors use it for looking at migration within the EU in a recent paper.[10]

12.4   Addressing International Technology Diffusion

I want to finish by addressing Ricardo's assumption that technologies differ internationally (a key difference with the factor endowments approach developed in the twentieth century, what Ron called the Swedish model). Evidence such as the data I showed you from CDK or MacDougall would seem first-level evidence that

---

[8]Worker l in country i has an efficiency (or psychic benefit) $e_i^j(l)$ working in sector j, that is drawn from the distribution $G_i^j(e) = \Pr\left[E_i^j(l) \le e\right] = \exp\left(-U_i^j e^{-\kappa}\right)$.

[9]See also Monte, Redding, and Rossi-Hansberg (2015).

[10]Caliendo, Opromolla, Parro, and Sforza (2017).

technologies aren't perfectly mobile. But technologies are not perfectly immobile either. Can we extend Ricardo to incorporate technology diffusion?

So far we have followed Ricardo in treating the productivity terms, z's or T's above, as exogenous. But they are the consequence of innovation and technology diffusion. Krugman (1979) provides a simple way to think about these forces. The static model is Ricardian. There are two countries, the North with a labor force L_N and the South with a labor force L_S. There are two types of varieties, which I'm going to call Exclusive (E) and Common (C): E are of measure n_E while C are of measure n_C. The total measure of varieties is $n = n_E + n_C$. Output per worker, the inverse of Ricardo's labor requirement, for a C variety is 1 in the North and the South, and for an E variety output per worker is 1 in the North and 0 in the South. That is, Southerners just don't know how to make the E varieties. Competition is perfect and there are no trade costs.

If the ratio n_E/n_C exceeds the ratio L_N/L_S and preferences are symmetric and CES (as above), with $\sigma > 1$, the relative northern wage is:

$$\frac{w_N}{w_S} = \left(\frac{n_E/L_N}{n_C/L_S}\right)^{\frac{1}{\sigma}} > 1, \qquad (12.20)$$

with the North producing only E varieties and the South producing all the C varieties.

Krugman embeds this static framework into a completely mechanical dynamic framework summarized by the two equations:

$$\dot{n}_E = \iota n, \qquad (12.21)$$

$$\dot{n}_C = \epsilon n_E. \qquad (12.22)$$

Here the parameter ι is the rate of innovation, the rate at which new varieties are introduced, which is proportional to the total stock of varieties n. New varieties start out as E, but then the ability to produce them leaks into the South. The parameter ϵ is the rate of diffusion of E varieties into C varieties. The measure of both types of varieties grows over time, with the share of E goods converging to:

$$\frac{n_E}{n} = \frac{\iota}{\iota + \epsilon}. \qquad (12.23)$$

If innovation is very large relative to diffusion, then there will be a lot of exclusive varieties relative to the total, and vice versa. If these technologies leak out very fast, then most varieties will be in the common pool.

What about welfare? Since innovation leads to more varieties and, because the CES assumption implies love of variety, everybody likes more innovation. The South also likes fast diffusion, for two reasons. It means that there are more goods that they can make more cheaply for themselves. And what they have to import from the North is also cheaper since the Northern wage is lower. What about the North? Does it benefit from faster diffusion? The answer is, at first, "yes". Starting from a situation with no diffusion, introducing a small mount allows the North to outsource production of some varieties to the South and have them made cheaper there. But as the rate of diffusion rises, the Southern wage creeps up, rendering varieties imported from the South more expensive. So, there's a non-monotonic relationship. The following equation shows the real wage in the North

$$\frac{w_N}{P} = n^{1/\sigma-1} \left[1 + \frac{n_C}{n} \left(\left(\frac{w_N}{w_S}\right)^{\sigma-1} - 1 \right) \right]^{\frac{1}{\sigma-1}}. \tag{12.24}$$

Substituting in Eq. (12.20) gives

$$\frac{w_N}{P} = n^{1/(\sigma-1)} \left[1 + \frac{n_C}{n} \left(\left(\frac{n}{n_C} - 1\right)^{(\sigma-1)/\sigma} \left(\frac{L_S}{L_N}\right)^{(\sigma-1)/\sigma} - 1 \right) \right]^{1/(\sigma-1)}. \tag{12.25}$$

This expression can increase or decrease in $\frac{n_C}{n}$, because the CES elasticity of substitution σ exceeds 1.

I wrote an Excel spreadsheet to see what level of n_C/n maximizes the real wage in the North. In a symmetric case in which the labor forces are the same, with $\sigma = 2$, the answer is 0.15: The North would like to have 15% of the goods in the common pool. Of course, once you go to 0.5, half of the goods are common, since that's the same as the Southerners' labor share, and wages are equalized. Beyond 0.5 the North becomes incompletely specialized and loses all its gains from trade.

Krugman applies his analysis to the universe of varieties. Kortum and I have been working on an extension of the Krugman model where we think of it as applying the analysis to different industries j with their own innovation and diffusion parameters.

I end with a quantitative exercise which I think is suggestive of the relative importance of innovation and diffusion in different industries. With apologies to Bela Belassa I refer to it as a calculation of comparative advantage as revealed by gravity.

Using data on bilateral trade in 21 different industries among 39 countries we estimate the following gravity equation

$$\ln X_{ni}^j = S_i^j + D_n^j + \gamma_{dist}^j \ln (dist_{ni}) + \gamma_C^j D_{ni}^{contiguity}$$
$$+ \gamma_l^j D_{ni}^{common\ language}, \tag{12.26}$$

where X_{ni}^j is exports from source i to destination n in industry j. The term S_i^j is a source effect for country i in industry j, D_n^j is a destination effect for country n in industry j, $dist_{ni}$ is the distance between i and n, $D_{ni}^{contiguity}$ is a dummy for the contiguity of i and n and $D_{ni}^{common\ language}$ is a dummy for i and n having a common language.

From expression (12.6) above, in terms of the Ricardian model we can interpret:

$$\exp\left(S_i^j\right) = T_i^j w_i^{-\theta}. \tag{12.27}$$

We then calculate, for each source i and industry j,

$$s_i^j = \frac{\exp\left(S_i^j\right)}{\sum_{i'}\exp\left(S_{i'}^j\right)}. \tag{12.28}$$

This measure gives us country i's share of world technology in industry j where countries are weighted by $w_i^{-\theta}$. Since these weights are the same across industries, we can compare the s_i^j across industries. We might infer that diffusion is more rampant in industries in which poorer countries have larger s_i^j's.

Figure 12.4 below report the measures for China, Japan and the United States in these 21 industries, the United States and Japan because they're the largest advanced economies and China because it's the largest developing economy.

For Textiles and Textile Articles China's share is 0.58. In Footwear, its share is even larger at 0.72. Japan and the United States are negligible in these industries. But then, if we look at optical, photographic, precision instruments, etc. China's share is only 0.13, while the US is at 0.33. With vehicles, China's is at 0.05 and Japan's is actually the largest at 0.28, and the US is at 0.24. One interpretation of these results in terms of the Krugman diffusion model is that diffusion is more prevalent, relative to innovation, in textiles and footwear, with the opposite the case in vehicles and in optical, photographic, precision instruments, etc. Hence differences in innovation and diffusion rates across industries can generate Ricardian comparative advantage.

Distance elasticity	China	Japan	USA	
-1.37	0.11	0	0.17	Live animals; Animal products
-1.38	0.09	0	0.26	Vegetable products
-1.42	0.01	0	0.08	Animal or vegetable fats, etc.
-1.29	0.06	0.01	0.16	Prepared foodstuffs; Beverages, etc.
-2.21	0.06	0.01	0.27	Mineral Products
-1.16	0.1	0.08	0.27	Chemicals
-1.36	0.17	0.13	0.2	Plastics
-1.2	0.62	0	0.04	Leather goods, etc.
-1.4	0.35	0	0.13	Wood and articles of wood; etc.
-1.5	0.12	0.03	0.26	Woodpulp paper; etc.
-1.3	0.58	0.01	0.05	Textiles and textile articles
-1.29	0.72	0	0.01	Footwear, etc.
-1.3	0.39	0.06	0.14	Stone, glass, porcelain, etc.
-1.36	0.25	0.02	0.19	Natural or cultured pearls, precious or semi-precious stones, etc.
-1.36	0.25	0.09	0.14	Base metals and articles of base metal
-0.99	0.28	0.13	0.17	Machinery and mechanical appliances; Electrical equipment, etc.
-1.34	0.05	0.28	0.24	Vehicles, Aircraft, Vessels and associated transport equipment
-0.78	0.13	0.14	0.33	Optical, photoraphic, precision, medical instruments; etc.
-0.58	0.04	0.01	0.39	Arms and ammunition; Parts and accessories thereof
-1.19	0.64	0.04	0.07	Miscellaneous manufactured articles
-0.52	0.08	0.01	0.58	Works of art, collectors pieces and antiques
-1.25	0.24	0.05	0.2	Averages

Fig. 12.4 Comparative advantage revealed through gravity. Source: Own calculations

12.5   Conclusion

We've explored three ways of going beyond Ricardo's simple example, allowing the model to accommodate smoother features of the world. But these extensions keep Ricardo's basic idea very much at their heart.

References

Alvarez, F., & Lucas, R. (2007). General equilibrium analysis of the Eaton-Kortum model of international trade. *Journal of Monetary Economics, 54*(6), 1726–1768.

Caliendo, L., Opromolla, L. D., Parro, F., & Sforza, A. (2017). *Trade and migration: A quantitative assessment.* Preliminary Working Paper.

Costinot, A., Donaldson, D., & Komunjer, I. (2012). What goods do countries trade? A quantitative exploration of Ricardo's ideas. *Review of Economic Studies, 79*, 581–608.

Eaton, J. & Fieler, A. C. (2017). *The gravity of unit values..* Preliminary Working Paper.

Eaton, J., & Kortum, S. (1999). International technology diffusion: Theory and measurement. *International Economic Review, 40*(3), 537–570.

Eaton, J., & Kortum, S. (2002). Technology, geography, and trade. *Econometrica, 70*(5), 1741–1779.

Finicelli, A., Pagano, P., & Sbracia, M. (2013). Ricardian selection. *Journal of International Economics, 89*, 96–109.

Krugman, P. (1979). A model of innovation, technology transfer and the world distribution of income. *The Journal of Political Economy, 87*(2), 253–266.

Lakagos, D., & Waugh, M. E. (2013). Selection, agriculture and cross-country productivity differences. *American Economic Review, 103*(2), 948–980.

Leontief, W. (1954). Domestic production and foreign trade: The American capital position reexamined. *Economia Internazionale, 7*(1), 9–45.

MacDougall, G. D. A. (1951). British and American exports: A study suggested by the theory of comparative costs. Part I. *The Economic Journal, 61*(244), 697–724.

Monte, F., Redding, S. J., & Rossi-Hansberg, E. (2015). *Commuting, migration and local employment elasticities.* NBER Working Paper, 21706.

Roy, A. (1951). Some thoughts on the distribution of earnings. *Oxford Economic Papers, 3*(2), 135–146.

Tombe, T. (2015). The missing food problem: Trade, agriculture and international productivity differences. *American Economic Journal, 7*(3), 226–258.

Chapter 13
Comments on "Putting Ricardian Trade Theory to Work in 2017: Current Empirical Analyses" by Jonathan Eaton

Peter H. Egger

Abstract This set of comments addresses some generic questions and problems of the "new" quantitative work. It is geared towards a reader looking at the respective work from an empirical rather than a theoretical angle.

Jonathan Eaton is one of the masterminds of the new quantitative literature in international economics. I will abstain from commenting on precisely his talk and presentation but will rather put forward a few generic comments that pertain to this very literature at large. In doing so, I will wear the chapeau of an empiricist. The reference work is very structural and well grounded in economic theory. In what follows, I will put forward thoughts on models, which generate aggregate (sector-country-pair) demand equations, so-called gravity equations, of the form

$$X_{j,ni} = B_{j,i} C_{j,n} D_{j,ni} (U_{j,ni}), \qquad (13.1)$$

where j denotes sectors, i denotes exporting countries and n denotes importing countries.

After defining sector-country aggregate expenditures, $E_{j,n} = \sum_i X_{j,ni}$, Eq. (13.1) may also be written as

$$X_{j,ni} = \pi_{j,ni} E_{j,n}, \qquad (13.2)$$

where $\pi_{j,ni} = X_{j,ni}/E_{j,n}$ is the bilateral trade (import or expenditure) share.

Furthermore, expenditure shares by importer n and sector j on the output from a given exporter i are:

Note: This chapter is based on a transcription of the presentation given at the conference "Celebrating 200 Years of Ricardian Trade Theory" on May 12, 2017, at the University of Basel, Switzerland. It is a comment to the presentation by Jonathan Eaton, i.e., to Chapt. 12 of this book.

P.H. Egger (✉)
Department of Management, Technology and Economics, ETH Zurich, Zurich, Switzerland
e-mail: egger@kof.ethz.ch

$$\pi_{j,ni} = \frac{B_{j,i}D_{j,ni}\left(U_{j,ni}\right)}{\sum_k B_{j,k}D_{j,nk}\left(U_{j,nk}\right)} \tag{13.3}$$

13.1 Model Calibration Versus Estimation

What the quantitative literature based on the above model type was mostly concerned with so far are three things: (i) estimating the parameter on sector-country-pair observable ad-valorem trade costs, $T_{j,ni}$, which is related to $D_{j,ni}$ through $D_{j,ni} = T_{j,ni}^{\alpha}$, where α is referred to as the so-called trade elasticity; (ii) decomposing $D_{j,ni}$ (or $T_{j,ni}$) into its components (assuming a multiplicative relationship); and (iii) gauging the effect of large or moderate changes in $T_{j,ni}$ on economic outcome such as real consumption, $E_{j,n}/\left[\sum_k B_{j,k}D_{j,nk}\left(U_{j,nk}\right)\right]^{\frac{1}{\alpha}}$.

In doing this, the calibrator will assume that $U_{j,ni} = 0$ for any j,ni so that there is no (or, more precisely, there cannot be any) gap between the quantitative model and the data. When resorting to estimation rather than calibration, one will have to make a choice whether $U_{j,ni}$ is a measurement error about trade flows (as, e.g., in Anderson & van Wincoop, 2003) or one about trade costs (as, e.g., in Eaton & Kortum, 2002), with the latter being problematic, as $U_{j,nk}$ enters in a non-loglinear fashion in the denominator of the empirical model (see Egger & Nigai, 2015).

What calibrators do is saying "let us 'invert' data to find out what $D_{j,ni}$ or $D_{j,ni}(U_{j,ni})$ is". However, the enterprise of decomposing trade flows $X_{j,ni}$ into their sector-exporter component $B_{j,i}$, their sector-importer component $C_{j,n}$, and their "residual" component $D_{j,ni}$ is not innocuous for various reasons. First of all, $B_{j,i}$, and $C_{j,n}$ are endogenous, in the sense that they both depend (non-linearly) on $D_{j,ni}$. In particular, the exogenous part of $B_{j,i}$ determines the "religion" of the economist, namely whether she goes to the church of Armington (goods are differentiated by country of origin), of Dixit, Stiglitz, and Krugman (goods are differentiated across firms and firms sell under monopolistic competition, producing at increasing returns to scale), or of Eaton and Kortum (sectors are differentiated, but firms differ by their random productivity and sell under perfect competition). However, one insight flowing from Arkolakis, Costinot and Rodríguez-Clare (2012) is that your religion does not matter for determining $D_{j,ni}$, as long as preferences, technology, or firm numbers are exogenous.

Staying ignorant about the exact specification of $B_{j,i}$ (by just considering as a ji-specific constant), and similarly, taking $C_{j,n}$ as such a jn-specific constant, and not measuring or estimating its components based on data comes at some cost, though: the level of $D_{j,ni}$ is fundamentally undetermined. To see this, assume an Eaton and Kortum world, where $B_{j,i}$ multiplicatively consists of the average productivity draw of firms in a country and sector and the wage costs (firm numbers and exporter-sector preference weights have been normalized to unity each). Then, as we cannot observe productivity, we have to make a decision of where to put the constant of the model, into productivity or trade costs. Hence, the level of both productivity across countries as well as of $D_{j,ni}$ is fundamentally undetermined. In any type of model—and independent of the religion of the researcher—$C_{j,n}$ depends on income spent on this sector and some reference price that is made up of the B's and the D's.

In any case the meaning of $B_{j,i}$ and $D_{j,ni}$ may be less important, if a focus is on the variance of these terms. However, as soon as we think of a world where firm numbers differ across countries and sectors, consumer preferences differ towards products from different countries and sectors, and the productivity of firms differ at least between countries and sectors, the decomposition of $B_{j,i}D_{j,ni}(U_{j,ni})$ in the numerator of Eq. (13.3) matters for a quantification of how important productivity differences versus trade costs are for economic outcome. If we call all differences across producer countries and sectors, i.e., $B_{j,i}$, productivity (and factor costs), we are inflating the importance of productivity. And if we call all of $D_{j,ni}$ just ad-valorem trade costs, when it might contain country-pair-sector productivity or preference differences, we are inflating the notion of trade costs.

In any case, when not operating with fixed effects but with observables, the gap between the model and the data will be found to be of nontrivial size. E.g., in Bergstrand, Egger, and Larch (2013) we illustrated that the structural parameterized model of Anderson and van Wincoop (2003) accounts for only two-thirds of the variation in the data as compared to a structural fixed effects version of the same model. Hence, there are important country(-sector) components in trade data that we tend to call either trade costs, productivity, endowments, or preferences, without paying much attention to what they really are.

13.2   Levels of Confidence

Unlike in traditional empirical work in economics, there is a certain lack of interest in levels of confidence in new quantitative work in international economics. Very much like the older—and in many ways closely related—literature on computable general equilibrium models of trade, calibrators are happy to take parameters from a host of different studies—with little interest in sample differences, differences in the underlying model ramifications, etc., between the studies the parameters come from and the data their model is calibrated to. Such practice is highly problematic: whenever parameters are estimated, there is a gap between the model and the data which is assumed to not exist for calibrators—hence, there is a fundamental inconsistency between the set-ups where parameters are estimated and the calibration exercise, which should cast doubt in the very estimates that are often used in calibration; and with any absence of residuals (a gap between the model and the data), we should not speak of empirical work but of theory with numbers.

In any case, with a structural estimation of multi-sector-multi-country trade models of the above kind, we should be aware of the variance-covariance matrix of the parameters not being straightforward, as the structural model involves (market-clearing) constraints that need to be properly taken into account. And these constraints are hard to avoid.

Some work has made use of ratio-type versions of the above structural model. E. g., Head and Ries (2001) proposed a ratio estimator with a product of two trade shares as in Eq. (13.3) in the numerator and another product of two trade shares in the denominator as the dependent variable. Caliendo and Parro (2015) proposed an alternative estimator with a product of three trade shares in the numerator and another product of three trade shares in the denominator. These estimators were proposed to estimate the trade elasticity α, while conditioning out the (sector-) country fixed effects. However, taking ratios in this way leads to a certain pattern of duplicity of variances and covariances in the variance-covariance matrix of the disturbances. If this is not taken into account properly, confidence levels about parameter point estimates will be biased (see Egger & Staub, 2016).

13.3   Gains from Trade

In their handbook chapter, Costinot and Rodríguez-Clare (2014) illustrate that the model structure—perfect versus monopolistic competition and final-goods-only versus input-output trade—matters a lot for the role of trade liberalization for real consumption.

What is traditionally done in related work is to shut down trade completely in the model—using its quantification based on data—and gauge the model-consistent difference in real consumption between autarky and the status quo.

It takes a lot to believe that everything that is constant in the model will be constant also in the data with large-scale experiments like switching from the status quo to autarky. Two things are important to note in this regard. First, "experiments" of the scale as done in this literature more or less completely lack support by the data. Second, even within the support of the data we know relatively little about the "stability" or "global applicability" of the model features.

Let me give a few examples. For instance, we tend to model consumer preferences as to be the same on a world-wide basis. Moreover, we tend to assume that production technologies (functions) are the same everywhere (maybe apart from total factor productivity). And we tend to assume that trade costs matter in the same way (in the sense of the trade elasticity a being the same) for high- versus low-sectors and country pairs.

All of that means that we can more or less "linearly" extrapolate wherever to and from wherever we start in terms of productivity, preferences, and trade costs. However, what we learn from the data based on the assumptions is a local linear approximation, and if we extrapolate to far from the status quo a small deviation from the assumptions may have gravid effects on the outcome. The models we tend to formulate will not lead to whole sectors becoming extinct and products to disappear in certain economies. However, we should see that this feature flows from (largely untested) assumptions we make, and it is not a feature of reality.

Overall, this practice may lead to a severe downward bias in the quantified effects of trade liberalization, something we should be very sensitive about at times where openness is under political attack.

References

Anderson, J. E., & Van Wincoop, E. (2003). Gravity with gravitas: a solution to the border puzzle. *The American Economic Review, 93*(1), 170–192.

Arkolakis, C., Costinot, A., & Rodríguez-Clare, A. (2012). New trade models, same old gains? *The American Economic Review, 102*(1), 94–130.

Bergstrand, J. H., Egger, P., & Larch, M. (2013). Gravity Redux: Estimation of gravity-equation coefficients, elasticities of substitution, and general equilibrium comparative statics under asymmetric bilateral trade costs. *Journal of International Economics, 89*(1), 110–121.

Caliendo, L., & Parro, F. (2015). Estimates of the trade and welfare effects of NAFTA. *The Review of Economic Studies, 82*(1), 1–44.

Costinot, A., & Rodriguez-Clare, A. (2014). Trade theory with numbers: Quantifying the consequences of globalization. In G. Gopinath, E. Helpmann, & K. Rogoff (Eds.), *Handbook of international economics* (Vol. 4). Amsterdam: Elsevier.

Eaton, J., & Kortum, S. (2002). Technology, geography, and trade. Econometrica, *70*(5), 1741–1779.

Egger, P. H., & Nigai, S. (2015). Structural gravity with dummies only: Constrained ANOVA-type estimation of gravity models. *Journal of International Economics, 97*(1), 86–99.

Egger, P. H., & Staub, K. E. (2016). GLM estimation of trade gravity models with fixed effects. *Empirical Economics, 50*(1), 137–175.

Head, K., & Ries, J. (2001). Increasing returns versus national product differentiation as an explanation for the pattern of US-Canada trade. *American Economic Review, 91*(4), 858–876.

Chapter 14
Short Discussion About "Putting Ricardian Trade Theory to Work in 2017: Current Empirical Analyses"

Nicolas Schmitt

Abstract This chapter includes the short discussion of the paper "Putting Ricardian Trade Theory to Work in 2017: Current Empirical Analyses" by Jonathan Eaton (Chap. 12 of this book) and of the comments to this paper by Peter H. Egger (Chap. 13 of this book). It is based on the transcription of the discussion. The session was chaired by Nicolas Schmitt, Professor of International Trade and Industrial Organization at Simon Fraser University. He has a PhD from the University of Toronto.

[This chapter starts with an introduction by Professor Schmitt to the third session of the conference entitled "Putting Ricardian Trade Theory to Work in 2017: Current Empirical Analyses" and then proceeds to the discussion.]

Nicolas Schmitt Ladies and Gentlemen, welcome to the third session of this conference. As you know research in international trade theory has been very dynamic during the last 30 years with intra-industry trade theories, the new developments with heterogeneous firms and the greater emphasis on empirical analyses in the field.

Therefore, the question we would like to ask is in which way the Ricardian trade theory is still important for these new developments and, also, in which way it may be different. Before we proceed to the discussion, let me briefly summarize what we just heard. In his talk, Jonathan Eaton, Distinguished Professor of Economics at Penn State, critically assessed the basic assumptions of the Ricardian Trade Model. He then showed how to extend the basic model to a continuum of countries and goods. Of course, Eaton and Kortum (2002) were crucial in this respect. Finally, Jonathan reviewed extensions of the basic Ricardian model that allow for imperfect labor mobility between sectors and technology diffusion.

Note: This chapter is based on a transcription of the discussion held at the Conference "Celebrating 200 Years of Ricardian Trade Theory" on May 12, 2017, at the University of Basel in Switzerland. The discussion in this chapter refers to the contents in Chaps. 12 and 13 of this book.

N. Schmitt (✉)
Department of Economics, Simon Fraser University, Burnaby, BC, Canada
e-mail: schmitt@sfu.ca

© Springer International Publishing AG 2017
R.W. Jones, R. Weder (eds.), *200 Years of Ricardian Trade Theory*,
https://doi.org/10.1007/978-3-319-60606-4_14

181

182 N. Schmitt

Jonathan's talk was commented by Peter Egger, Professor of Applied Economics at the ETH in Zurich, who assigned empirical trade economists to one out of three "religious" groups based on their assumptions about the sector-specific component of the gravity equation. He mentioned fundamental limitations of the current empirical analyses in international trade and urged caution about the use of ratios and fixed-effects estimation techniques.

[The following is the short discussion on both contributions (see Chaps. 12 and 13 in this book). We start with a reaction by Professor Jonathan Eaton to Professor Egger's comments.]

Nicolas Schmitt Jonathan, do you want to respond to these comments?

Jonathan Eaton Okay, just a few things. One point: I don't think of myself as at all religious. So, I would not agree of being categorized as a religion. I'm very adamant about that. In fact, you mentioned IRS as a kind of a competing framework. I love IRS. I find it hard to identify, but I'm a big fan of Bill's Frank Graham paper,[1] which I have taught many times. I just wanted to advertise a paper by a couple of former Penn State students and Andrés Rodríguez-Clare; they have a very nice paper.[2] It kind of integrates Eaton and Kortum (2002) with a framework like Bill's. I think that is still work in progress but the idea is to try to quantify the importance of IRS. I couldn't tell you where the identification clause is coming from, but they are smart guys—I'm sure they are doing a good job.

Gains from Trade: yes, a kind of an embarrassment with a lot of these models, is it that they are small. I think part of it is because we are so focused on many factors. I have a former student of mine, Farid Farrokhi, who did a job market paper on trade in oil[3] and was getting much larger gains from trade in that sector for I think reasons that aren't very surprising.

I'm totally fond of confidence levels, I'm not opposed to them. The only reason, we sometimes do what maybe you call the "mindless bootstrap", when we have done that in work with Kortum and Kramarz,[4] the standard errors were all very low. And I don't feel very confident reporting them, because it looks like I'm very confident, when I'm actually not confident. They are really about sampling error. When you have these kinds of data, sampling errors can't really generate that much in the way of lack of confidence, I guess.

Peter Egger That was coming from the idea that when we think the data is connected to everything else in general equilibrium then probably a bootstrap that assumes independence across observations is not the right thing to do.

Jonathan Eaton I believe that. I'm not an econometrician – but I certainly hope any of this stuff gives econometricians food for thought on how to better estimate these

[1]Ethier (1982).
[2]Arkolakis, Ramondo, Rodríguez-Clare, and Yeaple (2017).
[3]Farrokhi (2016).
[4]Eaton, Kortum, and Kramarz (2011).

kinds of models. I think it is a shame that the stuff, this new quantitative work, hasn't connected more with the old GTAP people. I talked with them a little bit. They seem to appreciate the stuff. It would be great if we could talk to them more. They were doing great work. In terms of this being theory with numbers: Yeah, that's probably the way we are starting. I'm not embarrassed or ashamed to be saying that it is what we are doing. Ricardo was theory with numbers. I think we are just going to data sources to get numbers from data sources rather than one from making them up. But I think there is a lot of work here. Maybe the theory and the data are a bit ahead of the econometrics. And you have been, I think, doing a lot of nice work on the econometrics of estimating these things. So I'm delighted to have econometricians to revisit stuff that, I think, a lot of us have been doing—to think about better estimation techniques. I think, there's still a bit of a disconnect between the theory and the data and standard econometrics. But thanks, those were great comments.

Ralph Ossa[5] I have some comments on the gains of trade. Both of you seem to share a popular perception that the gains of trade predicted by these models are very small and I mean it's correct, if you just use an aggregate model. But one could explore to consider a multi-sector extension in which case it's very easy to get much larger gains from trade. So, my best guess is that, if I do this, the gains from trade are about 50 percent of real income, if you look at the 50 largest countries of the world.[6] For the US of course you're never going to get big numbers. But it's not fair to say that these gravity models don't predict substantial gains.

Jonathan Eaton I think the point is, Ralph, that if you have multiple sectors of different elasticities, the gains from trade aren't determined by the average of those elasticities.

Ralph Ossa That's how you would think about the real world. What makes trade valuable is really stuff that you need. Either it's a critical input of production or it's a critical consumption good. Thinking about the gains from trade in some generic product, I don't think it's that unusual that they are small.

Peter Egger I think it's also true that when we do large scale experiments, you might want to have models that have more action on the extensive margins. Many products could, for example, just die out.

References

Arkolakis, C., Ramondo, N., Rodríguez-Clare, A., & Yeaple, S. (2017). *Innovation and production in the global economy*. NBER-Working Paper, No. 18972 (April 2013, revised May 2017). Cambridge, MA: NBER.

---

[5]Professor of Economics, University of Zurich.
[6]See Ossa (2015).

Eaton, J., & Kortum, S. (2002). Technology, geography, and trade. *Econometrica, 70*(5), 1741–1779.

Eaton, J., Kortum, S., & Kramarz, F. (2011). An anatomy of international trade: Evidence from French firms. *Econometrica, 79*(5), 1453–1498.

Ethier, W. J. (1982). Decreasing costs in international trade and Frank Graham's argument for protection. *Econometrica: Journal of the Econometric Society, 50*, 1243–1268.

Farrokhi, F. (2016). *Global sourcing in oil markets*. PhD dissertation, Pennsylvania State University.

Ossa, R. (2015). Why trade matters after all. *Journal of International Economics, 97*(2), 266–277.

Chapter 15
The Relevance of Ricardian Trade Theory for the Political Economy of Trade Policy

Wilfred J. Ethier

Abstract Ricardo's contribution to trade theory is commonly identified with the single-factor model that bears his name. But Ricardo's contribution to the theory of rent is also fundamental to the currently active literature on the political economy of trade policy. The multi-factor model often employed in this literature is thoroughly Ricardian.

Some years ago I attended a presentation by Murray Kemp. He was giving a paper and in his presentation he said that he was proud of the fact that a textbook on trade he wrote made no mention whatsoever of the "worthless" Ricardian Model. He then scolded me for not following his example. Of course, we know that the simple Ricardian model, using one factor of production, is a beautiful way of explaining production-based comparative advantage. Ron [Jones] has illustrated today that it is attractive and useful for a number of other reasons as well.

And Jon [Eaton] demonstrated its quantitative relevance. What I think Murray really had in mind, as he often did, was the gains-from-trade question, and in particular the possibility of generating a Pareto improvement in a situation where there would otherwise be both winners and losers. A single uniform factor of production is not really an effective way to approach this situation.

As Roy [Ruffin] pointed out in his presentation, though, Ricardo's concerns about international trade extended well beyond issues that are efficiently addressed in the context of a single uniform factor of production. More generally, a central contribution of Ricardo is his treatment of rents, and his concern over international trade was motivated to a significant degree by a concern about the effect of trade on the distribution of income between the rents of landowners and the profits of capitalists, labor being regarded as near a subsistence level, no matter what. So the distribution of income was basically a question of distribution between land-holders and capitalists.

Note: This chapter is based on a transcription of the presentation given at the Conference "Celebrating 200 Years of Ricardian Trade Theory" on May 12, 2017, at the University of Basel, Switzerland.

W.J. Ethier (✉)
Economics Department, University of Pennsylvania, Philadelphia, PA, USA
e-mail: ethierwj@msn.com

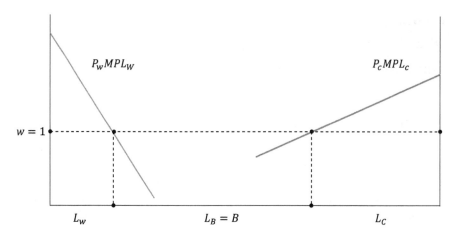

Fig. 15.1 A Ricardian model

I would like to draw attention to an area where I think Ricardo's approach to trade is still nevertheless pertinent to a significant policy-oriented part of the current literature. To approach this, think about a common version of the specific factors model (see Fig. 15.1).

A single mobile factor of production, labor (L), can be used for three purposes:

(1) Producing wheat (W) which also uses sector-specific land. Ricardo's law of diminishing returns therefore applies to labor in that sector.
(2) Producing cloth (C), which also utilizes capital that is sector-specific, so again the law of diminishing returns applies.
(3) Producing a numéraire good, ballast (B), which, as in the simple Ricardian model, is produced only by labor.

As long as ballast is actually being produced, the wage rate (w) is one—so labor is not a significant factor in distributional questions. Then, when international trade enters into the picture, global markets determine the two relative commodity prices and therefore position the diminishing-returns schedules. This determines the allocation of labor between the various sectors. (If the labor force is insufficient for ballast to be produced, the wage loses its anchor and the analysis becomes more complex). Anything that changes one or both of these international relative commodity prices will reallocate labor, and thus produce a magnified effect on either the rent of land or on that of capital, depending on the case.

There is a contemporary literature that is extremely dependent upon this, namely, the literature on the political economy on trade policy. It is based to a large extent on this model and so is thoroughly Ricardian. This literature basically began in the early 1980s with work by Hillman.[1] Its best known incarnation is the

---

[1]Hillman (1982).

Grossman-Helpman model developed in the 1990s.[2] The process it looks at, the effect of rent-seeking on determining trade policy, is not quite the one that Ricardo dealt with. However, the basic building blocks are extremely Ricardian and I regard this as an essentially Ricardian application.

This literature also has a quantitative component, which has largely taken the form of empirical testing of the Grossman-Helpman variant of the political-support model. On the whole, I think this has been very supportive of the overall political-support point of view, which, as I just said, is essentially based on Ricardian concepts—so therefore very kind to Ricardo. In particular, it supports those implications of the political-support model that were implicit in the pre-Grossman-Helpman era of the1980s. So, in that sense, it is supportive of the whole approach.

What it does not support are those predictions of the Grossman-Helpman model itself that are specific to that model. Most of the authors of these empirical works do interpret it as supportive of the Grossman-Helpman model (which illustrates the maxim that if you want to get published, do not start off by trashing the work of potential referees.) To be fair towards Grossman and Helpman, one can also make the criticism that the data used in this empirical work was inappropriate for interpreting the estimated equation as an implication of Grossman and Helpman.

To summarize, this political-economy literature, an application to issues in contemporary international trade with strong policy relevance, is based fundamentally on Ricardian ideas that are independent of a one-factor model. So fundamentally that we seldom bother to point this out. This aspect of Ricardo's thought remains very relevant today.

References

Ethier, W. J. (2012). The political-support approach to protection. *Global Journal of Economics, 1* (01), 1–14.

Grossman, G. M., & Helpman, E. (1994). Protection for sale. *American Economic Review, 84*(4), 833–850.

Hillman, A. L. (1982). Declining industries and political-support protectionist motives. *American Economic Review, 72*(5), 1180–1190.

---

[2]Grossman and Helpman (1994). Ethier (2012) provides an overview.

Chapter 16
What Next for Ricardo? Incorporating More Trade Distortions

Simon Evenett

Abstract Based on a dataset of over 11,000 government announcements and measures implemented, it is shown that trade distortions faced by exporters from G-20 nations have grown markedly since November 2008. In terms of trade coverage, the largest trade distortions are export incentives. Research findings concerning the impact of these export incentives estimated using modern versions of the Ricardian model are discussed.

My task is to try and relate the latest data we have on trade distortions to the Ricardian model and to see where we can shed further light on the trade barriers that matter. So, in this presentation, I will try the following questions:

(1) Which of trade distortions actually matter based on what we can see in the data?
(2) Can the Ricardian model shed light on the impact of the growing resort to trade distortions witnessed since the onset of the global economic crisis?

To do this, I am going to summarize the work of the team that I have in St Gallen that has been systematically collecting data on trade distortions for the past 8 years as part of the *Global Trade Alert* initiative, which we make available to others.[1]

Let me tell you a little bit about the data collection exercise and its origins. In 2009, you may remember people were nervous about a return of protectionism, and many people couched this in terms of us maybe seeing another Smoot-Hawley episode. I actually thought that was the wrong framing for the problem, because if you look at what happened in the early 1980s when we had a severe global downturn, we didn't see a resurgence in tariffs. Instead, we saw a huge number of voluntary export restraints used. So, a hypothesis that came to mind in 2009 was 'New Crisis, New Form of Prevalent Protectionism'.

Note: This chapter is based on a transcription of the presentation given at the Conference "Celebrating 200 Years of Ricardian Trade Theory" on May 12, 2017, at the University of Basel, Switzerland. It also incorporates information from Chap. 4 of the latest (July 2017) report of the Global Trade Alert (Evenett & Fritz, 2017).

[1]This data can be downloaded at http://www.globaltradealert.org/data_extraction

S. Evenett (✉)
Department of Economics, University of St. Gallen, St. Gallen, Switzerland
e-mail: simon.evenett@unisg.ch

© Springer International Publishing AG 2017
R.W. Jones, R. Weder (eds.), *200 Years of Ricardian Trade Theory*,
https://doi.org/10.1007/978-3-319-60606-4_16

If you want to explore that hypothesis, you have to say "right, where are we going to get data on what governments are doing?" We then run into a problem because outside of the agricultural sector, while we do have good data on tariffs and on anti-dumping actions, in fact we have very little data on other forms of trade distortion. So the first task was to collect this data, which could also be used to inform policymakers.

We have tried to collect data on trade or policy decisions that alter the relative treatment of domestic firms compared to their foreign rivals, whatever the form of trade policy is. We have now documented over 11,000 government announcements and measures implemented. A government announcement could be as small as a single presidential decree to raise a tariff on butter, or it could be an Indian budget with thousands of policy interventions. So we have 10,000 of these, all available on our website. We have collected 175% more data on crisis-era policy interventions than the World Trade Organization has managed to collect in its Trade Monitoring Database.[2]

For each policy intervention that we document, we identify the implementing country, the policy instrument that they have used, and whether the policy instrument relates to trade in goods, trade in services, foreign direct investment, or migrant workers. We then look at the products and the sectors and, where appropriate, using United Nations trade data at the six-digit level we identified the potentially affected trading partners. Consequently, this is a sizable data set. Already this data set has been mentioned in nearly 1200 studies in Google Scholar.

Let me show you how we thought about the taxonomy of possible trade policy instruments. Most people's mental mindset is that you have an exporter who is shipping to an importer who might face some traditional market access barrier, like a tariff or anti-dumping measure. We certainly capture that, but we should also be aware that exporters can compete in an importing country against a firm that has received a bailout or some type of subsidy. Then there is a further type of trade distortion, and that is that exporter i may be competing in market j against exporter k, and exporter k has received some type of export incentive. Now, formally, export subsidies of the government to manufacturing are banned. However, if you create the export incentive through the tax system, then the rules are much more ambiguous. So there is this possibility as well (See Fig. 16.1).

In the preparation for the last Global Trade Alert report, published in July 2017, Johannes Fritz and I revisited how we assess the trade affected by crisis-era discriminatory government policies. Much of our original approach was retained—namely, using published trade data to conservatively identify the trading partners affected by a trade distortion[3]—but here we employed more disaggregated trade data

---

[2]This WTO database can be accessed at http://tmdb.wto.org/SearchMeasures.aspx?lang=en-US

[3]Some examples may be helpful. In the case of an import restriction being imposed by country A in product B, we use trade data to identify which foreign trading partners exported more than $1 million dollars of product B to country A in the year before the import restriction was implemented. In the case of an export subsidy offered by country C in product D, then we used trade data to identify the foreign trading partners (E,F,G. ...) where C exports more than $1 million of product D in the year before the subsidy was offered. Call those foreign trading partners'

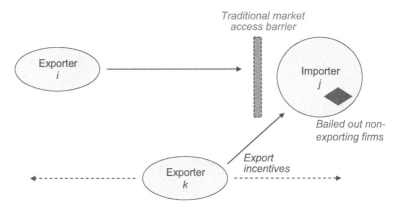

Fig. 16.1 Impact of foreign trade distortions (and reforms) on an exporter. Source: Own figure

to estimate the trade covered by crisis-era commercial distortions.[4] Doing so involved reviewing every since measure in our database and updating measures where necessary. Wherever possible, the identification of trading partners and computations of the size of trade flows affected have been automated, substantially reducing the potential for human error in classification.

In Table 16.1 we report, for 38 different policy instruments whose implementation treats foreign commercial interests worse than domestic rivals, the percentages of G20 exports that compete in markets where a given discriminatory policy instrument was in force. To get a sense of how those percentages varied over time, those calculations were made for each year 2009–2016. We can then compare across policy instruments and over time.

Moreover, bearing in mind that an exporter can face more than one discriminatory policy instrument when competing in a market abroad, we also calculated the total percentage of G20 exports that face some form of crisis-era protectionism (these statistics were presented in Table 16.1). Lastly, we stress that only policy instruments implemented after 1 November 2008 count towards these totals. To the extent that pre-crisis protectionism exists, it does not influence the calculations presented here.

---

markets the destination markets. Then we further consult trade data to see which other nations export (X,Y,Z etc.) more than $1 million of product D to those destination markets. We then identify nations X, Y, and Z as the trading partners affected by the export subsidy implemented by country C.

[4]Specifically, we changed from using four-digit to six-digit classification of products, according to the United Nations Harmonized System.

Table 16.1 Breakdown of G20 export exposure to discriminatory policies, by policy instrument

Discriminatory policy instrument	2009	2010	2011	2012	2013	2014	2015	2016
Tax-based export incentive	33.87	40.28	45.58	54.22	57.48	55.67	54.20	56.23
Trade finance	0.40	1.13	3.10	3.82	3.97	20.20	21.93	24.63
Other export incentive	2.39	3.62	3.63	3.98	14.71	5.64	11.40	15.39
Tax or social insurance relief	1.79	3.08	6.02	7.73	8.64	8.94	9.25	9.53
Import tariff	0.85	1.73	1.82	2.04	3.43	6.81	7.92	8.67
Public procurement localisation	1.31	2.38	2.57	5.52	6.25	6.54	7.38	7.50
Export subsidy	1.76	8.10	13.64	17.85	23.54	23.72	10.80	7.09
Financial grant	0.47	2.71	3.04	3.71	4.77	5.99	6.49	6.83
Public procurement access	3.41	4.32	4.59	4.60	5.00	5.15	5.17	5.19
State loan	0.30	0.55	0.33	0.21	0.35	0.62	2.21	3.73
Bailout (capital injection or equity participation)	2.17	3.05	3.12	3.30	3.62	3.60	3.61	3.69
Import-related non-tariff measure	0.15	0.63	0.66	0.81	1.36	1.64	3.29	3.36
Local sourcing	0.17	0.97	1.31	1.50	1.54	1.99	2.54	2.67
Import ban	0.02	0.38	0.51	0.49	0.69	0.68	2.00	2.06
Production subsidy	0.23	0.44	0.60	0.65	0.62	1.14	1.41	1.62
Import quota	0.24	1.23	1.22	1.27	1.34	1.36	1.29	1.27
Import licensing requirement	0.33	0.25	0.35	0.53	0.62	0.87	1.09	1.17
Anti-dumping (AD) duties	0.17	0.42	0.63	0.77	0.88	0.98	1.03	1.12
Internal taxation of imports	0.43	0.43	0.47	0.53	0.54	0.71	0.98	1.06
Loan guarantee	0.24	0.41	0.41	0.42	0.66	0.75	0.78	0.81
Localisation incentive	0.19	0.34	0.22	0.23	0.22	0.22	0.29	0.71
Instrument unclear	0.00	0.12	0.18	0.25	0.46	0.73	0.77	0.62
Anti-subsidy duties	0.04	0.08	0.15	0.20	0.23	0.29	0.36	0.44
Financial assistance in foreign market	0.00	0.05	0.08	0.08	0.08	0.09	0.22	0.31
Local operations required	0.00	0.00	0.00	0.01	0.02	0.02	0.25	0.30
Interest payment subsidy	1.58	1.77	0.17	0.18	0.20	0.20	0.25	0.28
Import tariff quota	0.24	0.01	0.13	0.23	0.42	0.18	0.21	0.23
In-kind grant	0.00	0.00	0.00	0.00	0.02	0.11	0.14	0.17
Trade balancing measure	0.00	0.00	0.05	0.07	0.07	0.07	0.14	0.16
State aid	0.00	0.00	0.00	0.00	0.01	0.01	0.05	0.13
Public procurement preference margin	0.08	0.07	0.00	0.07	0.10	0.16	0.17	0.12
Consumption subsidy	0.08	0.10	0.10	0.10	0.10	0.10	0.10	0.10
Safeguards	0.03	0.05	0.06	0.06	0.06	0.08	0.08	0.07
Trade payment measure	0.00	0.00	0.00	0.00	0.00	0.00	0.04	0.05
Price stabilisation	0.00	0.00	0.00	0.00	0.00	0.00	0.00	0.00
Local labour use	0.00	0.00	0.00	0.00	0.00	0.00	0.00	0.00
Import incentive	0.00	0.00	0.00	0.00	0.00	0.00	0.00	0.00

(continued)

Table 16.1 (continued)

Discriminatory policy instrument	2009	2010	2011	2012	2013	2014	2015	2016
Anti-circumvention in trade defence	0.00	0.00	0.00	0.00	0.00	0.00	0.00	0.00
All	41.79	52.20	58.09	64.07	67.08	69.91	71.52	73.46

The data in this table refers to the percentage of G20 exports facing a given discriminatory policy instrument that was in effect at the end of the year in question. Note that some policy instruments appear nationality blind but are implemented in a manner that worsens the relative treatment of foreign commercial interests. The entries in this table have been sorted in descending order according to the G20 export exposure at the end of 2016, the final column of this table

16.1 Beggar-Thy-Neighbour Export Measures and Government Subsidies More Generally Are Where the Action Really Is

The policy instruments in Table 16.1 are ranked in descending order in terms of the percentage of G20 exports affected during 2016, helping to identify the crisis-era policy interventions of greatest concern. Interestingly import tariff increases–which as noted earlier in this report get a lot of attention–is "only" the fifth most important trade distortion, affecting 8.67% of G20 exports by the end of 2016.[5] The top four discriminatory policy interventions in terms of G20 export coverage relate to various forms of state fiscal incentives. The top three relate to measures to promote national exports as the expense of other countries' exporters.

By far the most prevalent trade distortions are those associated with tax-based incentives for exporters. These may involve lower taxes on inputs, rebates of other kinds, and provisions that ultimately reduce the taxes on profits earned from exporting. There was a significant expansion in the range of such tax-based export incentives early in the crisis; so much so that by the end of 2009, already a third of G20 exports competed in overseas markets against foreign firms eligible for export-related tax breaks. By 2016 that percentage had risen to 56%.[6]

Reinforced by other forms of export incentives and a ramping up of trade finance over time—much of the latter appears to have departed considerably from its original purpose and increasingly looks like export subsidisation through the back door–the total amount of G20 exports facing various forms of crisis-era

---

[5]Trade defence measures (antidumping and anti-subsidy duties) are even lower down the list. Despite the considerable attention given to these measures in the media and in the academic literature, they are simply not where the trade policy action is.

[6]China's considerable contribution to the expansion in exports competing against subsidised rivals is documented and discussed in Evenett, Fritz, and Yang (2012).

Table 16.2 Breakdown of G20 export exposure to discriminatory policies, by United Nations MAST classification of trade measures

MAST chapter	Policy instruments	2009	2010	2011	2012	2013	2014	2015	2016
D	Contingent trade protection	0.20	0.48	0.70	0.83	0.95	1.05	1.11	1.22
E	Non-automatic licensing, quotas	0.83	1.86	2.14	2.44	2.99	3.01	4.52	4.57
F	Price control measures	0.43	0.43	0.47	0.53	0.54	0.71	0.98	1.06
G	Finance measures	0.00	0.00	0.00	0.00	0.00	0.00	0.04	0.05
I	Investment measures	0.36	1.16	1.41	1.64	1.67	2.10	2.78	3.23
L	Subsidies (except export subsidies)	5.43	7.78	9.44	11.88	13.39	14.67	15.89	17.21
M	Government procurement	4.54	6.38	6.64	9.59	10.73	11.04	11.31	11.39
P	Export measures	34.47	42.80	49.78	56.74	59.01	58.84	60.22	62.86
	Import tariff measures	0.85	1.73	1.82	2.04	3.43	6.81	7.92	8.67
	Instrument unclassified	0.15	0.76	0.84	1.00	1.66	2.37	4.06	3.98

The data in this table refers to the percentage of G20 exports facing a given class of discriminatory policy instrument that was in effect at the end of the year in question. The entries in this table have been sorted in descending order according to the G20 export exposure at the end of 2016, the final column of this table

protectionism has reached 73% by the end of 2016.[7] That percentage is ten times the headline percentage found in WTO monitoring reports.

It should now be apparent why looking at the current era through a Smoot-Hawley lens is inappropriate. Governments can distort international commerce in many different ways and there is no reason why governments must respond in the same way to each global economic crisis. The reality is that, since the onset of the most recent global economic crisis, governments have put most of their efforts in stealing market share for their exporters away from foreign rivals rather than shutting down imports.

Moreover, rather than face the pain and reality of adjustment, in a wide range of sectors governments have sought to prop up firms with all manner of state largesse.[8] By the end of 2016, one-sixth of all G20 exports[9] competed in foreign markets

[7]Had we kept working at the more aggregate four-digit product classification this percentage would be closer to 90%.

[8]See the data in row L, relating to non-export related subsidies, in Table 16.2.

[9]To be clear, the many bailouts of financial institutions during the crisis era do not count towards this estimate. Effectively, only subsidies to farmers and manufacturers will affect trade in goods and so the estimates presented here.

against a domestic firm that had received some form of state financial assistance (excluding export-related assistance.) While overcapacity in certain sectors (steel and aluminium being leading examples) has received attention among trade policy-makers and at the G20, the problem of state largesse affects a far wider swathe of global agriculture and manufacturing.

16.2 Implications for Research Using the Ricardian Model

As far as crisis-era trade distortions are concerned, the action is in state financial support, not import restrictions. Fortunately, the modern version of the Ricardian model (Eaton & Kortum, 2002) can be readily adapted for econometric purposes to accommodate different types of trade distortion, including export and production subsidies.[10] In two studies with Johannes Fritz–one on the exports of Least Developed Countries and one on extra-exports of the European Union–we have estimated the effects of different crisis-era trade distortions using Ricardian theory-founded gravity equations. Interestingly, in both cases export incentives to rival firms were the biggest factor holding back sales abroad (Evenett & Fritz, 2015, 2016). The overall effect of such export incentives has been to reshuffle global trade flows, reminding us that trade distortions can affect both the distribution as well as the level of world trade.

References

Eaton, J., & Kortum, S. (2002). Technology, geography, and trade. *Econometrica, 70*(5), 1741–1779.

Evenett, S. J., & Fritz, J. (2015, June 16). *Throwing sand in the wheels: How foreign trade distortions slowed LDC export-led growth*. London: CEPR.

Evenett, S. J., & Fritz, J. (2016). *Europe fettered: The impact of crisis-era trade distortions on exports from the European Union*. Prepared for the Sweden's National Board of Trade.

Evenett, S. J., & Fritz, J. (2017). *Will awe Trump rules?* The 21st report of the global trade alert. London: CEPR Press.

Evenett, S. J., Fritz, J., & Jing, Y. C. (2012). Beyond dollar exchange-rate targeting: China's crisis-era export management regime. *Oxford Review of Economic Policy, 28*(2), 284–300.

---

[10]Care is needed here. The general equilibrium effects of various trade distortions still need further work.

Chapter 17
200 Years of Ricardian Theory: The Missing Dynamics

Esteban Rossi-Hansberg

Abstract In recent years, trade economists have started to incorporate dynamics in international trade models, using frameworks that are at their core Ricardian. Using a quantitative model to estimate the effect of dynamic knowledge innovation, I argue that reducing trade barriers leads to large gains from trade as a result of these dynamics. I illustrate these effects with a quantification of the impact of trade barrier reduction between Latin American countries. Productivity levels and their distribution in space are estimated to be much greater when including the dynamic effects that result from the trade liberalization.

I am not a classically trained trade economist. I studied at Chicago when there were really no trade economists there, so I studied macroeconomics and got interested initially in trade as a secondary topic, and so it is excellent (and somewhat surprising) to be here with all of you. When I think about Ricardian trade theory and the kind of work I have been interested in during the last few years, the key aspect that I think requires more attention is dynamics. So I will use my talk to make the case for that.

I came to trade theory because I was interested in the distribution of economic activity in space, and trade was just an example where the economic activity in space matters. I was also very interested in regional economics, and urban economics. In fact, since Eaton and Kortum's famous paper,[1] we have experienced the explosion of a set of frameworks that have at their core this Ricardian theory, but that can be used for international trade, but also for urban economics and regional economics, once you sprinkle in a little bit of agglomeration and congestion.

A group of us have been using these models, along with a lot of data, to try to think about general equilibrium counterfactuals in all these spatial dimensions.

Note: This chapter is based on a transcription of the presentation given at the Conference "Celebrating 200 Years of Ricardian Trade Theory" on May 12, 2017, at the University of Basel, Switzerland.

[1]Eaton and Kortum (2002).

E. Rossi-Hansberg (✉)
Department of Economics and Woodrow Wilson School, Princeton University, Princeton, NJ, USA
e-mail: erossi@princeton.edu

Eaton and Kortum showed us how to do it for trade, and since then, we have expanded the set of economic situations in which we can use them to perform general equilibrium counterfactuals, as many of you have already mentioned today. Most of these counterfactuals are, of course, computed conditional on the local characteristics at the country level, the regional level or, maybe, the block level if we are thinking about a city. One of those characteristics is productivity. The conclusion from these models, keeping fixed these local characteristics, is that the gains from trade are in general small. Think about voters living in some region that has been completely changed over a decade. As a trade economist, you may say to those voters "if you shut down trade, you will have 2 percent lower consumption". They may say, "Well, I'll take it, I'll take my old town with 2 percent less consumption".

So the question is, do we believe these numbers, or do we think these numbers are missing important channels? I believe that we are missing some channels. Ralph [Ossa] mentioned one of these channels. Namely, that we should considers substitution across sectors with elasticities of substitution that are potentially a lot lower than the ones we use in some of these calculations. Costinot and Rodriguez-Clare have some estimations of the resulting gains if we do so[2] and Ralph has a paper on that, too.[3] There are two other channels that I would like to underscore here:

(1) Internal trade: That, is, the fact that there is a lot of trade interactions within countries. We should take into account how the internal distribution of economic activity varies with trade barriers.
(2) Dynamics: That is, the fact that productivity levels are not constant. We think that when we open up a market, productivity levels will be affected.

Let me focus on productivity dynamics. There is a good reason to think that there are important dynamics going on here. The basic argument is simply that if you are thinking about undertaking some costly innovative activity, you need to understand your market and the size of it in order to make that decision; understand whether it is profitable to invest or not. And so there is this very basic logic in economics that tells you that, inevitably, these dynamic effects have to be there.

There is also a question, of course, of how large these dynamic effects are. Now, writing models with dynamics that are quantitatively flexible, such as the Eaton-Kortum model and the follow-up models, is very hard. Part of the reason why it is so hard is that the state space includes the characteristics of all countries and regions. The set of state variables in the dynamic investment problem is extremely large. Therefore, there have been very few attempts to try to do this. And most of the papers that have attempted this have had to take some short-cuts. You can add dynamics in different ways and there is some literature, or some emerging literature, that has been trying to do this, but as you can see, all this literature is very recent (see Fig. 17.1).

---

[2]Costinot and Rodriguez-Clare (2014).
[3]Ossa (2015).

- Hard problem since dynamic investment problem has dynamic characteristics of all countries / regions as state variables

- Important, though, since trade frictions likely affect investment decisions as they affect profitability of investments
    - » Same with mobility frictions and more generally any spatial friction

- Dynamics can be the result of:
    - » Capital accumulation: Eaton, Kortum and Nieman (2016) and Anderson, Larch and Yotov (2015)
    - » Improvements in technology through innovation and diffusion: Desmet and Rossi-Hansberg (2015) and Desmet, Nagy and Rossi-Hansberg (2017)
    - » Transitional dynamics from mobility: Caliendo, Dvorkin and Parro (2015)

Fig. 17.1 Incorporating dynamics: a few attempts. Source: Illustration based on the presentation slide of the Conference

You can try to add dynamics to capital accumulation, to improvements in technology, or to diffusion—Jonathan [Eaton] talked a little bit about that and I'm going to talk more about it today—or you can think about transitional dynamics caused by mobility and the effect that workers moving to different regions is going to have over time, which Lorenzo Caliendo and Fernando Parro[4] have been working on.

I have been thinking about the effect of trade on technology and the fact that the investment decisions of firms are going to be affected by market size. When you think about technology and the fact that it is endogenous, you can think about diffusion, which is complicated. That does not mean that it is not present or not important, but it is complicated because it is so hard to measure and see. You can think about patents. However, when we talk about innovation, we talk about all improvements in technology, so you do not want to limit yourself to patents. We are also talking about small improvements in technology, better techniques, so thinking only about patents is going to miss a lot of the real effects.

In my view the more important economic mechanism here is market size. If a firm is thinking about innovating, its market size is going to determine whether it will do so or not. The key aspect of this is the replicability of technology: The fact that when I invent that one thing, I want to use it as many times as I can. What trade does, at the end of the day, is that it allows me to use that invention many times over. So the key implication from reducing trade frictions is that it allows producers to invent things and use them more often; exploit the replicability of technology.

---

[4]Caliendo, Dvorkin, and Parro (2015).

- In the aggregate, correlation between income per capita and population density increases with development.

  » -0.11 in Africa but 0.5 in North America

  » Also evident across U.S. counties and zip codes

- Suggests that innovation happens in places with larger market size.

Fig. 17.2 Dynamic Ricardian comparative advantage: market size. Source: Illustration based on the presentation slide of the Conference

There are some smoking guns that tell you that this is important: One is, for example, the fact that the correlation between income per capita and population density increases with development. So, in areas that are more developed, the correlation between income per capita and density is high, suggesting that some of this innovation may be happening at a local level. Something similar happens when you look at the data of firms in cities (Fig. 17.2).

It is very hard to pin down and be very precise about measuring this exactly, because these technologies are sometimes a little bit elusive, but when you try to organize the local data through these ideas, there seems to be something there.

Together with Klaus Desmet and Dávid Kristián Nagy,[5] I have tried to use one of these quantitative models to think about the effect of trade and migration on dynamic knowledge innovation, and whether reducing trade barriers will have a much greater impact if we incorporate some of these effects. We have measured it as well as we can, given the available data on growth, migration, production, etc. We try to do the best job possible in quantifying these models and although we're not going to test them, we're going to use all the data that we can to get the best number we can put on the table.

That number may be imperfect in all sorts of ways, but it is the best number that we can come up with. And let me say that this exercise passes one test. If I use all these data to quantify the model for the year 2000, then I can move backwards in time using the model to try to predict the past. When I run it backwards and see how the model does in terms of explaining population counts across regions in 1950, it does really well. The good fit gives us some confidence in the model.

The implication of this model is that we have large gains from trade due to the dynamic effect on innovation. In particular, the elasticity of the present discounted value (PDV) of real GDP to trade costs is about 0.75. You can also think about gains from relaxing migration restrictions and those are also very large [elasticity of the PDV of real GDP to migration costs is 1.24] (Fig. 17.3).

---

[5]Desmet, Nagy, and Rossi-Hansberg (2017).

- In Desmet, Nagy and Rossi-Hansberg (2017) we incorporate this mechanism in a quantitative dynamic spatial framework

  » Spatial resolution of 1x1 degrees for whole world

  » Innovation due to market size, diffusion, costly trade, and costly migration

  » Quantified using local population and output, trade, migration, wellbeing, and growth data

---

- Fairly successful in backcasting exercise from 2000

  » Correlation between population in 1950 is 0.97 and in population changes is 0.74

- Leads to large *gains from trade* due to dynamic gains

  » Elasticity of the PDV of real GDP to trade costs is 0.75

- Leads to large *gains from migration*

  » Elasticity of the PDV of real GDP to migration costs is 1.24

Fig. 17.3 Are dynamic effects large? Source: Illustration based on the presentation slide of the Conference

17.1   A Free Trade Agreement for Latin America

Let me illustrate with one particular exercise. It gives me the opportunity to show you some nice maps with lots of colors as well as the level of heterogeneity that you can incorporate into these models. We quantify a model of the whole world economy at a 1×1 degree level; so each one of these squares is 1×1 degree. We have some data from [William D.] Nordhaus (G-Econ 4.0) at that level, so it has some internal trade and some international trade, of course.

Now imagine the following exercise. Assume that, perhaps motivated by Trump's election, Latin American countries sign a trade agreement between themselves. The countries in Latin America reduce trade costs between them by 35 percent. Internal country trade costs remain the same. We want to think about the technology implications of this reduction. What I have here [in Fig. 17.4] is the change in productivity at impact when you sign that agreement. It doesn't include the U.S., so, it's from Mexico southwards. This is, of course, a policy that has been under discussion many times in Latin America. You can see the productivity increases that come as a result of the policy. They are very varied across regions. Some regions gain a lot, in particular Argentina and some regions of Peru. Mexico gains very little, because it trades a lot with the U.S. already. These are the gains in productivity; but note that these numbers are really small. The largest number on this scale is 0.009 (9×10^{-3}). This means that the impact on those regions that

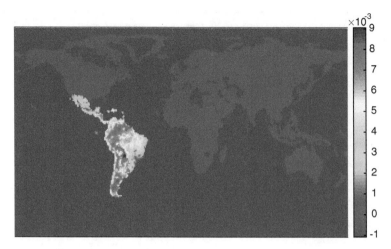

Fig. 17.4 Latin American trade agreement: productivity change at impact. Source: Illustration based on the presentation slide of the Conference

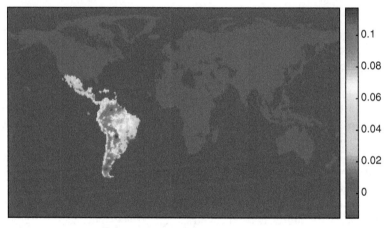

Fig. 17.5 Latin American trade agreement: productivity change after 50 years. Source: Illustration based on the presentation slide of the Conference

gained the most is close to 1% and a lot of the other regions gained essentially nothing in terms of productivity. Furthermore, if you are outside of Latin America, this is a policy that essentially does not affect you.

Now I'm going to move forward in time. Fifty years later, what do these gains in productivity look like? The numbers in Fig. 17.5 are no longer multiplied by 10^{-3}. They tell me that the regions gaining the most are now improving their productivity

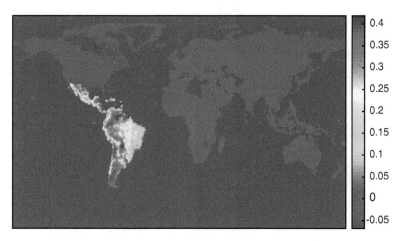

Fig. 17.6 Latin American trade agreement: productivity change in balanced growth path. Source: Illustration based on the presentation slide of the Conference

by about 10% as a result of the free trade agreement that was signed. The color pattern is very similar, though, which means that the relative effects do not change that much. Mexico still looks as if it does not gain that much, whereas Peru and Argentina are seen to gain more.

In the model the distribution of economic activity will converge eventually to a balanced growth path. Figure 17.6 shows the spatial productivity distribution in the balanced growth path. The highest numbers are now in the region of 40%. Countries are now saying "so we signed this free trade agreement and productivity started to improve, and now these are serious numbers". These incentives to innovate created an improvement in productivity over time. But more importantly, look at the North of Mexico. Eventually, the North of Mexico became the connection between the United States and the block of countries in the free trade area. So productivity started to increase there. Of course, in a model where there are no dynamics, we are going to completely miss this type of effect. And so the question is, how much of the gains from trade are coming from these dynamic productivity changes.

Figure 17.7 shows the level and growth effects. The growth effects disappear over time, but it takes a long time for that to happen. Why is this? Well, how much you want to invest depends on what others have invested in the past, so that creates the sequentiality that leads to very protracted effects from these trade agreements. Importantly, the numbers showing the increases in the present discounted value of real GDP and welfare are of an order of magnitude greater than what you would get in a model without any dynamics. Thus, a lot of the gains are further in the future. They are much larger, because now you are impacting the growth rate, and so the effects on technology and output accumulate over time. As I mentioned before, there are a lot of issues with these numbers, and we can question them in all sorts of

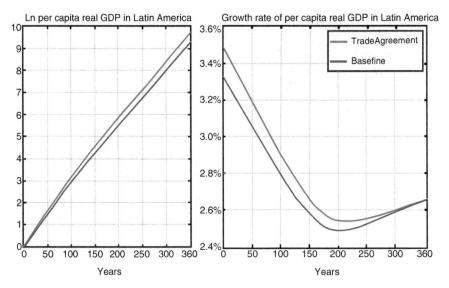

Fig. 17.7 Latin American trade agreement: real GDP percentage growth. Source: Illustration based on the presentation slide of the Conference

ways, but it is some indication that focusing more on some of these dynamics is a good idea.

17.2   Conclusion

To conclude, we need more work on establishing more exactly this link between market size and innovation, and to measure in a better way the parameters that govern this relationship. We need more models that have dynamics and that allow us to introduce capital, through consumption and savings decisions, together with these innovation decisions. There is a lot to develop here and I think this is one of the areas in which we can push these Ricardian theories quite a bit further. There are a lot of smoking guns around that show us that this is important. One of those smoking guns can be found next to Bill Gates, when he said, "I wish for a week that we could shut down trade and then, you know, Boeing, Microsoft, Hollywood, pharma would resize their R&D departments for a couple of weeks for fun. And then two weeks later people would go 'Holy smokes, that was not a very good deal'."[6]

---

[6]Financial Times, April 18, 2016.

References

Anderson, J. E., Larch, M., & Yotov, Y. V. (2015). *Growth and trade with frictions: A structural estimation framework*. NBER: National Bureau of Economic Research, No. w21377.

Caliendo, L., Dvorkin, M., & Parro, F. (2015). *Trade and labor market dynamics*. RIETI Discussion Paper Series, 16-E-050.

Costinot, A., & Rodriguez-Clare, A. (2014). Trade theory with numbers: Quantifying the consequences of globalization. In G. Gopinath, E. Helpman, & K. Rogoff (Eds.), *Handbook of international economics* (Vol. 4). Amsterdam: Elsevier.

Desmet, K., Nagy, D. K., & Rossi-Hansberg, E. (2017). The geography of development. *Journal of Political Economy* (forthcoming).

Desmet, K., & Rossi-Hansberg, E. (2015). On the spatial economic impact of global warming. *Journal of Urban Economics, 88*, 16–37.

Eaton, J., & Kortum, S. (2002). Technology, geography, and trade. *Econometrica, 70*(5), 1741–1779.

Eaton, J., Kortum, S., & Neiman, B. (2016). Obstfeld and Rogoff's international macro puzzles: A quantitative assessment. *Journal of Economic Dynamics and Control, 72*, 5–23.

Ossa, R. (2015). Why trade matters after all. *Journal of International Economics, 97*(2), 266–277.

Chapter 18
Final Panel Discussion: Wilfred J. Ethier, Simon Evenett, Esteban Rossi-Hansberg and Rolf Weder

Andrew Lee

Abstract This chapter records the panel discussion that took place with Wilfred J. Ethier, Simon Evenett and Esteban Rossi-Hansberg, chaired by Rolf Weder. It includes comments and questions from the audience regarding these presentations (Chaps. 15, 16 and 17, respectively) and emphasizes the main challenges faced by Ricardian trade theory today. It deals with topics such as how to develop the Ricardian model to reflect contemporary issues, the backlash against international trade within societies, the potential long-run impact of President Trump's policies on international trade, the implications of uncertainty for production and trade patterns, the testing of the proposition that there are gains from trade, and the subject of international trade and migration.

18.1 Questions on Ethier's, Evenett's and Rossi-Hansberg's Presentations

Rolf Weder (chair of the panel discussion) Before we start the panel discussion, I would like to open the floor by asking you for questions and comments regarding the presentations we have seen from Wilfred Ethier [Chap. 15], Simon Evenett [Chap. 16] and Esteban Rossi-Hansberg [Chap. 17]. If I may, I will begin by asking a question to you, Bill [Wilfred Ethier]. The model you spoke about looks like the specific factors model. Is that correct?

Wilfred J. Ethier Yes, it is the even version of the specific factors model, i.e. the version where there is an equal number of factors and goods. Another variant is uneven, where it does not have ballast [see Chap. 15].

Note: This chapter is based on a transcription of the discussion held at the Conference "Celebrating 200 Years of Ricardian Trade Theory" on May 12, 2017, at the University of Basel in Switzerland. The discussion in this chapter refers, in particular, to the contents in Chaps. 15, 16 and 17 of this book.

A. Lee (✉)
Cooperative State University Karlsruhe, Karlsruhe, Germany
e-mail: lee@dhbw-karlsruhe.de

© Springer International Publishing AG 2017
R.W. Jones, R. Weder (eds.), *200 Years of Ricardian Trade Theory*,
https://doi.org/10.1007/978-3-319-60606-4_18

Rolf Weder So your argument is basically that the whole distributional issue—focusing on labor and rent of different types of land—is, in principle, already embedded in the model. Right?

Wilfred J. Ethier Yes, the political economy of trade policy is all about Ricardian concerns. One interesting point, though, is that most of the papers in this area never refer at all to Ricardo, even though I think it is the intellectual basis of all of this. I guess this is a situation where if a contribution is so fundamental and is so ubiquitously adopted, then a certain intellectual winners' curse applies: Nobody bothers to refer to you!

Harris Dellas Why do you need the Ricardian element at all in this? What is the difference to the standard specific factors model that appears, for example, in Ron's textbook [pointing to Ron Jones]?

Wilfred J. Ethier A natural question to ask is about the distribution of income between land, capital and labor. Ricardo's concern was between land and capital, and labor was basically at the subsistence level.

Scott Taylor So, if what you showed us is a Ricardian model and what we saw earlier today is a Ricardian model, then I guess it's really true that Ricardo was extremely smart in picking the one-factor model to make his gains from trade argument.

Wilfred J. Ethier Yes. He chose the most appropriate vehicle for what he wanted to do.

Rolf Weder Thank you, Bill. Do we have any questions or comments on Simon Evenett's presentation [in Chap. 16]?

Jonathan Eaton Looking at some data you mentioned relating to trade distortions, does this include elements such as U.S. EXIM [Export-Import Bank of the United States] bank loans?

Simon Evenett It does for other countries, but we don't have much recorded for the U.S. EXIM Bank, although we do have some loans. I'm glad you raised export finance. There has been a huge amount of very bad policy innovation in export financing. A great example is the United Kingdom, which now has a scheme that will actually give foreigners money to buy British goods. So you don't give the export subsidy directly to the British exporter, you give it to the customer. That's an area of innovation, and you will find similar innovations from Japan and South Korea as well.

Peter Egger You mentioned Chinese exports being eligible for export-related tax breaks. Does this also cover foreign firms based in China that re-export?

Simon Evenett Yes. They are eligible as well. So, of course, any Chinese firm which exports to a foreign market will be competing against other countries and, of course, these Chinese firms have an advantage here, being able to win larger market shares. These policies have been copied by the Brazilians, by the Indians, by the South Africans, so this is a disease that is spreading.

Rolf Weder Thank you, Simon. Before we proceed to the panel discussion, I have a question for you, Esteban, about your presentation [in Chap. 17]. In the past, we have always said that as soon as you allow for changes in the labor coefficient in a Ricardian model, as soon as you allow for endogenous innovation—and this is part of your model—we are in an area of great uncertainty, because we do not really fully understand how firms do this kind of thing. So, how solid are these numbers?

Esteban Rossi-Hansberg We do one check with the data, which is that we use growth experiences across regions and calibrate so that the model gets increases in GDP roughly correct in the world. We then match migration costs, so that the movements of people and economic activity that this generates are exactly consistent with what we observe in the real world for a period. And so, it's an aggregate calibration in the sense that it's not a micro-calibration at the firm level. In some sense, I would argue that we want something like this [aggregate calibration], because these productivity levels hide a lot of actions, such as entry, decisions of the individual firms, etc. There are all kinds of things that are summarized by these productivity levels. The moment that you go to a firm and you say, "OK, I want to try to exactly measure your innovation or your patent creation", you narrow the interpretation to a point that you're leaving a lot of other things behind. And so, in some sense, I'm a little partial towards this kind of local, but aggregate type of quantification, rather than the micro-, firm-level quantification.

Rolf Weder Thank you, Esteban. OK, I would now like to start the panel discussion.

18.2   Panel Discussion

Rolf Weder The idea of this final panel is not to solve all the problems in the world, but to ask the question what we as trade theorists can contribute to this, and maybe consider how we should adjust trade theory to cope with all these challenges. So my question to you panelists is the following: when you think about what each of you presented and we compare this with what we have heard throughout the whole day, does this basically imply that we should just make numerous refinements? We started with a very simple theory two hundred years ago, and now we are refining the model more and more, so that it becomes much closer to the real world, without really fundamentally changing how we think about international trade. Is that basically the message that you are giving, or do you see a challenge in that we have to take things into account that are radically different from what we did in the past? This is what I would like to ask you, the panelists, before we open up the discussion.

Wilfred J. Ethier My reaction would be to say that we are not concentrating on refining and developing the Ricardian model. We're concentrating on addressing real issues, and we're finding that basic Ricardian ideas turn out to be accurate, which is sort of the reverse of your suggestion.

Esteban Rossi-Hansberg I agree with that.

Simon Evenett I think that the answer to your question is yes and no. In the context of my specific presentation, for sure, given the spread of these export incentives, they must be affecting competition with trillions of dollars of trade. And presumably these are very wide-ranging so that they must have general equilibrium effects. So, one refinement would be the systematic inclusion of export subsidies in figuring out what this is doing in international trade, what kind of knock-on effects we have on labor market, you can see where this is going. So I think that is a clear refinement there. And then the answer "no" to the question "is there something profound we are missing"? Well, if you want to look at the crisis era seriously, I think you have to take finances and input. Because the reality is that most firms have to pay their suppliers and their staff before they receive revenue. So the guys in macro are a long way down the road. They forecast this years ago; cash-in-advance models, and things like this. But I wonder if you really want to understand the crisis response on the trade side, one should think about the consequences of finance drying up and the public policy interventions to reintroduce finance. So that might require a much more elaborate re-do of the model, but again, the fundamental insight is right, the Ricardian insight is there.

Esteban Rossi-Hansberg My view is that I would not characterize what we are doing as some kind of refinement of Ricardo. I think one of the components of it is Ricardo, but these models now are much richer than that, and have many other elements. I would say they have Ricardo, and they have Krugman, and they have Ethier, and they have Jones, and they have Eaton and all sorts of people in them that have contributed to the ideas, and Ricardo is one of them. It is a core idea and an important idea for the trade component of it, but there are many other components of these models. I think that the key is that we now have the methods and the data to combine these different forces and get some results out of them.

Rolf Weder Is your message that we have been underestimating the gains from trade, so we basically have to tell the world that exchange of the factors of production and goods is much more important than previously thought? And we do this in order to support, let's say, a situation where we still have open borders? Is that what you mean?

Esteban Rossi-Hansberg From my perspective, and from the numbers that come out of the frameworks that I have been analyzing and quantifying, the answer is clearly yes. That is, the gains are larger, and to the extent that this matters for the public and in the public debate, to understand how large those gains are, you should definitely say so.

Rolf Weder   But why, then, do we have this kind of backlash where people have become more critical? Is it because we have not been convincing enough in showing the importance of it to society, or is it because we have maybe overlooked something?

Esteban Rossi-Hansberg   Or maybe because our politicians are not looking at the future benefits, but are short-sighted and evaluate only the immediate effects, which are perhaps large, but not as large.

Rolf Weder   Do you agree, Simon?

Simon Evenett   Yes, when I try to listen to what the critics are saying, I get the sense that they equate trade liberalization with substantial redistributions of income. If there are extra gains, those gains are seen to be very narrowly shared, and we, by arguing that the pie is larger, come across as being quite naïve advocates of essentially a small minority that are receiving a lot of extra benefits. In that sense we've come across as 'useful idiots' in the eyes of some of the critics. And no one wants to feel like a useful idiot. But I do think that is a large part of it.

Rolf Weder   Bill, would you like to add something?

Wilfred J. Ethier   Well, I agree with that. It's not just, though, that there's the perception of a small number of people capturing most of the benefit. It's also the exact opposite, that there is this relatively small pot of people taking a big hit.

Esteban Rossi-Hansberg   There is another aspect of this discussion, which occurs within a country where there is a segregation issue. If a group that is affected is in a particular location, how you deal with that location matters a lot, which is why researchers have been studying certain cities that have been declining. Therefore, incorporating all these issues about local segregation and the decline of cities is as important as, or perhaps more important than the fact that trade policy is going to have a direct effect on these people. At the same time, we need to really try to understand the key problem of local prices. I don't think we understand local prices and the local effects on real wages, because we don't have very good price data at a local level that includes the basket of products that is actually consumed. And so because of that, we don't have a good sense, a good measurement of the real effects that this is having. If we want to make progress in understanding the effects of trade on income distribution, we need to collect prices and talk about real wages and actual consumption in these locations.

Rolf Weder   OK, do we have any questions from the audience?

Ralph Ossa[1]   I agree with the panelists that if you ask why there is so much skepticism of world trade and globalization, a lot has to do with adjustment costs, especially in the U.S. with the import competition from China. But if you think more broadly about skepticism towards trade agreements, I think another important element is that there are all sorts of policies in these trade agreements that are just

---

[1]Professor of Economics, Department of Economics, University of Zurich.

not classic trade liberalization measures: investor-state dispute settlement, intellectual property protection, standards, all sorts of things that we haven't captured in any of our models. I think we run the risk of instinctively saying that we love trade agreements, because they're called trade agreements, but what is controversial about them is not really the trade aspect but rather the other elements. If you listen to the critics, they will often explicitly say this. I think that this needs to be studied and we haven't done much about that.

Rolf Weder I agree. Kurt?

Kurt Schmidheiny[2] Esteban, you mentioned migration and its welfare implication. In my view, migration and labor protection are where we have a deviation from Ricardian theory. When you look at welfare, do you distinguish between the welfare effect on migrants and the welfare effect on a country level, on those who do not leave?

Esteban Rossi-Hansberg You can measure the welfare effects for different types of people and these are models in which welfare is not going to equalize because there are mobility costs. So you can calculate different statistics. The ones that I gave you in terms of those elasticities are averages, but you can definitely decompose them. In these models we have large endowment effects; if you are a person who was born in beautiful Switzerland and you get to live here and work here, you get an endowment effect that other people who were not born here don't have. By way of migration costs, they would need to pay in order to 'get in', and so there are going to be big welfare differences as a result of that. The changes in welfare frictions take some of these away, so some people are going to lose as a result of losing those endowment effects. But that is all taken into account in these numbers that I gave you.

Rolf Weder Yes, Scott.

M. Scott Taylor Esteban showed us the long-run effects of trade liberalization and Simon was talking about how protection changed with the crisis. So I guess what I'm wondering now is if you put those two together, will there be a long-run effect of Donald Trump? Will, in twenty years from now, the world have gravitated to a different place than it would have otherwise? Esteban, it looked like your model wasn't very homeostatic. Where you end up depends on where you started and maybe some short-run deviations would alter that, so what do we think of the long-run effects of protection in the era of Trump?

Wilfred J. Ethier Each crisis generates its own response, and that response in turn generates subsequent constraints. So, Smoot-Hawley and all of that protection in the Great Depression generated more bilateral liberalization, which generated voluntary export restraints, which led to the Uruguay Round. So the question is

---

[2]Professor of Economics, Faculty of Business and Economics, University of Basel.

what type of damage will President Trump do that will generate responses to that. The thing about it is that he seems inherently unpredictable.

Simon Evenett To go on from exactly that point and to bring in Esteban's point as well: I think we need to think about scenarios. One scenario is that the rest of the world thinks that Trump is unreliable, and so they form their own regional blocs. Another response might be to say there won't be any big trade deals, because the U.S. won't want to be part of any and it doesn't look like the Chinese are serious about doing genuine trade reform in trade deals. In this case, we're in a world of unilateral trade reform. I would then go back to Esteban's model and say that if I want to expand the market size for my innovative firms, I'll start giving them export incentives. The potential market size increases the incentive to innovate, and so, in that scenario, you might actually combine what I've found with Esteban's logic, and that might be a way of building a more sophisticated answer to the Trump question.

Harris Dellas Do your models account for the possibility that we have relocation of economic activity as a result of uncertainty? Think what happened in the 1990s when we had voluntary export restraints and Japanese car manufacturers shifted production to the U.S.

Simon Evenett Yes, and to reinforce your point, last year General Electric's CEO announced publicly that they would localize production. They used to produce railway locomotives at one place in the United States and they now have five production facilities near to governments that buy huge numbers of locomotives, mainly in emerging markets. I think if you dig further, you will find in a number of sectors companies with very active so-called localization policies, which are essentially moving production facilities closer to the customers. So I think you're on to something, and we just haven't modeled it.

Harris Dellas You don't have any quantitative information?

Simon Evenett No, but there are clearly enough examples out there to motivate someone who wanted to research in that area.

Harris Dellas It is interesting to start thinking about the implications of uncertainty for production and trade patterns. Now, Trump is just an example of this. As I have not followed the literature, I am curious to know what is happening in this area or whether people think this is secondary in comparison to other things we have heard about.

Esteban Rossi-Hansberg My reading of the literature, which may be wrong, is that there was a literature on uncertainty in trade, but this died out because it was not reaching very different conclusions or anything that was particularly insightful, relative to thinking of it as some form of trade friction. I don't know of any efforts to combine uncertainty as a concept with this quantitative framework to revisit that question again. There are people at the LSE, [Francesco] Caselli and Silvana [Tenreyro], who have studied some of the implications of uncertainty in these models, but it is under-researched, I would agree.

Rolf Weder Roy?

Roy J. Ruffin There seems to be a disconnect between what we do about gains from trade and the Barro approach, which does not analyze the gains from trade by looking at the models in international trade that say there are gains from trade. The approach of "I want to test the model and make sure that the model is right"—we are not asking that question. But then the question is how do we test this proposition that there really are trade gains? How would we then go about actually testing the model?

Jonathan Eaton There are different ways of testing and we tend to go back to econometrics and look at standard errors, but I think there's another type, which is very much the physics model; here's a parsimonious paradigm, let's see how far we can push it. And let's take it to new data. We can reconcile the model with bilateral trade data, but now let us look at price data, because the model also has implications for price data. So, I think that's a more robust way of testing, which is to move the model ahead. I think this is the nice thing about this experiment; there is something wrong, the model is failing, but then, what's parsimonious fits. Peter [Egger] would be able to formalize this much more. But what I read about, although I don't understand physics very well, is that this seems to be the way a lot of the physics models get tested. So Newtonian physics may be doing fine here, but if somebody takes a photograph from outer space and something is wrong, they have to start rethinking. I think that's the different ways these models work.

Peter Egger Where physics has an easier life than we do is that it never has to deal with counterfactuals. We have to think ex-ante, before changing variables, and reflect on how it would eventually affect the world, so in some way, we have a more difficult task than physics.

Lukas Hohl[3] However, some issues of the Ricardian model have already been tested in economic experiments.

Simon Evenett I know nothing about physics so I'm only going to talk about economics. You may remember the Leamer and Levinsohn survey on testing trade theory from the mid-1990s.[4] One point they made, which I thought made a lot of sense, was that you need to test a theory and see its performance in its domain, where you think it's most likely to work. And that is quite a useful principle: if you really think that the absence of labor mobility across borders is an absolutely critical feature of the Ricardian model, then data sets where that's more likely to be found is a better place to test a Ricardo model than data sets with much more cross-border mobility. So you can start thinking about performance inside the domain or outside the domain. You may recall that in the late 1990s there was a big fight about which theory was behind the success of the gravity equation. And, of course, it turns out

---

[3]PhD student, Faculty of Business and Economics, University of Basel.
[4]Leamer and Levinsohn (1995).

that it was everything, and so everyone wanted to claim that this is their prize! However, one way of looking at this was testing each of those theories in their own domain, where they are supposed to work. And that, I thought, was a useful way of thinking about the problem.

Esteban Rossi-Hansberg I think another answer to this is the aspect of specificity. The fact that these models are connected to very particular circumstances that are quantified with current data can help us make predictions about very particular policy experiments. We can then observe the outcome of this policy experiment in practice, and gauge the success of these models in explaining what actually happens. Therefore, having that level of specificity, I think, allows us to provide counterfactuals that can then be compared to what actually happened in certain circumstances. When you state things at a very abstract level that is not as specific, it is very hard to do that. But I think we are getting to a level where we can have that specificity and therefore test the theory in that way.

Roy J. Ruffin We do that because the gains from trade seem so obvious in the countries that were highly protectionist versus countries that have open borders. Look what happened to Argentina. At one time they were as rich as the United States, they then turned protectionist and now they are way down here and the United States is way up there. So, we tend to take it for granted that, yes, there are gains from trade.

Harris Dellas All this requires that we have a good measure of the gains from trade. The only way to do this is to take a model, because there it is clear. We need to have a way to measure gains from trade empirically, in a way that is independent of a model.

Rolf Weder So, we have another question. Please?

Madeleine Schmidt[5] I actually wanted to ask the same thing. What are actual measures for gains from trade? How do we define these in research?

Harris Dellas In the model, it is very easy. [People laugh]

Ralph Ossa It's true that it is model-dependent to some extent, but you can measure things like real income, you can measure wages divided by prices, and you can get good results when countries shut down. Haggay Etkes and Assaf Zimring, for example, have a really interesting paper on the Israel-Palestine conflict, how Israel's blockade of Gaza reduced trade.[6] Yes, I agree, it's still model-specific to some extent because income was set equal to utility, but I don't think it's quite as bad as we make it sound.

---

[5]Master student at the University of Basel.
[6]Etkes and Zimring (2015).

Peter Egger Well, with heterogeneous agents it becomes difficult.

Esteban Rossi-Hansberg But to the extent that we have models that can show what happened, there is nothing wrong with measuring gains from trade from a model perspective. OK, it may be model-specific, but if we have a good model, so what?

Rolf Weder May I ask another question before we close, as you are all here. Think about issues from the perspective of society, or at least the way we perceive it. One issue is environment. Now, the relationship between international trade and the environment is taken care of by Scott Taylor, we all know that! [People laugh] However, if you take another topic such as migration, it seems that this is something that, in addition to international trade, people are concerned about or look at very differently. So my question to you is this: are we good enough as trade theorists to explain the effects of migration and international trade separately, and maybe even combined? Is there maybe something here that we haven't fully understood that is preventing us from providing good insights and answers when this topic is discussed? For example, I know that Bill has written papers on trade and migration, and you, Esteban, emphasized that you estimate everything at the same time, didn't you?

Wilfred J. Ethier Yes.

Rolf Weder So, is there a kind of gap, maybe because Ricardo assumed that there is no factor mobility so we have waited for too long to think about it? Or is there no need to dig further and think more theoretically about this?

Esteban Rossi-Hansberg I think there's a great need to come up with models that can deal with mobility of people and trading goods at the same time. This model [referring to model presented in Chap. 17] has it, but it does so in a particular way, and I think that there's a lot more room to think about this. I happen to believe that if you're going to think about mobility, introducing within-country mobility is very important if you want to address these issues. We were talking about discontentment, and some of these local issues are essential. Mobility is therefore not only cross-county, but also within-country. Introducing this also means including local agglomeration effects, local congestion effects, etc, and so all of this comes with a whole baggage of parameters. It's hard to estimate and it's hard to quantify, and so this is the agenda: put better numbers on the table for all of this, and slowly improve the quantification. I think the agenda is nicely laid out for us, we just have to work our way through it.

Rolf Weder OK, lots to do!—Yes, Beat?

Beat Spirig[7] I have a question not only for the panelists, but for all the speakers today. Ariel Rubinstein, in a recent edition of the *Journal of Economic Literature*,

---

[7]Lecturer, Faculty of Business and Economics, University of Basel.

wrote the following: "I like a formal model when a beautiful, original and clever story about life miraculously emerges from the symbols."[8] And so I would like to hear some beautiful, original and clever Ricardo stories from today's guests.

Roy J. Ruffin The 2×2 model! [People laugh]

Ralph Ossa Was there not a famous quote about Samuelson saying something ...

Ronald Jones In 1968, there was a meeting known then as the Third Congress of the International Economic Association, of which Paul Samuelson was the president. He was giving a talk, and said, and I'm now quoting,

> Our subject puts its best foot forward when it speaks out on international trade. This was brought home to me years ago when I was in the Society of Fellows at Harvard along with the mathematician Stanislaw Ulam. Ulam, who was to become an originator of the Monte Carlo method and co-discoverer of the hydrogen bomb, was already at a tender age a world famous topologist. And he was a delightful conversationalist, wandering lazily over all domains of knowledge. He used to tease me by saying, "Name me one proposition in all of the social sciences which is both true and non-trivial". This was a test that I always failed. But now, some thirty years later, on the staircase so to speak, an appropriate answer occurs to me: the Ricardian theory of comparative advantage; the demonstration that trade is mutually profitable even when one country is absolutely more—or less—productive in terms of every commodity. That it is logically true need not be argued before a mathematician; that it is not trivial is attested by the thousands of important and intelligent men [Ronald Jones: by the way, later on he would say "people"] who have never been able to grasp the doctrine for themselves or to believe it after it was explained to them.[9]

I finished my paper I gave this morning with: If Ricardo could speak after 200 years, he might say "Thank you Professor Samuelson, this proves my case!"

Rolf Weder This is actually a very good final statement by Ron Jones to conclude this conference. To finish off, let me thank each and every one of you for coming here to Basel for this conference to think about international trade. It was an incredibly exciting day—for me, it really was a dream come true. I will have to ask my wife tomorrow morning, "Did this really happen?" Many thanks to all of you for your excellent contributions and discussions!

References

Etkes, H., & Zimring, A. (2015). When trade stops: Lessons from the Gaza blockade 2007–2010. *Journal of International Economics, 95*(1), 16–27.

Leamer, E. E., & Levinsohn, J. (1995). International trade theory: The evidence. In G. M. Grossman & K. Rogoff (Eds.), *Handbook of international economics* (Vol. 3, pp. 1339–1394). Amsterdam: Elsevier Science Publishers B.V.

---

[8]Rubinstein (2017), p. 166.
[9]Samuelson (1969), p. 9.

Rubinstein, A. (2017). Comments on economic models, economics, and economists: Remarks on economics rules by Dani Rodrik. *Journal of Economic Literature, 55*(1), 162–172.

Samuelson, P. A. (1969). The way of an economist. In P. A. Samuelson (Ed.), *International economic relations: Proceedings of the third congress of the international economic association* (pp. 1–11). London: Macmillan.

Part III
Back to the Future: Challenges of 2017 and the Original Idea of 1817

Part III starts with a short reflection on the challenges of globalization in 2017 and discusses some of them in the light of Ricardian trade theory. We then present the original Chapter VII "On Foreign Trade" written by David Ricardo and published in 1817 in his book *On the Principles of Political Economy and Taxation*.

The editors together with the "Jubilee" (the original book, extracts from Chapter VII "On Foreign Trade" and associated correspondence written by David Ricardo) in the showcase

Globalization—Quo Vadis? A panel discussion on the challenges of globalization in the Aula of the University of Basel, April 19, 2017—exactly 200 years after David Ricardo's book *On the Principles of Political Economy and Taxation* was published in London

Celebration dinner after the Scientific Trade Conference at the river Rhine in Basel (Switzerland) on May 12, 2017

Chapter 19
Current Challenges of Globalization in the Light of the Ricardian Trade Theory

Ronald W. Jones and Rolf Weder

Abstract This concluding chapter of the book starts with the observation that many problems in the world economy are not or only loosely related to globalization and thus could be solved by self-responsible countries. An important challenge of globalization is, however, caused by the frictions and the churning process of international trade that requires constant adjustments and flexibility by individuals. In the first part, we touch on this aspect in the light of an increasing fragmentation of the production process. In the second part, we extend the Ricardian model by allowing for international mobility of some inputs and argue that this fosters the churning process. In the third part, we emphasize that as countries are countries for a reason, they are likely to continue limiting the accessibility of some of their markets. We conclude that the study of "markets with overlapping domains" lies at the heart of Ricardian trade theory.

"What challenges of globalization?", one may ask. Obviously, there are many *problems* in the world economy. There are still many poor people who live and work under very bad, precarious conditions—particularly in low-income countries. There is continuing environmental degradation in many nations. Natural resources are overused. Species of flora and fauna become extinct. Oceans are overfished.

And there are clear signals of global warming with all its potentially very negative impact on our planet, as a whole, and on many equilibria related to the climate, the oceans, the mountains, the glaciers and the geography of world population.

These problems are, however, to a large extent not or only indirectly related to globalization. They are mainly caused by the inability or unwillingness of individual countries' governments to do their homework: To establish property rights, to provide a basic and well-working public infrastructure financed by a broad tax base

R.W. Jones (✉)
Department of Economics, University of Rochester, Rochester, NY, USA
e-mail: ronald.jones@rochester.edu

R. Weder (✉)
Faculty of Business and Economics, University of Basel, Basel, Switzerland
e-mail: rolf.weder@unibas.ch

© Springer International Publishing AG 2017
R.W. Jones, R. Weder (eds.), *200 Years of Ricardian Trade Theory*,
https://doi.org/10.1007/978-3-319-60606-4_19

and to internalize negative externalities to solve the "tragedy of the commons" problem. The countries are engaged in producing and using weapons instead of fighting against poverty within their boundaries. For some issues, such as the over-fishing of the oceans or global warming, cooperation and commitment among nations is, indeed, mandatory. For most of the challenges, individual countries should and can, however, be self-responsible.

Globalization can sometimes aggravate these problems. Open-access resources may be quickly depleted through exports. Pollution may rise due to countries' specialization in pollution-intensive export industries and increasing transportation. Foreign capital may be used to finance wars or a below-standard production. Globalization can sometimes reduce these problems. Imports from resource-abundant countries can put a halt on domestic degradation. Countries may get access to environmentally friendly goods or technology. Foreign capital may be used to finance the opposition against wars, be invested in above-standard production methods and promote innovation.

There is a quickly growing literature in international trade that evaluates and integrates these contradictory and partly compensating effects into a framework that allows to going beyond the elaboration of (extreme) examples. Professor M. Scott Taylor is a pioneer in the area of international trade, renewable resources and the environment. He often uses the Ricardian trade model (see Chap. 7 of this book) as a foundation of the analysis. Whereas the fate of open-access resources through international trade may indeed be grim (e.g., Taylor, 2011), it turns out that the effect of trade on pollution created through production may be positive (e.g., Antweiler, Copeland, & Taylor, 2001). The reason is that it increases efficiency and the demand for less-polluting production techniques. Looking at the relationship between international trade and poverty, there is evidence for poverty-reducing effects of globalization (e.g., Dollar & Kraay, 2004).

What international trade and the exchange of factors of production, however, also do: They create frictions. This is, what we want to emphasize in the following—in the light of the Ricardian trade theory. It is something which, in our view, many people all over the world have become more aware of during the last decades. It is an aspect that has made many people more critical about free-trade agreements and globalization in general, despite their awareness of the large gains from trade. In the first section, we start with a short reflection on the nature of international trade. We then introduce the notion of "markets with overlapping domains" to discuss an important extension of the Ricardian model towards factor mobility. Finally, we emphasize that "countries are countries for a reason" and conclude with a short outlook.

19.1   The Nature of International Trade

David Ricardo insisted on a very important characteristic of international trade. That is—as discussed from different perspectives in this book—the notion of *comparative advantage*. The surprising implication of this Ricardian idea is that a country may be willing to import a good that is produced abroad less efficiently than at home. The reason is that this allows the country to use its released resources in what it can produce *relatively* better. And the foreign country can compete by focusing on what it can produce relatively well—even though it has an absolute disadvantage in everything it does.[1] Note that this was—and still is—extremely liberating, because no country is left out. No matter how "poorly trained" an economy is, it has a comparative advantage in something.

Trade theorists by and large tended to focus on the aspect that countries will, with trade, concentrate their activities into those in which they have a comparative advantage. How much concentration? According to the Ricardian trade model, concentration could go from, let us say, a hundred goods in autarky to a very few in trade if transportation costs were low enough. The degree of concentration can thus be rather stark. The story often ends at this point and does not pursue one consequence of this which is very important for the kind of situation that we have encountered in the past and that we will face in the future.

If a country is growing and developing or if it is embedded in a global market in which there can be big changes in relative prices and world demand, the small set of goods or industries in which the country has a comparative advantage may shift. There is a difference between the relatively balanced and broadly based consumption structure in a country and what the country chooses to produce in a world in which there is relatively free and open international trade. That means it is a natural consequence of being in a trading situation that there is a *churning process* going on in the identification of what goods are the country's best goods and what goods used to be the best in the past and are no longer produced in the country. This fundamental process is part of the nature of international trade.

This characteristic also applies to a world economy with a much finer division of labour as a consequence of outsourcing or offshoring individual stages of the production processes. In the trade literature, these stages are called fragments, production blocks, intermediate goods, tasks or jobs which can be dislocated to different countries or regions.[2] The coordination of these decentralized activities requires some efforts and thus causes some costs (we may call them "service link costs") which are likely to have a fixed cost component. This implies, however, that international outsourcing increases if these coordination costs fall due to quickly decreasing communication and transportation costs (e.g., the internet). The fragmentation of the production process has also been promoted because of technological changes, the reduction of trade barriers and the rise of output in combination with service link costs that are prone to increasing returns.

What is the implication if more and more things are internationally traded? Does this mean that comparative advantage "goes out of the window"? No, it just means that what you identify as the "thing" that gets traded changes. But the principle of

---

[1]The fundamentals which lead to these implications are explained in detail in Chaps. 4 and 5 of this book.

[2]See, e.g., Jones (2000, Chap. 7), Grossman and Rossi-Hansberg (2008) or Antràs (2016).

comparative advantage to explain the pattern of trade, i.e., what is produced and what is imported, works just as well as it did for (final) goods. The variety of what gets traded increases. It includes services. Research & Development may be "produced" in one location, whereas production may take place at another one. Locations of the individual production stages may even differ for different products within an industry or firm. Countries'—or individual regions'—relative productivities in all of these activities determine what is produced where.

This could, however, imply a greater demand for government interference by those who are negatively affected by this increased churning process. They may be worried and thus become constrained in their productivity because of the permanent uncertainty they face regarding what they do, for whom they work and where they live. The process may, of course, offer a lot of opportunities for flexible minds. But it also can be experienced as a constant threat or danger by risk-averse and less flexible individuals. It may lead to a conflict between generations, even a kind of "civil war scenario" (see Jones, 2000, p. 149). Thus, the question arises what the government's role should be in all of this.

Governments may not be able to ignore this demand in order to make sure that the gains from specialization can also be realized in future. There will, however, be a fine line between two strategies: (1) to allow for this highly fragmented international trade with a "minimal social safety net" for those who need it and (2) to constrain this process through a reduction of competition with "maximal personal security". There are, in principle, considerable Ricardian gains from trade to be made in this "new fragmented environment". The question is whether societies and their governments find a continuous way to realize them.[3]

19.2 Markets with Overlapping Domains

The discipline of international trade is fundamentally concerned with the co-existence of markets that have overlapping domains (Jones, 1995). In David Ricardo's theory, factors of production are internationally immobile and thus national, whereas the goods produced with those factors enjoy global markets. As important as the doctrine of comparative advantage is, it is thus based on an assumed international immobility of factors of production.

Suppose we have—in addition to immobile labour—capital that is free to move from one country to another and the owners of capital ask where they should invest. Then the question of absolute advantage becomes important. But it does not obliterate comparative advantage. The reason is that as long as we have inputs

---

[3]David Ricardo was aware of the frictions caused by international trade. He seems to have implicitly argued that trade liberalization should not happen too quickly and that some abrupt change on world markets might be cushioned through temporary protection. See Chap. 2 in this book and the quote with respect to temporary duties on imports of corn in Ricardo's *Essay on Profits*.

such as labour that are relatively (not completely) immobile between countries, then comparative advantage as regards those factors can co-exist with the question of absolute advantage for capital that is mobile. Factors that cannot move, ask: "What can we do?" And there will be a good answer for it. Factors that are internationally mobile, say: "Where should we go?" And there will be a good answer for them.

The consideration of some mobile factors of production obviously increases the complexity of markets with overlapping domains in a Ricardian trade model. There may be a national (or even regional) mobility of labour, combined with goods being traded on world markets and a further input (e.g., capital) being exchanged between regions, but not globally. Thus, regional labour markets overlap with international capital markets, and both overlap with the world market for goods. The question we want to pursue in the following is: What are the implications of the international mobility of some (not all) inputs for the nature of trade discussed above? The simplest way to study the issue is offered by the "Augmented Ricardian Trade Model" as proposed in Jones (1980, 2000) in which one of the two industries not only uses labour, but also an internationally mobile factor of production.[4]

Suppose a Ricardian model with two countries, Home and Foreign, producing two goods, 1 and 2, for the world market with labour that is internationally immobile. We now assume that to produce a unit of good 1 requires not only a_{L1} units of labour, but also a_{K1} units of physical capital which is internationally mobile. Wages (w, w^*) are determined endogenously in the two national labour markets. These national markets overlap with, first, the world market for the two goods where the relative price, p_1/p_2, is determined and, second, the international market for capital with r being the rental on a unit of capital. We will be assuming that the countries are embedded in a large world economy, so that they are price takers both for the two goods they produce as well as for the internationally mobile input. In a variant of our discussion of the model's implications we will assume that K is only mobile between the two countries and thus is not shared with the rest of the world.

In competitive markets, firms in any industry cannot make profits. Thus the following inequalities, (19.1) and (19.2), can be established for the home country and analogously for Foreign:

$$a_{L2}w \geq p_2 \tag{19.1}$$

$$a_{L1}w + a_{K1}r \geq p_1 \tag{19.2}$$

If unit costs are greater than the price, the good will not be produced. Under which conditions does the home country produce both goods in equilibrium? The answer is: When the unit costs shown in (19.1) and (19.2) just equal the price in each industry. Dividing (19.2) by (19.1), now requiring that price equals cost, yields

---

[4]The following is based on Sect. 2.1 "An Augmented Ricardian Model" in Jones (2000) on *Globalization and the Theory of Input Trade*. The model and a first version of Fig. 19.1 appeared in Jones (1980).

combinations of the relative price of the two goods, p_1/p_2, and the return of capital (deflated by the price of good 2) in which the home country would produce both goods in a competitive equilibrium. Thus,

$$\frac{a_{L1}}{a_{L2}} + a_{K1}\frac{r}{p_2} = \frac{p_1}{p_2}. \tag{19.3}$$

This equation is quite revealing. Given the prices of the two goods on the world market (p_1, p_2), the answer to the question whether a country can attract the mobile input, K, and thus produce good 1 depends on (a) the country's relative labour productivity with respect to producing good 1 (a_{L1}/a_{L2}), (b) its productivity in using capital in the production of good 1 (a_{K1}), and (c) the price of capital (r). If the price of the mobile factor is high, a country's input coefficient for capital (a_{K1}) becomes more relevant.

Figure 19.1 plots the relationship expressed in Eq. (19.2) for both the home country (H) and the foreign country (F), with the relative price of the two goods on the vertical and the price of capital (deflated by p_2) on the horizontal axis. Note that we assumed that Home has a comparative advantage in good 1 with respect to labour (the factor trapped by national boundaries) and an absolute disadvantage in the productivity of capital (the internationally mobile factor).[5] Thus, the vertical intercept of Home's relative cost line is smaller than that of the foreign country, whereas its slope is larger.

The exogenous prices of the two goods and of capital on the world market can be illustrated by any point in Fig. 19.1. If this point lies in region II, both countries are

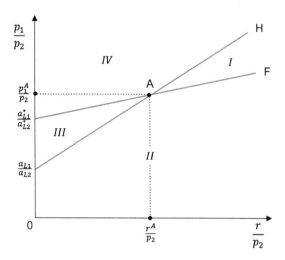

Fig. 19.1 The joint role of comparative and absolute advantage

---

[5]Thus, $a_{L1}/a_{L2} < a_{L1}^*/a_{L2}^*$ and $a_{K1} > a_{K1}^*$.

only producing good 2 as p_1 is too low to cover unit cost at the given rental rate, r, which has to be paid to attract internationally mobile capital. If, on the other hand, the price vector is located in region IV, both countries are completely specialized in good 1. Why? Given the relatively high price of good 1, the countries want to produce more of it. But this implies that wages in industry 1 are bidden up such that the unit costs in industry 2 become greater than the price of good 2. As implied by Eq. (19.1), the countries become completely specialized in good 2.

A price combination in region III implies that the home country specializes in good 1, attracting the international mobile capital. The foreign country is completely specialized in good 2. Note that good 1 is the industry in which Home uses relatively less labour than Foreign, i.e., in which it has a comparative advantage. Suppose r and p_1 rise to a price vector in region I: The pattern of production switches. Why? As the price of capital rises Foreign's absolute advantage in using the mobile factor becomes more important. As we reach region I, Foreign produces good 1 and Home loses industry 1. Home loses it because its comparative advantage in the use of labour has become less relevant and is, in fact, outweighed by its absolute disadvantage in using the internationally mobile input.

This implies that with international factor mobility, absolute advantage in attracting the mobile factor becomes important, but comparative advantage with respect to the internationally immobile factor remains relevant. This creates, however, a bigger role for country-specific characteristics in affecting trading patterns. Note that changes in countries' overall levels of taxation or regulation typically do not affect the pattern of production in the standard Ricardian trade model: It depends on comparative advantage and remains unaffected if, e.g., taxes on labour income rise. With some factors being internationally mobile, these type of changes affect countries' absolute advantage in attracting the mobile factors and thus have an impact on trade and production patterns.

We therefore conclude that in a world that is increasingly characterized by some internationally mobile inputs, patterns of production are more likely to be affected by changes in economic policies or prices on the world market. This is the result of comparative advantage as a determinant of trade patterns being complemented by absolute advantage in attracting internationally mobile factors of production. An example may help to illustrate this point. Suppose the two goods are only produced with internationally immobile labour. We continue to assume that the home country has a comparative advantage in good 1. Let us start with a situation in which Home is producing both goods. If p_1 gradually increases, Home will increase its production of good 1 and completely specialize in this industry. Foreign may eventually also start to produce good 1 if p_1 rises enough. If p_1 is high enough, both countries only produce good 1 (see Chap. 4 in this book).

Compare this with the situation in the augmented Ricardian trade model presented above, with capital being internationally mobile and, in combination with labour, being used in industry 1. As a variant of our interpretation we assume now that the two countries are the only ones in which capital can be invested. Consequently, they compete for capital. We assume again that p_1 is low, but gradually increases. As can be seen from Fig. 19.1, Home will be the first one to start to produce good 1. What is the intuition of this? The home country enjoys a comparative advantage in labour. However, as p_1 continues to rise towards $p_1{}^A/p_2$, the relevance of Foreign's comparative disadvantage is more and more reduced thanks to its absolute advantage in attracting the mobile factor. It eventually starts to produce good 1 in point A in Fig. 19.1. If p_1 increases further, Home loses its industry 1 because it cannot compete against Foreign to attract the mobile factor; with a rental rate above r^A its unit cost of producing good 1 turns out to be too high compared to Foreign's with its absolute advantage in using K.

This *non-monotonic behaviour of capital flows* may be surprising. But it is quite typical in a situation where comparative and absolute advantages jointly determine the patterns of production and trade.[6] The interesting insight is that workers in a country's industry producing a good for the world market may happily observe that its price rises. This is a signal that the world wants more of this good. As they expand production and thus try to attract more of the internationally mobile factor whose price keeps rising, they may suddenly realize that they are outcompeted by the foreign country's industry which has an absolute advantage in using the—now more expensive—mobile factor. This example serves as a confirmation of our argument above that, with some factor mobility, changes in the world market can foster the churning process with all the challenges coming with it.

19.3 Countries are Countries for a Reason

International trade theory is typically occupied with the interaction between markets that are national and those which are international. Trade economists then analyze the gains from trade which result from moving from autarky (where residents only trade in national markets) to free trade. By free trade we mean unimpeded trade in final and intermediate goods and services as well as raw materials between countries.

Trade models may sometimes be extended by assuming that *some* factors of production may be mobile between countries. An example is the augmented Ricardian model, discussed above in Sect. 19.2, in which labour is assumed immobile and capital—only used in one industry—mobile internationally. This allows for studying frictions that arise from changes of prices of goods and inputs on the world market in a more realistic scenario. How about going to the extreme where all goods and services are freely traded as well as all factors of production are internationally mobile? Such a vision may be attractive to some, but this is not the typical subject of the discipline of international trade.[7] As one of us wrote some time ago:

---

[6]Jones (2000, pp. 20–34) discusses this nonmonotonic behavior of capital flows in the Heckscher-Ohlin framework.

[7]For example, the former president of the Commission of the European Union, José Manuel Barroso, said in 2014 with an eye on Switzerland that "It cannot be that there is free movement for carrots, but not for people." (See Neue Zürcher Zeitung, 17.2.2014; translation by the authors).

> What is often missing in discussions of gains from free trade is an explicit recognition that countries are countries for a reason. They are like clubs, with certain rules generally agreed upon and restrictions placed as to the conditions under which others may participate, if at all, in national markets. (Jones, 1995, p. 274)

Autarky is obviously not a desirable policy. It would sacrifice the large (Ricardian) gains from trade and specialization emphasized in this book and above. But neither is a policy which would open up all markets—in goods, services, raw materials, intermediates, capital and labour. We believe there is a trade-off between these two extreme policies. The gains from being able to trade with other countries and exchange factors of production have to be balanced by the loss of control over some domestic markets and thus the marginal loss of sovereignty.

This creates some tension and ambiguity in the discussion of a country's attitude with respect to trade policy and to a membership to, for example, regional economic agreements. Companies and their employees are anxious to get access to other markets for their products and services and thus to capture gains from trade in a variety of industries in the manufacturing and service sector. But, at the same time, to open markets in "critical" areas (such as food or culture) or to allow for unlimited international mobility of labour is likely to be felt by many as a threat to the particular characteristics and identity of a country. An "optimal trade policy" is, therefore, not a policy that completely opens all markets.

The nonchalance with which many policy-makers consider these fundamental feelings of residents seems to be one reason why we have experienced some backlash in the support of globalization in many countries in the last years. Pursuing a strategy that intends to open all markets and, as a consequence or an alleged necessity, envisions a harmonization of all sorts of regulations (in labour markets, product requirements and production methods) ignores some fundamental desire of human beings. It may also threaten the great diversity among countries.

David Ricardo assumed international trade in goods, but an international immobility of the factors of production. His defense of this assumption alluded also to "a natural disinclination which every man has to quit the country of his birth and connections" (see Chap. 3 of this book). It is an extreme assumption in the Ricardian model. In today's real world, capital has attained a high international mobility and also labour is to some extent internationally mobile. However, in *relative terms* the Ricardian assumption seems still to be appropriate, at least for many countries. Most markets in goods and services are much more open than the national labour markets. Moreover, the mobility of people within countries is typically much larger than the mobility between countries.[8]

Thus, the world of David Ricardo 200 years ago was in many ways similar to the world of today. In addition to the lower degree of exchange of labour between countries *relative* to the exchange of goods and services, it is also the countries which are still important. In fact, the number of countries has increased from less than 100 around 1817 to more than 200 in 2017.[9] We interpret this as a sign that

---

[8]See, for example, World Bank (2009, p. 147).

[9]See Mac Gregor (1854, pp. 9 ff.) and United Nations (2017).

there is a reason for countries to be countries. Some harmonization took place, but countries still want to deliberately set their own rules and regulations and social agenda. Visions that globalization will lead to a world-wide harmonization of markets with easy access to all participants are likely to prove unrealistic.

19.4   Concluding Remarks

There are a number of problems in the world economy. Many of them can and should be solved by self-responsible countries within their boundaries. Globalization may sometimes increase, sometimes reduce these problems. We emphasize in this concluding chapter of the book that the Ricardian gains from international trade through specialization may be amplified through the fragmentation of the production process of goods and services and the associated international trade in intermediates, fragments, production blocks or tasks—whatever we may call them. The churning process which is fundamental to international trade thereby tends, however, to be fostered. This process may be further accelerated through the increased international mobility of some factors of production.

This requires a high flexibility among individuals within countries as they have to constantly adjust to the associated changes in the patterns of production and trade. Once countries are highly integrated into world markets, they are also in exposed positions. As countries are countries for a reason they are likely to limit the accessibility of foreigners to some markets and to pursue their own agenda in regulation and social protection. This has been the case 200 years ago when David Ricardo wrote his still highly relevant chapter "On Foreign Trade". It is true today and may not be much different 200 years from now.

References

Antras, P. (2016). *Global production: Firms, contracts, and trade structure*. Princeton, NJ: Princeton University Press.

Antweiler, W., Copeland, B., & Taylor, M. S. (2001). Is free trade good for the environment? *American Economic Review, 91*(4), 877–908.

Dollar, D., & Kraay, A. (2004). Trade, growth, and poverty. *The Economic Journal, 114* (February), F22–F49.

Grossman, G. M., & Rossi-Hansberg, E. (2008). Trading tasks: A simple theory of offshoring. *The American Economic Review, 98*(5), 1978–1997.

Jones, R. W. (1980). Comparative and absolute advantage. *Swiss Journal of Economics and Statistics (SJES), 116*(2), 272–288.

Jones, R. W. (1995). The discipline of international trade. *Swiss Journal of Economics and Statistics, 131*(3), 273–288.

Jones, R. W. (2000). *Globalization and the theory of input trade*. Cambridge, MA: MIT Press.

Mac Gregor, J. (1854). *The resources and statistics of nations. Exhibiting the geographical position and natural resources, the area and population*. London: Routledge.

Taylor, M. S. (2011). Buffalo hunt: International trade and the virtual extinction of the North-American Bison. *American Economic Review, 101*(7), 3162–3195.

United Nations. (2017). *Overview*. New York: United Nations. Accessed July 22, 2017, from http://www.un.org/en/sections/about-un/overview/

World Bank. (2009). *Reshaping economic geography*. World Development Report 2009. Washington, DC: World Bank.

Chapter 20
On Foreign Trade

David Ricardo

Abstract This chapter contains a reprint of David Ricardo's Chapter VII "On Foreign Trade". The reprint is from the third edition of *On the Principles of Political Economy and Taxation*. Note that this is Ricardo's final version of his text that remained unchanged. The book was published by John Murray in London in 1821 with an edition of 1000 copies. The first edition appeared on April 19, 1817 by the same publisher.

This chapter starts with the front matter and the list of contents of David Ricardo's *On the Principles of Political Economy and Taxation*. These are followed by Chapter VII "On Foreign Trade" which is reproduced here in full length.

Originally published in: Ricardo, D. *On the Principles of Political Economy and Taxation*, 3rd ed., John Murray, London, 1821.

D. Ricardo
Gatcombe Park (near Minchin Hampton), Gloucestershire, UK

233

ON

THE PRINCIPLES

OF

POLITICAL ECONOMY,

AND

TAXATION.

ON

THE PRINCIPLES

OF

POLITICAL ECONOMY,

AND

TAXATION.

BY DAVID RICARDO, ESQ.

THIRD EDITION.

LONDON:

JOHN MURRAY, ALBEMARLE-STREET.

1821.

CONTENTS.

CHAPTER VII.

ON FOREIGN TRADE.

No extension of foreign trade will immediately increase the amount of value in a country, although
it will very powerfully contribute to increase the
mass of commodities, and therefore the sum of enjoyments. As the value of all foreign goods is
measured by the quantity of the produce of our
land and labour, which is given in exchange for
them, we should have no greater value, if by the
discovery of new markets, we obtained double the
quantity of foreign goods in exchange for a given
quantity of our's. If by the purchase of English
goods to the amount of 1000*l.*, a merchant can obtain a quantity of foreign goods, which he can sell
in the English market for 1,200*l.*, he will obtain
20 per cent. profit by such an employment of his
capital; but neither his gains, nor the value of the
commodities imported, will be increased or diminished by the greater or smaller quantity of foreign
goods obtained. Whether, for example, he imports twenty-five or fifty pipes of wine, his interest
can be no way affected, if at one time the twenty-
five pipes, and at another the fifty pipes, equally
sell for 1,200*l.* In either case his profit will be
limited to 200*l.*, or 20 per cent. on his capital;

and in either case the same value will be imported
into England. If the fifty pipes sold for more
than 1,200*l.*, the profits of this individual merchant
would exceed the general rate of profits, and capital would naturally flow into this advantageous
trade, till the fall of the price of wine had brought
every thing to the former level.

It has indeed been contended, that the great
profits which are sometimes made by particular
merchants in foreign trade, will elevate the general rate of profits in the country, and that the ab-
straction of capital from other employments, to
partake of the new and beneficial foreign commerce, will raise prices generally, and thereby increase profits. It has been said, by high autho-
rity, that less capital being necessarily devoted to
the growth of corn, to the manufacture of cloth,
hats, shoes, &c. while the demand continues the
same, the price of these commodities will be so
increased, that the farmer, hatter, clothier, and
shoemaker, will have an increase of profits, as well
as the foreign merchant*.

They who hold this argument agree with me,
that the profits of different employments have a
tendency to conform to one another; to advance
and recede together. Our variance consists in
this: They contend, that the equality of profits

* See Adam Smith, book i. chap. 9.

will be brought about by the general rise of profits; and I am of opinion, that the profits of the favoured trade will speedily subside to the general level.

For, first, I deny that less capital will necessarily be devoted to the growth of corn, to the manufacture of cloth, hats, shoes, &c. unless the demand for these commodities be diminished; and if so, their price will not rise. In the purchase of foreign commodities, either the same, a larger, or a less portion of the produce of the land and labour of England will be employed. If the same portion be so employed, then will the same demand exist for cloth, shoes, corn, and hats, as before, and the same portion of capital will be devoted to their production. If, in consequence of the price of foreign commodities being cheaper, a less portion of the annual produce of the land and labour of England is employed in the purchase of foreign commodities, more will remain for the purchase of other things. If there be a greater demand for hats, shoes, corn, &c. than before, which there may be, the consumers of foreign commodities having an additional portion of their revenue disposable, the capital is also disposable with which the greater value of foreign commodities was before purchased; so that with the increased demand for corn, shoes, &c. there exists also the means of procuring an increased supply, and therefore neither prices nor profits can permanently rise. If more of the produce of the land and labour of England be employed in the purchase of foreign commodities, less can be employed in the purchase of other things, and therefore fewer hats, shoes, &c. will be required. At the same time that capital is liberated from the production of shoes, hats, &c. more must be employed in manufacturing those commodities with which foreign commodities are purchased; and consequently in all cases the demand for foreign and home commodities together, as far as regards value, is limited by the revenue and capital of the country. If one increases, the other must diminish. If the quantity of wine, imported in exchange for the same quantity of English commodities, be doubled, the people of England can either consume double the quantity of wine that they did before, or the same quantity of wine and a greater quantity of English commodities. If my revenue had been 1000*l.*, with which I purchased annually one pipe of wine for 100*l.* and a certain quantity of English commodities for 900*l.*; when wine fell to 50*l.* per pipe, I might lay out the 50*l.* saved, either in the purchase of an additional pipe of wine, or in the purchase of more English commodities. If I bought more wine, and every wine-drinker did the same, the foreign trade would not be in the least disturbed; the same quantity of English commodities would be exported in exchange for wine, and we should receive double the quantity, though not double the value of wine. But if I, and

others, contented ourselves with the same quantity
of wine as before, fewer English commodities
would be exported, and the wine-drinkers might
either consume the commodities which were before exported, or any others for which they had
an inclination. The capital required for their production would be supplied by the capital liberated
from the foreign trade.

There are two ways in which capital may be
accumulated : it may be saved either in consequence of increased revenue, or of diminished
consumption. If my profits are raised from 1000*l.*
to 1200*l.* while my expenditure continues the same,
I accumulate annually 200*l.* more than I did before. If I save 200*l.* out of my expenditure, while
my profits continue the same, the same effect will
be produced; 200*l.* per annum will be added to
my capital. The merchant who imported wine
after profits had been raised from 20 per cent. to
40 per cent., instead of purchasing his English
goods for 1000*l.* must purchase them for 857*l.* 2*s.*
10*d.*, still selling the wine which he imports in return for those goods for 1200*l.*; or, if he continued to purchase his English goods for 1000*l.* must
raise the price of his wine to 1400*l.*; he would
thus obtain 40 instead of 20 per cent. profit on his
capital; but if, in consequence of the cheapness of
all the commodities on which his revenue was expended, he and all other consumers could save the
value of 200*l.* out of every 1000*l.* they before ex-

pended, they would more effectually add to the
real wealth of the country; in one case, the savings would be made in consequence of an increase
of revenue, in the other, in consequence of diminished expenditure.

If, by the introduction of machinery, the gene-
rality of the commodities on which revenue was
expended fell 20 per cent. in value, I should be
enabled to save as effectually as if my revenue had
been raised 20 per cent.; but in one case the rate
of profits is stationary, in the other it is raised 20
per cent.—If, by the introduction of cheap foreign
goods, I can save 20 per cent. from my expenditure, the effect will be precisely the same as if machinery had lowered the expense of their production, but profits would not be raised.

It is not, therefore, in consequence of the extension of the market that the rate of profit is
raised, although such extension may be equally
efficacious in increasing the mass of commodities,
and may thereby enable us to augment the funds
destined for the maintenance of labour, and the
materials on which labour may be employed. It is
quite as important to the happiness of mankind,
that our enjoyments should be increased by the
better distribution of labour, by each country producing those commodities for which by its situation,
its climate, and its other natural or artificial advantages, it is adapted, and by their exchanging

them for the commodities of other countries, as
that they should be augmented by a rise in the
rate of profits.

It has been my endeavour to shew throughout
this work, that the rate of profits can never be increased but by a fall in wages, and that there can
be no permanent fall of wages but in consequence
of a fall of the necessaries on which wages are expended. If, therefore, by the extension of foreign
trade, or by improvements in machinery, the food
and necessaries of the labourer can be brought to
market, at a reduced price, profits will rise. If,
instead of growing our own corn, or manufacturing
the clothing and other necessaries of the labourer,
we discover a new market from which we can supply ourselves with these commodities at a cheaper
price, wages will fall and profits rise ; but if the
commodities obtained at a cheaper rate, by the extension of foreign commerce, or by the improvement of machinery, be exclusively the commodities consumed by the rich, no alteration will take
place in the rate of profits. The rate of wages
would not be affected, although wine, velvets, silks,
and other expensive commodities should fall 50
per cent., and consequently profits would continue
unaltered.

Foreign trade, then, though highly beneficial to
a country, as it increases the amount and variety
of the objects on which revenue may be expended,
and affords, by the abundance and cheapness of

commodities, incentives to saving, and to the accumulation of capital, has no tendency to raise the
profits of stock, unless the commodities imported
be of that description on which the wages of
labour are expended.

The remarks which have been made respecting
foreign trade, apply equally to home trade. The
rate of profits is never increased by a better distribution of labour, by the invention of machinery,
by the establishment of roads and canals, or by any
means of abridging labour either in the manufacture or in the conveyance of goods. These are
causes which operate on price, and never fail to be
highly beneficial to consumers; since they enable
them with the same labour, or with the value of
the produce of the same labour, to obtain in exchange a greater quantity of the commodity to
which the improvement is applied; but they
have no effect whatever on profit. On the other
hand, every diminution in the wages of labour
raises profits, but produces no effect on the price
of commodities. One is advantageous to all classes,
for all classes are consumers; the other is beneficial only to producers; they gain more, but every
thing remains at its former price. In the first
case they get the same as before; but every thing
on which their gains are expended, is diminished
in exchangeable value.

The same rule which regulates the relative value of commodities in one country, does not regu-

late the relative value of the commodities exchanged between two or more countries.

Under a system of perfectly free commerce, each
country naturally devotes its capital and labour to
such employments as are most beneficial to each.
This pursuit of individual advantage is admirably
connected with the universal good of the whole.
By stimulating industry, by rewarding ingenuity,
and by using most efficaciously the peculiar powers
bestowed by nature, it distributes labour most effectively and most economically: while, by increasing
the general mass of productions, it diffuses general
benefit, and binds together by one common tie of
interest and intercourse, the universal society of
nations throughout the civilized world. It is this
principle which determines that wine shall be
made in France and Portugal, that corn shall be
grown in America and Poland, and that hardware and other goods shall be manufactured in
England.

In one and the same country, profits are, generally speaking, always on the same level; or differ
only as the employment of capital may be more or
less secure and agreeable. It is not so between
different countries. If the profits of capital employed in Yorkshire, should exceed those of capital employed in London, capital would speedily
move from London to Yorkshire, and an equality
of profits would be effected; but if in consequence

of the diminished rate of production in the lands of England, from the increase of capital and population, wages should rise, and profits fall, it would not follow that capital and population would necessarily move from England to Holland, or Spain, or Russia, where profits might be higher.

If Portugal had no commercial connexion with other countries, instead of employing a great part of her capital and industry in the production of wines, with which she purchases for her own use the cloth and hardware of other countries, she would be obliged to devote a part of that capital to the manufacture of those commodities, which she would thus obtain probably inferior in quality as well as quantity.

The quantity of wine which she shall give in exchange for the cloth of England, is not determined by the respective quantities of labour devoted to the production of each, as it would be, if both commodities were manufactured in England, or both in Portugal.

England may be so circumstanced, that to produce the cloth may require the labour of 100 men for one year; and if she attempted to make the wine, it might require the labour of 120 men for the same time. England would therefore find it her interest to import wine, and to purchase it by the exportation of cloth.

To produce the wine in Portugal, might require only the labour of 80 men for one year, and to produce the cloth in the same country, might require the labour of 90 men for the same time. It would therefore be advantageous for her to export wine in exchange for cloth. This exchange might even take place, notwithstanding that the commodity imported by Portugal could be produced there with less labour than in England. Though she could make the cloth with the labour of 90 men, she would import it from a country where it required the labour of 100 men to produce it, because it would be advantageous to her rather to employ her capital in the production of wine, for which she would obtain more cloth from England, than she could produce by diverting a portion of her capital from the cultivation of vines to the manufacture of cloth.

Thus England would give the produce of the labour of 100 men, for the produce of the labour of 80. Such an exchange could not take place between the individuals of the same country. The labour of 100 Englishmen cannot be given for that of 80 Englishmen, but the produce of the labour of 100 Englishmen may be given for the produce of the labour of 80 Portuguese, 60 Russians, or 120 East Indians. The difference in this respect, between a single country and many, is easily accounted for, by considering the difficulty with which capital moves from one country to another,

to seek a more profitable employment, and the activity with which it invariably passes from one province to another in the same country*.

It would undoubtedly be advantageous to the
capitalists of England, and to the consumers in
both countries, that under such circumstances, the
wine and the cloth should both be made in Portugal, and therefore that the capital and labour of
England employed in making cloth, should be re-
moved to Portugal for that purpose. In that case,
the relative value of these commodities would be
regulated by the same principle, as if one were the
produce of Yorkshire, and the other of London:
and in every other case, if capital freely flowed towards those countries where it could be most pro-
fitably employed, there could be no difference in
the rate of profit, and no other difference in the

---

* It will appear then, that a country possessing very considerable advantages in machinery and skill, and which may
therefore be enabled to manufacture commodities with much
less labour than her neighbours, may, in return for such commodities, import a portion of the corn required for its consumption, even if its land were more fertile, and corn could be grown
with less labour than in the country from which it was imported. Two men can both make shoes and hats, and one is superior to the other in both employments; but in making hats, he
can only exceed his competitor by one-fifth or 20 per cent., and
in making shoes he can excel him by one-third or 33 per cent.;
—will it not be for the interest of both, that the superior man
should employ himself exclusively in making shoes, and the inferior man in making hats?

real or labour price of commodities, than the additional quantity of labour required to convey them to the various markets where they were to be sold.

Experience, however, shews, that the fancied or real insecurity of capital, when not under the immediate control of its owner, together with the natural disinclination which every man has to quit the country of his birth and connexions, and intrust himself with all his habits fixed, to a strange government and new laws, check the emigration of capital. These feelings, which I should be sorry to see weakened, induce most men of property to be satisfied with a low rate of profits in their own country, rather than seek a more advantageous employment for their wealth in foreign nations.

Gold and silver having been chosen for the general medium of circulation, they are, by the competition of commerce, distributed in such proportions amongst the different countries of the world, as to accommodate themselves to the natural traffic which would take place if no such metals existed, and the trade between countries were purely a trade of barter.

Thus, cloth cannot be imported into Portugal, unless it sell there for more gold than it cost in the country from which it was imported; and wine cannot be imported into England, unless it will sell for more there than it cost in Portugal. If the trade were purely a trade of barter, it could only continue whilst England could make cloth so cheap as to obtain a greater quantity of wine with a given quantity of labour, by manufacturing cloth than by growing vines; and also whilst the industry of Portugal were attended by the reverse effects. Now suppose England to discover a process for making wine, so that it should become her interest rather to grow it than import it; she would naturally divert a portion of her capital from the foreign trade to the home trade; she would cease to manufacture cloth for exportation, and would grow wine for herself. The money price of these commodities would be regulated accordingly; wine would fall here while cloth continued at its former price, and in Portugal no alteration would take place in the price of either commodity. Cloth would continue for some time to be exported from this country, because its price would continue to be higher in Portugal than here; but money instead of wine would be given in exchange for it, till the accumulation of money here, and its diminution abroad, should so operate on the relative value of cloth in the two countries, that it would cease to be profitable to export it. If the improvement in making wine were of a very important description, it might become profitable for the two countries to exchange employments; for England to make all the wine, and Portugal all the cloth consumed by them; but this could be effected only by a new distribution of the precious metals, which should raise the price of cloth in England, and lower it in Portugal. The relative price of wine would fall in England in consequence of the real advantage from the improvement of its manufacture; that is to say, its natural price would fall; the relative price of cloth would rise there from the accumulation of money.

Thus, suppose before the improvement in making wine in England, the price of wine here were 50*l.* per pipe, and the price of a certain quantity of cloth were 45*l.*, whilst in Portugal the price of the same quantity of wine was 45*l.*, and that of the same quantity of cloth 50*l.*; wine would be exported from Portugal with a profit of 5*l.* and cloth from England with a profit of the same amount.

Suppose that, after the improvement, wine falls to 45*l.* in England, the cloth continuing at the same price. Every transaction in commerce is an independent transaction. Whilst a merchant can buy cloth in England for 45*l.* and sell it with the usual profit in Portugal, he will continue to export it from England. His business is simply to purchase English cloth, and to pay for it by a bill of exchange, which he purchases with Portuguese money. It is to him of no importance what becomes of this money: he has discharged his debt by the remittance of the bill. His transaction is undoubtedly regulated by the terms on which he

L

can obtain this bill, but they are known to him at
the time; and the causes which may influence the
market price of bills, or the rate of exchange, is no
consideration of his.

If the markets be favourable for the exportation
of wine from Portugal to England, the exporter of
the wine will be a seller of a bill, which will be
purchased either by the importer of the cloth, or
by the person who sold him his bill; and thus
without the necessity of money passing from either
country, the exporters in each country will be paid
for their goods.   Without having any direct transaction with each other, the money paid in Portugal by the importer of cloth will be paid to the
Portuguese exporter of wine; and in England by
the negotiation of the same bill, the exporter of
the cloth will be authorized to receive its value
from the importer of wine.

But if the prices of wine were such that no wine
could be exported to England, the importer of
cloth would equally purchase a bill; but the price
of that bill would be higher, from the knowledge
which the seller of it would possess, that there was
no counter bill in the market by which he could
ultimately settle the transactions between the two
countries; he might know that the gold or silver
money which he received in exchange for his bill,
must be actually exported to his correspondent in
England, to enable him to pay the demand which

he had authorized to be made upon him, and he might therefore charge in the price of his bill all the expenses to be incurred, together with his fair and usual profit.

If then this premium for a bill on England should be equal to the profit on importing cloth, the importation would of course cease; but if the premium on the bill were only 2 per cent., if to be enabled to pay a debt in England of 100*l.*, 102*l.* should be paid in Portugal, whilst cloth which cost 45*l.* would sell for 50*l.*, cloth would be imported, bills would be bought, and money would be exported, till the diminution of money in Portugal, and its accumulation in England, had produced such a state of prices as would make it no longer profitable to continue these transactions.

But the diminution of money in one country, and its increase in another, do not operate on the price of one commodity only, but on the prices of all, and therefore the price of wine and cloth will be both raised in England, and both lowered in Portugal. The price of cloth, from being 45*l.* in one country and 50*l.* in the other, would probably fall to 49*l.* or 48*l.* in Portugal, and rise to 46*l.* or 47*l.* in England, and not afford a sufficient profit after paying a premium for a bill to induce any merchant to import that commodity.

It is thus that the money of each country is ap-

portioned to it in such quantities only as may be
necessary to regulate a profitable trade of barter.
England exported cloth in exchange for wine, because, by so doing, her industry was rendered
more productive to her; she had more cloth and
wine than if she had manufactured both for herself; and Portugal imported cloth and exported
wine, because the industry of Portugal could be
more beneficially employed for both countries in
producing wine. Let there be more difficulty in
England in producing cloth, or in Portugal in
producing wine, or let there be more facility in
England in producing wine, or in Portugal in
producing cloth, and the trade must immediately
cease.

No change whatever takes place in the circumstances of Portugal; but England finds that she
can employ her labour more productively in the
manufacture of wine, and instantly the trade of
barter between the two countries changes. Not
only is the exportation of wine from Portugal
stopped, but a new distribution of the precious
metals takes place, and her importation of cloth is
also prevented.

Both countries would probably find it their interest to make their own wine and their own cloth;
but this singular result would take place: in England, though wine would be cheaper, cloth would
be elevated in price, more would be paid for it by

the consumer; while in Portugal the consumers, both of cloth and of wine, would be able to purchase those commodities cheaper. In the country where the improvement was made, prices would be enhanced; in that where no change had taken place, but where they had been deprived of a profitable branch of foreign trade, prices would fall.

This, however, is only a seeming advantage to Portugal, for the quantity of cloth and wine together produced in that country would be diminished, while the quantity produced in England would be increased. Money would in some degree have changed its value in the two countries it would be lowered in England and raised in Portugal. Estimated in money, the whole revenue of Portugal would be diminished; estimated in the same medium, the whole revenue of England would be increased.

Thus then it appears, that the improvement of a manufacture in any country tends to alter the distribution of the precious metals amongst the nations of the world : it tends to increase the quantity of commodities, at the same time that it raises general prices in the country where the improvement takes place.

To simplify the question, I have been supposing the trade between two countries to be confined to

two commodities—to wine and cloth; but it is
well known that many and various articles enter
into the list of exports and imports. By the ab-
straction of money from one country, and the accumulation of it in another, all commodities are
affected in price, and consequently encouragement
is given to the exportation of many more commodities besides money, which will therefore prevent
so great an effect from taking place on the value of
money in the two countries as might otherwise be
expected.

Beside the improvements in arts and machinery,
there are various other causes which are constantly
operating on the natural course of trade, and which
interfere with the equilibrium, and the relative
value of money. Bounties on exportation or importation, new taxes on commodities, sometimes
by their direct, and at other times by their indirect operation, disturb the natural trade of barter,
and produce a consequent necessity of importing
or exporting money, in order that prices may be
accommodated to the natural course of commerce;
and this effect is produced not only in the country
where the disturbing cause takes place, but, in a
greater or less degree, in every country of the
commercial world.

This will in some measure account for the different value of money in different countries; it
will explain to us why the prices of home commo-

dities, and those of great bulk, though of comparatively small value, are, independently of other
causes, higher in those countries where manufactures flourish. Of two countries having precisely
the same population, and the same quantity of land
of equal fertility in cultivation, with the same
knowledge too of agriculture, the prices of raw
produce will be highest in that where the greater
skill, and the better machinery is used in the manufacture of exportable commodities. The rate
of profits will probably differ but little; for wages,
or the real reward of the labourer, may be the
same in both; but those wages, as well as raw produce, will be rated higher in money in that country, into which, from the advantages attending
their skill and machinery, an abundance of money
is imported in exchange for their goods.

Of these two countries, if one had the advantage in the manufacture of goods of one quality,
and the other in the manufacture of goods of another quality, there would be no decided influx of
the precious metals into either; but if the advantage very heavily preponderated in favour of either,
that effect would be inevitable.

In the former part of this work, we have assumed,
for the purpose of argument, that money always
continued of the same value; we are now endea-
vouring to shew that besides the ordinary variations
in the value of money, and those which are com-

s

mon to the whole commercial world, there are also partial variations to which money is subject in particular countries; and to fact, that the value of money is never the same in any two countries, depending as it does on relative taxation, on manufacturing skill, on the advantages of climate, natural productions, and many other causes.

Although, however, money is subject to such perpetual variations, and consequently the prices of the commodities which are common to most countries, are also subject to considerable difference, yet no effect will be produced on the rate of profits, either from the influx or efflux of money. Capital will not be increased, because the circulating medium is augmented. If the rent paid by the farmer to his landlord, and the wages to his labourers, be 20 per cent. higher in one country than another, and if at the same time the nominal value of the farmer's capital be 20 per cent. more, he will receive precisely the same rate of profits, although he should sell his raw produce 20 per cent. higher.

Profits, it cannot be too often repeated, depend on wages; not on nominal, but real wages; not on the number of pounds that may be annually paid to the labourer, but on the number of days' work, necessary to obtain those pounds. Wages may therefore be precisely the same in two countries; they may bear too the same proportion to rent, and to the whole produce obtained from the land, although in one of those countries the labourer should receive ten shillings per week, and in the other twelve.

In the early states of society, when manufactures have made little progress, and the produce of all countries is nearly similar, consisting of the bulky and most useful commodities, the value of money in different countries will be chiefly regulated by their distance from the mines which supply the precious metals; but as the arts and improvements of society advance, and different nations excel in particular manufactures, although distance will still enter into the calculation, the value of the precious metals will be chiefly regulated by the superiority of those manufactures.

Suppose all nations to produce corn, cattle, and coarse clothing only, and that it was by the exportation of such commodities that gold could be obtained from the countries which produced them, or from those who held them in subjection; gold would naturally be of greater exchangeable value in Poland than in England, on account of the greater expense of sending such a bulky commodity as corn the more distant voyage, and also the greater expense attending the conveying of gold to Poland.

This difference in the value of gold, or which is

the same thing, this difference in the price of corn
in the two countries, would exist, although the facilities of producing corn in England should far exceed those of Poland, from the greater fertility of
the land, and the superiority in the skill and implements of the labourer.

If however Poland should be the first to improve
her manufactures, if she should succeed in making
a commodity which was generally desirable, including great value in little bulk, or if she should
be exclusively blessed with some natural production, generally desirable, and not possessed by other
countries, she would obtain an additional quantity
of gold in exchange for this commodity, which
would operate on the price of her corn, cattle, and
coarse clothing. The disadvantage of distance
would probably be more than compensated by the
advantage of having an exportable commodity of
great value, and money would be permanently of
lower value in Poland than in England. If, on the
contrary, the advantage of skill and machinery
were possessed by England, another reason would
be added to that which before existed, why gold
should be less valuable in England than in Poland,
and why corn, cattle, and clothing, should be at a
higher price in the former country.

These I believe to be the only two causes which
regulate the comparative value of money in the
different countries of the world ; for although tax-

ation occasions a disturbance of the equilibrium of money, it does so by depriving the country in which it is imposed of some of the advantages attending skill, industry, and climate.

It has been my endeavour carefully to distinguish between a low value of money, and a high value of corn, or any other commodity with which money may be compared. These have been generally considered as meaning the same thing; but it is evident, that when corn rises from five to ten shillings a bushel, it may be owing either to a fall in the value of money, or to a rise in the value of corn. Thus we have seen, that from the necessity of having recourse successively to land of a worse and worse quality, in order to feed an increasing population, corn must rise in relative value to other things. If therefore money continue permanently of the same value, corn will exchange for more of such money, that is to say, it will rise in price. The same rise in the price of corn will be produced by such improvement of machinery in manufactures, as shall enable us to manufacture commodities with peculiar advantages: for the influx of money will be the consequence; it will fall in value, and therefore exchange for less corn. But the effects resulting from a high price of corn when produced by the rise in the value of corn, and when caused by a fall in the value of money, are totally different. In both cases the money price of wages will rise, but if it be in consequence of the fall in the value of

money, not only wages and corn, but all other commodities will rise. If the manufacturer has more
to pay for wages, he will receive more for his manufactured goods, and the rate of profits will remain unaffected. But when the rise in the price
of corn is the effect of the difficulty of production,
profits will fall; for the manufacturer will be obliged to pay more wages, and will not be enabled
to remunerate himself by raising the price of his
manufactured commodity.

Any improvement in the facility of working the
mines, by which the precious metals may be produced with a less quantity of labour, will sink the
value of money generally. It will then exchange
for fewer commodities in all countries; but when
any particular country excels in manufactures, so
as to occasion an influx of money towards it, the
value of money will be lower, and the prices of
corn and labour will be relatively higher in that
country, than in any other.

This higher value of money will not be indicated
by the exchange; bills may continue to be nego-
ciated at par, although the prices of corn and labour should be 10, 20, or 30 per cent. higher in
one country than another. Under the circumstances supposed, such a difference of prices is the
natural order of things, and the exchange can only
be at par, when a sufficient quantity of money is
introduced into the country excelling in manufac-

tures, so as to raise the price of its corn and labour.
If foreign countries should prohibit the exportation
of money, and could successfully enforce obedi-
ence to such a law, they might indeed prevent the
rise in the prices of the corn and labour of the manufacturing country; for such rise can only take
place after the influx of the precious metals, supposing paper money not to be used; but they could
not prevent the exchange from being very unfavourable to them.   If England were the manufacturing country, and it were possible to prevent the
importation of money, the exchange with France,
Holland, and Spain, might be 5, 10, or 20 per
cent. against those countries.

Whenever the current of money is forcibly stopped, and when money is prevented from settling
at its just level, there are no limits to the possible
variations of the exchange. The effects are similar
to those which follow, when a paper money, not
exchangeable for specie at the will of the holder is
forced into circulation.   Such a currency is necessarily confined to the country where it is issued : it
cannot, when too abundant, diffuse itself generally
amongst other countries.   The level of circulation
is destroyed, and the exchange will inevitably be
unfavourable to the country where it is excessive in
quantity : just so would be the effects of a metallic
circulation, if by forcible means, by laws which
could not be evaded, money should be detained in

a country, when the stream of trade gave it an impetus towards other countries.

When each country has precisely the quantity of money which it ought to have, money will not indeed be of the same value in each, for with respect to many commodities it may differ 5, 10, or even 20 per cent., but the exchange will be at par. One hundred pounds in England, or the silver which is in 100*l.* will purchase a bill of 100*l.*, or an equal quantity of silver in France, Spain, or Holland.

In speaking of the exchange and the comparative value of money in different countries, we must not in the least refer to the value of money estimated in commodities, in either country. The exchange is never ascertained by estimating the comparative value of money in corn, cloth, or any commodity whatever, but by estimating the value of the currency of one country, in the currency of another.

It may also be ascertained by comparing it with some standard common to both countries. If a bill on England for 100*l.* will purchase the same quantity of goods in France or Spain, that a bill on Hamburgh for the same sum will do, the exchange between Hamburgh and England is at par; but if a bill on England for 130*l.*, will purchase no more than a bill on Hamburgh for 100*l*., the exchange is 30 per cent. against England.

In England 100*l*. may purchase a bill, or the right of receiving 101*l*. in Holland, 102*l*. in France, and 105*l*. in Spain. The exchange with England is, in that case, said to be 1 per cent. against Holland, 2 per cent. against France, and 5 per cent. against Spain. It indicates that the level of currency is higher than it should be in those countries, and the comparative value of their currencies, and that of England, would be immediately restored to par, by abstracting from theirs, or by adding to that of England.

Those who maintained that our currency was depreciated during the last ten years, when the exchange varied from 20 to 30 per cent. against this country, have never contended, as they have been accused of doing, that money could not be more valuable in one country than another, as compared with various commodities; but they did contend, that 130*l*. could not be detained in England, unless it was depreciated, when it was of no more value, estimated in the money of Hamburgh, or of Holland, than the bullion in 100*l*.

By sending 130*l*. good English pounds sterling to Hamburgh, even at an expense of 5*l*., I should be possessed there of 125*l*.; what then could make me consent to give 130*l*. for a bill which would

give me 100*l.* in Hamburgh, but that my pounds
were not good pounds sterling?—they were dete-
riorated, were degraded in intrinsic value below
the pounds sterling of Hamburgh, and if actually
sent there, at an expense of 5*l.*, would sell only
for 100*l.* With metallic pounds sterling, it is not
denied that my 130*l.* would procure me 125*l.* in
Hamburgh, but with paper pounds sterling I can
only obtain 100*l.*; and yet it was maintained that
130*l.* in paper, was of equal value with 130*l.* in
silver or gold.

Some indeed more reasonably maintained, that
130*l.* in paper was not of equal value with 130*l.* in
metallic money; but they said that it was the metallic money which had changed its value, and not
the paper money. They wished to confine the
meaning of the word depreciation to an actual fall
of value, and not to a comparative difference between the value of money, and the standard by
which by law it is regulated. One hundred pounds
of English money was formerly of equal value with,
and could purchase 100*l.* of Hamburgh money : in
any other country a bill of 100*l.* on England, or
on Hamburgh, could purchase precisely the same
quantity of commodities. To obtain the same
things, I was lately obliged to give 130*l.* English
money, when Hamburgh could obtain them for
100*l.* Hamburgh money. If English money was
of the same value then as before, Hamburgh money must have risen in value. But where is the

proof of this? How is it to be ascertained whether English money has fallen, or Hamburgh money has risen? there is no standard by which this can be determined. It is a plea which admits of no proof, and can neither be positively affirmed, nor positively contradicted. The nations of the world must have been early convinced, that there was no standard of value in nature, to which they might unerringly refer, and therefore chose a medium, which on the whole appeared to them less variable than any other commodity.

To this standard we must conform till the law is changed, and till some other commodity is discovered, by the use of which we shall obtain a more perfect standard, than that which we have established. While gold is exclusively the standard in this country, money will be depreciated, when a pound sterling is not of equal value with 5 dwts. and 3 grs. of standard gold, and that, whether gold rises or falls in general value.

M

Acknowledgments We are indebted to the University of Basel Library which is in possession of one book of this rare edition of 1821 and made it available to us. We thank Claire-Lise Dovat for her support in photo printing the individual pages of Chapter VII.

CPSIA information can be obtained
at www.ICGtesting.com
Printed in the USA
LVHW081227170520
655852LV00002B/127